Contents

Introduction 2
Chapter One: June/Jul 4
Chapter Three: Noven 34
Chapter Six: April-June 2018 96
Chapter Eight: October-December 2018 138
Chapter Ten: January 2019 238
Chapter Eleven: February 2018 261
Chapter Twelve: March 2019 279
Chapter Thirteen: April 2019 293
Chapter Fourteen: Exclusive Reviews 312
Mr Opinionated's Top 25 Films 340
Acknowledgements 342
Collaborator Links 343

1,

To
John

Introduction

Way back in 2017, even though it feels a lot longer, I started putting my inane opinions of film on the internet. What started then as something to pass my time, at a time when I was at a bit of a loose end permanently, has now become somewhat of an obsession. Reviewing films got my back on my feet, off to university to do something with my life, and ultimately, makes me a lot happier.

Not all films make me happy, as you will soon see by reading on, some make me despair for whoever makes decisions in Hollywood, and some just make me depressed (looking at you Boss Baby).

So, this is a journey through all my writing up to this point, as well as some exclusive reviews I've written just for this book, as if I didn't spend enough of my life writing about film, so at least that gives you somewhat of a reason to buy this rather than read them all online.

It's also interesting for me to look back at my writing and see for myself how its evolved in two years' worth of university education, and a whole lot of time spent watching films.

I will say though, I have presented these reviews as they were originally written, and in some cases, especially in the earlier reviews, my viewpoint may have softened, or hardened, depending on the movie. I also feel that the quality of the critique improves as I go on. Not that the earlier reviews are bad, just time spent watching films and experience eventually shows.

I'll also include my opinion pieces that I've written on-and-off at the end of the book, just in case those are of any interest, this will be the definitive collection of my writing thus far.

Thanks for reading, and here's to many more years!

Nathan x

Chapter One: June/July 2017

Pirates of the Caribbean: Salazar's Revenge (Originally published on June 23rd, 2017)
Directed by Joachim Ronning and Espen Sandberg
Starring: Johnny Depp, Javier Bardem, Brenton Thwaites and Kaya Scodelario

So, I went into this movie not expecting much. I'd enjoyed the first Two Pirates movies years ago, mostly for the swashbuckling adventure and Jack Sparrow, of course. But time was not kind to this franchise.

It's third and fourth instalments both range from over-long to downright unnecessary. So will this fifth adventure bring life back to the franchise. Well, in many ways yes, it does.

Story

Permanently drunk pirate Jack Sparrow has made his fair share of enemies over the years, including Davy Jones at one point. But now his enemies are coming back from the grave for their revenge.

Following the story of Will Turner's son searching for the Trident of Poseidon, to save his father from a cursed life aboard The Flying Dutchman. Thinking his best route of action is to seek out his father's former friend Jack Sparrow, the journey takes his through the feared 'Devil's triangle' where his Navy crew mates are killed by a ship sailed by the undead, led by the vengeful Captain Salazar, who gives Henry Turner a warning to take to Jack Sparrow.

Meanwhile, a young woman due to be hanged for being a witch escapes, convinced she holds the map that leads to the Trident, she spends the movie on the run from the law. On the same island, coincidentally, Jack Sparrow is pulling off an elaborate bank heist, which ultimately proves unfruitful, resulting in his crew leaving.

Through a series of contrivances Henry comes across Sparrow and the woman (named Carina) and the three plot to go after the Trident together, soon after Catrina and Jack are captured and set to be executed, only to be rescued by Henry and Jack's former crew.

They take to the seas in a barely floating old ship where they encounter Salazar at every turn, who is at times aided by Jack's best 'frenemy' Captain Barbosa.

Verdict

I want to avoid spoilers if I can in my reviews, so I'll leave the summary of the plot there before I give away any big twists or plot points.

Seeing Johnny Depp play Jack Sparrow is like slipping into an old, comfy t-shirt. It's a welcome sight to see Depp return to this character after a few years of shall we say, mixed verdicts. For what it's worth he looks like he relishes stepping back into the part and jumps back into it with gusto, giving us moments of humour at the captain's expense.

Henry Turner and Catrina are the new additions in this film, and Catrina in particular stands out as strong, independent character, often resulting in her being called a witch and sent to the gallows, she sticks to her guns and principles, and it's nice to see them move away from a 'damsel in distress' archetype, even though there is an undercurrent of romance between her and Henry.

Henry himself has his moments of greatness, but overall is probably the least fleshed out of the characters, as a result can come across as quite generic, but his goals and ambitions are believable, and he shows just enough character to get behind.

The villain is where this movie comes alive however, Javier Bardem is quite brilliant as a bad guy, as seen in Skyfall, and here portrays a villain who for all intents and purposes is of a heroic nature, he believes he is in the right and that's what makes him, there are many angles from which it is to see him as a good guy in another story, but this being a story focusing on typically rule-breaking, rum-swilling pirates our interpretation of 'good' is somewhat skewed.

Elsewhere, Geoffrey Rush looks typically comfortable as Barbosa, this time cast as a somewhat 'king of the seas' before being dragged back into Jack Sparrow's life, and there's also a highly amusing cameo from Sir Paul McCartney, of all people.

At the end of the day, this movie isn't going to win any Oscars', but we knew that. It's very enjoyable and very well directed and it more than steadies the ship (see what I did there?) but it feels like it should definitely be the last one, however talk has already started for a sixth instalment so there's not much chance of that, however, that doesn't make this movie any worse, in fact I'm willing to recommend it, which I never thought I would going in.

The Boss Baby (Originally published June 25th, 2017)
Directed by: Tom McGrath
Starring: Alec Baldwin, Steve Buscemi, Jimmy Kimmel and Lisa Kudrow.

So, from time to time, my fiancée chooses our film at the cinema, after this choice however, she might not for a long time.

A film I was expecting less than nothing from somehow managed to still be disappointing even with the lowest possible expectations. I don't think I've ever sat through worse dross in a cinema before, yes, it is terrible, extremely so, yes, it's for kids, but that's no excuse. Zootropolis was for kids and that managed to have a great message and be incredibly smart, this movie has no such merits.

Story

Tim is a normal kid with a great life with loving parents, until his perfect life is thrown into disarray with the arrival of a baby brother, conspicuously dressed in a suit. Ultimately suspicious of his new brother, Tim vows to bring him down.

After discovering that his baby brother has the mind of an adult middle manager, representing Baby co. he soon finds himself embroiled in the feud between babies and puppies, as the titular Boss Baby brings his older brother along to bring down Puppy Co.

Verdict

Did any of that sound entertaining to you? Throw in a voice performance from Alec Baldwin and a cornucopia of bodily functions jokes (fart jokes etc.) you have the lowest denominator of a kid's movie, one that your little devil might enjoy while it's on but is entirely without substance. It's highly unlikely it will remain a favourite they take through childhood, in the same way my generation took Toy Story through theirs.

Unfunny and predictable is not a great combination for any movie. Not least a movie like this with such utterly inconsequential stock characters, there's not one shred of creativity in any character, whereas other better movies have taken such stock characters and built on them (for example Inside Out) this movie just languishes in its comfort zone like a baby carries a blanket.

In short, it's been a long time since DreamWorks has come out with anything that in any way challenges Disney's monopoly on great family movies, and with this it looks like their several universes away from doing so anytime soon, especially with a sequel announced for this movie, despite it not needing one in any conceivable way. Avoid this movie, even if your kids want to see it, there is much better for them to see, it's not worth losing the brain cells.

Hampstead (Originally published June 26th, 2017)
Directed by Joel Hopkins

Starring: Diane Keaton, Brendan Gleeson, Lesley Manville and Jason Watkins.

Was a tough one to name, this. Without the word 'movie' thrown in there it may have looked like a review of a place, and seeing as I've never visited Hampstead, neither know particularly where it is (although I've an inkling that it may be near London) that would be quite misleading.

Anyway, Hampstead. You can give this movie one thing right out of the gate, you couldn't exactly call it over hyped, I think I remember seeing one trailer in the lead up to release, I thought it looked pretty charming but nonetheless forgot about it until I was scheduling my latest cinema visit. Among the latest blockbusters sat this movie, so I thought I'd practice what I preach and support a smaller movie.

Story

An American widower living in Hampstead has a rather dull life, she spends it around overbearing middle-class women, who could be charitably described as 'busybodies' campaigning for the latest cause of the day, she is also having money troubles on account of the husband leaving her in debt.

All this leads to her being propositioned by an accountant, and shortly after involved in the life of an Irish vagabond named Donald who lives in a shack on the Heath, she begins to campaign against one of her friends to save Donald's shack as their friendship blossoms.

Verdict

That short summary may not sell you very much on the movie, I've left out a few details to avoid spoilers as I always do, but it's sweet of nature and simple of setup, a promising premise is played off well by its characters.

The movie as a whole, however, is rather a mixed bag, it seems in the middle to have a fair amount of pacing issues, as it does start to feel as though it's dragging, especially as the movie enters what feels like it's final act, it overreaches itself at times with repeated arguments that seem to exist purely to pad out the running time, and some fringe characters remain underdeveloped, leaving two strong leads and a supporting cast that are rather interchangeable.

The positive side of that coin being it's two leads, played by Diane Keaton and Dominic Gleeson, Gleeson especially gives a very personal performance, sometimes understated in the best possible way, it's a performance that would bring great acclaim if there were more eyes on the film, somewhat disappointingly. Diane Keaton also gives a strong performance, portraying a woman in the middle of her humanity, a worried son and overbearing friends and neighbours, she brings a fish-out-of-water feel from the off and carries her struggles very well.

If you overlook its length and occasional duller moments, at the heart of this film is a sweet tale of a man's right to live as he pleases. It's strong lead characters vastly overshadow supporting players and on balance that's not a bad thing as it invests it's time in getting us invested in Donald's struggles by not casting a broad net, it instead tells a personal, contained tale of unlikely acquaintance and as a whole is not a bad movie, if anything it has shot for the moon and miscalculated it's trajectory. It's not the best thing you'll see this year, but you'll leave happy for the experience and that's all you can ask for really.

Gran Torino (Originally published June 28th, 2017)
Directed by Clint Eastwood
Starring: Clint Eastwood, Bee Vang, Ahney Her and Christopher Carley

So, I've done a few current movie reviews, I thought I'd branch out and add my comments on an older film that I find particularly interesting, in one way or another.

So, Clint Eastwood then, he's a bit of a Marmite actor by all accounts, some like him, some don't, personally I can take or leave him, I like his old 'Man With No Name' films, but sometimes find him somewhat samey, I do think however that he is a very talented director as well as actor, so how appropriate that he was behind the camera for this too.

Story

Walt Kowalski (Eastwood) is a recently widowed, ill-tempered Korean War veteran living in a neighbourhood predominantly occupied by members of the Hmong community (an Asian people native to Southern China, Vietnam and Thailand) a community in turmoil at the hands of a gang of Hmong's one of whom is the cousin of Walt's next-door neighbours.

After Thao, one of Walt's next-door neighbours is coerced into his cousin's gang, he's challenged with stealing Walt's prized possession, his Gran Torino, Thao is caught in the act by Walt and ran off.

Later on, Walt runs off the gang from his next-door neighbour's lawn after they attempt to force Tao into their gang, he then learns it was Thao who tried to steal his car and warns him from ever stepping on his property. However, Walt again becomes entangled with his neighbours lives as he saves Thao's sister, Sue, from a black gang's unwanted sexual advances, he finds that he is growing fond of Sue, and eventually takes Thao under his wing, to help him find his way in the world.

Verdict

Despite this film being nine years old, I've chosen to refrain from including spoilers, as it really is a movie that has to be experienced, it's somewhat of a 'hidden gem' even though it was met with a fair amount of acclaim following its release it has now been forgotten to history, which is a shame because I think it's one of Eastwood's best efforts, as both a director and actor.

His portrayal of Walt is so believable in its delivery you feel at times that you are looking into a person's life, as opposed to a character on screen, he shines most in the screen time shared with Thao or Sue, as seeing the affection his character has for the two youngsters grow is endearing in a character that at the start of the film, showed no endearing qualities to any outsiders. The insults still remain, but as the film goes on, they're fired behind a wall of affection as opposed to real prejudice.

Another commendable part of the movie is it's supporting players, specifically Sue and Thao, who are played by Ahney Her and Bee Vang respectively. Both have key parts of the plot to carry and to their credit they carry it incredibly well, the stand-out moments for me are the scenes where Walt takes Thao to the barbers and to a prospective job, trying to educate him on how red-blooded American males communicate.

It's also a movie well realised in its direction, Eastwood has a penchant for a dark, gritty, realistic directing style that is recognizable here, he creates a downtrodden atmosphere, not only in the Hmong characters but in Walt himself as he adjusts to life without his wife.

There's also a great symmetry between the first speech of the movie, given by a priest at Walt's wife's funeral and the movies conclusion, one which I'll leave you all to discover yourself as I highly recommend this film, especially if you're only aware of Eastwood as the Western actor with squint-y eyes, you'll come out of this with a whole new perception of him as both an actor and director, and a feeling of bittersweet triumph as the film reaches its conclusion, it's one that I think is essential viewing, it would be a real shame for this movie to be forgotten.

Spider-Man: Homecoming (Originally published July 13th, 2017)
Directed by Jon Watts
Starring: Tom Holland, Michael Keaton, Robert Downey Jr and Zendaya

The MCU soldiers on in this entry, the first solo outing for the web-slinger in the MCU, after making his long-awaited debut in the franchise in Captain America: Civil War, we're nine years on from the start of the MCU and the quality hasn't seemed to drop in the last few years, so let's get down to it.

Story

Following the events of Captain America: Civil War, Peter Parker is balancing his life at home and school, and his life as Spider-Man, constantly waiting for the call of Tony Stark for his next assignment, meanwhile killing time by stopping petty criminals and helping little ladies across the street.

Meanwhile, a new threat has emerged as a weapons trader dons a strong wingsuit and becomes a thorn in Spider-Man's side as he attempts to stop this new threat against the advice of Tony Stark, who doesn't think he's ready.

While balancing this, he juggles his school life, around which is his friendship with Ned, a tech proficient student and eventual aid to Peter's alter ego and his love for Liz, a popular classmate.

Verdict

First off, let me state that I adored this film while I was watching, and still think it's pretty great afterward, I'm saying this now to counter-balance the criticism I will level at it. Tom Holland might just have been born to be Spider-Man and builds upon his well-received debut in Civil War with aplomb, he's such a natural in the suit and out of it that it almost makes you forget that he is the third man to don the costume in 15 years.

Elsewhere in the cast, Michael Keaton shines as the wing-suited villain The Vulture/Adrian Toomes and is a rare villain in that you can sometimes sympathise with his struggles and from a certain angle it almost seems like he is justified, making him a more complex villain than most we've seen in the MCU. Also, Jacob Batalon gives a stellar performance as Ned, who becomes Spidey's 'man in the chair' and has just enough charisma to make the characters 'nerdiness' not overbearing, keeping him well in the likable category.

Now for the not so nice stuff, firstly Tony Stark comes off as a real jerk in this movie in most of his scenes, coming off as unappreciative of Peter's help during the events of Civil War, becoming almost like an overbearing asshole dad, especially in a scene where he takes Spidey's suit where you just want Spidey to sucker-punch Tony, overall it comes off as very disingenuous and seems like writers struggling to create tension chose to make Tony an asshole.

I also never bought for a minute that Peter was the nerd and outcast he was made out to be, firstly because he's without a doubt the best looking of the male classmates, enough to turn the heads of the movies female characters in fact, also add the fact that he has a body to die for, he's not someone you could see the Jock's picking on too often, seeing as he's in better shape. I get that in the comics he was portrayed as this, but when you look at it logically, there's no way someone who looks like Peter looks like here would be an outcast, it just doesn't ring true.

Finally, and this is really nit-picky, and I suspect more down to ego than the movie's doing, but it annoyed the hell out of me and that's that Gwyneth Paltrow gets fourth or fifth billing at the end of the movie, despite having approximately five lines and appearing in exactly one scene. It really rankled me because the supporting cast worked so hard in fleshing out the film's world, yet here they get credited below someone who was as significant to the film as a fly that might have landed on the camera, she added nothing and quite easily could have been cut, and her high billing just smacks of over-inflated egos.

After all that criticism though, I can't get past the fact that I really enjoyed this movie, it isn't my favourite of the MCU, or my favourite Spider-Man movie, but it's a hell of an effort from Tom Holland especially, if his upwards trajectory continues, we could have the best Spider-Man on our hands, and most definitely a very welcome addition to the MCU.

Baby Driver (Originally published July 14th, 2017)
Directed by Edgar Wright
Starring: Ansel Elgort, Jon Hamm, Jamie Foxx and Kevin Spacey

One of the greatest thrills I can imagine is a movie that takes you by surprise, I was exposed to zero build-up to this movie, didn't see a trailer and don't think I saw a poster, all I knew when I went in was it was directed by Edgar Wright (whose work I'm a fan of) and that a few people I knew spoke very highly of it, and I have a feeling I'll be adding my voice to the chorus of positivity before this review is out... have I said too much already?

Story

Baby is a talented young getaway driver working for crime boss Doc to pay off a debt he owes after trying to steal one of Doc's cars. Due to severe tinnitus he is constantly listening to his iPod, lost in his own world. Along the way he'll mix with eccentric criminals to help pull off heists.

After paying off his debt, he swears off his life as a getaway driver, instead getting a job as a pizza delivery guy and sparking a relationship with a girl he meets at his favourite diner, however he is coerced back into driving by Doc, and the situation soon breaks down...

Verdict

I apologise that the plot synopsis I gave there is short, but it really is a film you must experience first-hand, and reading it here would most certainly spoil the experience, but take my word for this, it is an incredible movie, all the better for the fact that I didn't know what to expect going in, and hopefully by retaining certain details anyone who may read this will enjoy it just as much.

Make no mistake, this is a good movie, no not good, great, it's slick direction and cinematography compliment the killer soundtrack and aid a talented cast in giving great performances all around. There are times where the direction will take you back to Wright's earlier efforts alongside Messrs Pegg and Frost, specifically in its depiction of action and violence, the action peaks during one of the few gunfights, where the sounds of the action seamlessly mix with the soundtrack as if it was written specifically for it.

The soundtrack is comprised of both classics and modern efforts covering everything from Run the Jewels to The Damned, and like certain movies in the Marvel Universe, is made all the better for it. Scenes are presented in synchronicity with the music giving the impression of a character lost in a world of music.

Speaking of characters, there are some real stand-out performances in this movie, starting with the lead character for who the film is named, Baby, who is played by Ansel Elgort, a young actor with an undoubtedly bright future. Pulling off a character like Baby couldn't have been an easy task, the character is exactly talkative so you have to bring it out in his body language and behaviour, Ansel dives into this challenge with a triple-somersault pike and wins the proverbial gold medal (please pardon that tortured metaphor) elsewhere, Kevin Spacey plays crime lord Doc, and inhabits every scene he's in and injects it with the grit it needed, there's a part of Kevin Spacey that I think really enjoys being a villain, so imagine his disappointment when he found out that the character inhabits a shade of Grey, and straddles the line of villainy effortlessly.

Among the few characters he drives to heists the characters of Buddy and Bats, played by John Hamm and Jamie Foxx respectively, stand out, Jamie revels in playing the unhinged criminal, turning in a performance to put alongside his great turns in Django and Ray to name but a few. Hamm goes through a devastating arc in the run-time of the movie, which to say that he seemed like a throwaway side character for most of the run time is rare in movies, the part was always in capable hands with the talented Hamm, who borders on stealing the show.

There is so much more I could say but risk bordering cheer leading at this point, the only criticism I can think of was in its marketing, as a movie this good should have way more coverage than it has, so I'm going to do the movie a solid and recommend that you make time to see this movie, you won't be disappointed.

Logan (Originally published July 21st, 2017)
Directed by James Mangold
Starring: Hugh Jackman, Patrick Stewart, Dafne Keen and Stephen Merchant

I remember when the first trailer for this was released, I usually don't get hung up on trailers as they can colour your view of a movie, and don't usually tell you much about the film, so when I saw the trailer and it instantly made me 100 times more interested in the movie you know how different and impressive the trailer was.

Ever since The Dark Knight was released, it rocketed to near the top of my all-time films and sitting proudly as my all-time favourite comic book movies, and Logan is the first film since to come anywhere near challenging it, not quite surpassing it you understand, as I haven't re-watched it nearly as much as I have The Dark Knight but after a few re-watches it just might threaten The Dark Knight's long held place at the top of my list.

Story

In the year 2027, mutants have all but died out, Logan is surviving just over the border in Mexico, caring for an elderly Professor X, who is suffering from dementia, which has catastrophic effects due to his telekinesis.

Logan is getting by driving a limo and drinking, his regeneration ability also seems to be diminishing, he is approached by a former nurse at an illegal facility that appears to be growing mutants, she asks him to take a young girl with very similar abilities to Logan, he refuses, however after encouragement from Charles, Logan takes the girl on the run from the company that grew her, in an attempt to take her to a safe 'Eden' near the Canadian border.

Verdict

Logan instantly catches the eye by having a strikingly different visual style to almost any comic book movie, especially those in the X-Men universe, having the feel of a classic Western in terms of style. This stylistic changes suits the darker tone the movie is aiming for, this being an R-Rated effort, the language and violence is ramped up to new levels, although it is worth noting that the focus is more on the characters themselves as opposed to balls-out action, as a result most of the action feels sluggish as a result of Logan's diminished abilities, he no longer regenerates as fast, and the simple act of drawing his claws causes him extreme pain.

Hugh Jackman truly has Logan down to a fine art at this point, after 17 years with the claws his last effort stands as a testament to his acting ability as Old Logan struggles across America, exhaustedly fighting off pursuers at every turn, it almost feels as though it's a parallel to Jackman's own ageing, being quoted before that he was getting too old for the part, it feels like he's added that to his performance.

His supporting cast is stellar too, with the typically great performance from Sir Patrick Stewart, as well as a surprisingly grounded performance from Stephen Merchant as Logan's albino assistant helping him with Xavier's care, Caliban. On the villainous side, Boyd Holbrook plays Donald Pierce the head of security for the company responsible for X-23's creation (we'll get to her) a ruthless character who will stop at nothing to catch up to Logan and X-23, as with the rest of the cast, it's a grounded and exceptional performance, creating a truly unlikeable character.

So onto X-23 (Laura) she is portrayed by the young actress Dafne Keene who really must be commended for bringing this pivotal character to life so brilliantly despite her relative inexperience, she truly stands out during the more action packed sequences, with the film not containing as much action as previous movies they had to stand out as different, and whereas Logan's fighting style had become slower and encumbered, Laura isn't in that situation, she brings the Wolverine fire to fights, and hopefully it leads to more for this talented young woman.

Of course all this in insubstantial if the story doesn't hold up and luckily it does, a much smaller scale more personal story surrounding the future of mutant-kind and morality, and rest assured there are a few gut-punches of emotion in this movie, none of which will be spoiled here, the effect of such brings emotion to a genre that rarely strays into tear-jerking territory, but there are several moments in this directly aimed at the heart-strings.

It is truly hard to find something that jumps out as a fault, because of the movie's overall quality, however the movie did seem to contrive a solve-all MacGuffin towards the plots end, which while being needed for the film to reach a conclusion, did feel a tad contrived. All that aside, spare a few hours in your life to watch Logan, long time X-Men fans will love it for the sense of closure to the story, while it doesn't quite exist in the same timeline as the other movies, it's still worth seeing for the closure to a story and it's accessible for new viewers who are put off by the usual comic book movie tropes. I cannot recommend this movie enough for those who enjoy a compelling narrative, as Logan will take you on a ride that will stay for you for years to come.

Chapter Two: August-October 2017

War for the Planet of the Apes (Originally published August 1st, 2017)
Directed by: Matt Reeves
Starring: Andy Serkis, Woody Harrelson and Steve Zahn

Let it first be said that I'm late to this particular Simian bandwagon. It was only a few months ago that I first watched Rise (of the Planet of the Apes) and Dawn (see past brackets) and was utterly astounded at the level of storytelling achieved by CG Apes (led by Andy Serkis, natch) and a few stand out human performances. I loved both films, but felt Dawn was an improvement over its predecessor for fleshing out the world the Apes create and the characters of the Apes themselves.

Story

After the events of Dawn the Apes find themselves hunted by a human army led by a ruthless Colonel (played by Woody Harrelson) the Apes must face the onslaught of the humans and find a new home before their complete annihilation.

Verdict

First off, this film is bloody beautiful. The direction, the effects around the Apes, the locations. Matt Reeves truly brought this world to life, his director of photography also deserves a mention for finding the perfect angle for every shot, under the instruction of Reeves I'm certain, not a second of screen-time is wasted.

Of course, a special mention must be given to Andy Serkis, who has brought the franchise's main primate, Caesar to life so effortlessly and skilfully, he had well and truly staked his claim as the king of

MoCap long before this trilogy even arrived, but his reputation has been bolstered no end by his career-making (had it not been for Gollum) turn in these films, Caesar has had more of an arc in three films than many human characters go through in many other efforts from Hollywood.

So after blowing smoke up the director and star's arse for two paragraphs, is War any good? Yes, incredibly so. I can't remember a trilogy of such ascending quality, maybe Lord of the Rings, but that had the advantage of a stellar story already being there, this series has built everything it has from scratch, and how rare is it in Hollywood that sequels are made because they had a story to tell and not as a blind attempt at making money? It truly is a special series of such high quality that anyone attempting to make a fourth must be brave or mad to carry the weight of this near-perfect trilogy on his/her back.

It also must be mentioned, that the score for this movie is incredible. Scored by Michael Giacchino, he who scored Star Wars: Rogue One to great success, again succeeds greatly here in creating the atmosphere required to carry the weight of this story, it's worth noting that his score for Dawn was stellar too.

I don't do scores for reviews, as I don't believe a complex opinion can be boiled down to a number, so I depend on recommending a movie or not, informing cinema visits for all who read, and my advice here would be, if you've seen the first two, go as soon as possible, if you haven't, watch the first two, then go and watch this, you will thank me later.

Dunkirk (Originally published August 10th, 2017)
Directed by Christopher Nolan
Starring: Fionn Whitehead, Tom Glynn-Carney, Jack Lowden and Harry Styles

I have to admit to some trepidation going into this movie. After all with a subject like World War II, and one so grounded in realism is unlikely to surprise, after all the war has been over for 70+ years so it's safe to say we know who came out victorious. However, there is one thing Christopher Nolan does well it's surprised his viewers, with his casting and filmmaking, with that said let's dive into it.

Story

It's 1940 and the British Army is pinned down by advancing German forces in the French town of Dunkirk, under fire from air and from land, they begin the perilous evacuation mission.

Told from the perspective of three main sides, a soldier stranded on Dunkirk beach, a civilian sailing his private ship to aid the evacuation and an RAF pilot, flying over the channel and keeping the skies clear of German bombers. It tells the remarkable story of the civilian help to evacuate Dunkirk.

Verdict

This film is really something special. It grabs you by the scruff of the neck in the very first minute and doesn't let go until the credits roll, using an effective mix of orchestral score (provided by Nolan regular Hans Zimmer) and the soundtrack of war, that is bullets and bombs it makes you feel like you are stood on the beach. It drips with an intense atmosphere. Intense is probably the best word, but it's the best possible tension, a feeling of unknowing, unknowing that these characters that we've grown to like will make it home unscathed, unknowing of the threat of any number of German planes ready to emerge from the clouds.

Nolan really is a filmmaker at the top of his game, never more is this apparent than in the beauty of some shots in this movie, whether they be encompassing shots of the beach itself, or a view from the cockpit of a spitfire, it could not look crisper and more refined if it were a drawing in an art gallery, every frame jumps from the screen to tell its own story, plenty of column-inches have been dedicated in the past to the merits of Christopher Nolan, but he really is that good, how he makes a movie feel alive and jump off the screen without need for gimmicks like 3D or the latest CGI, filmmaking this good can only be achieved with passion and painstaking skill.

Now onto the performance side; what is great about the casting is Nolan's casting of young, unknown actors (paralleling the young age of many soldiers too young to have taken part in this war but still did) and compliments it by adding great experience on top, Tom Hardy receives top billing in this movie, yet despite this he has less than ten lines, and the truth is he didn't need any more lines, the nuances in his performance come in the tension of the moment, and the way he acts with his eyes is just incredible, he has more range in just his eyes than many actors do in their entire bodies. Overall the movie is light on dialogue, which doesn't really hamper the movie in any way. It builds effective tension by actions, by scene after scene of seemingly never-ending trials and tribulations for his characters to conquer, it's simply astounding.

Let's address the elephant in the room while I'm on the topic of acting. Harry Styles. Was I sceptical when I heard he'd be in this movie? Yes, but also optimistic, after all Heath Ledger was seen as a strange choice when he was cast as The Joker ten plus years ago. Is his performance as good as Ledger's? No, but it's no less surprising. He delivers lines and carries scenes like someone who's been acting for years also, and I will stop using the word I promise, his character drips with tension, as one would when they've been stood on a beach being bombarded by German bombs. I don't know what lies ahead for Mr Styles in terms of acting, but I hope he sticks at it, he really looks like he has something to add.

In conclusion then, if any movie were to convince you that movies are art, this is the one, not only does it look beautiful, it sounds beautiful, it feels beautiful, hell IT IS beautiful, in every sense that a movie can be. I know it's early to be throwing around Oscar rumours, but this is one movie that deserves a nomination for at least direction and cinematography, if not more. So to wrap-up, put aside a few hours and treat yourself, film-making doesn't get any better than this.

Atomic Blonde (Originally published August 16th, 2017)
Directed by David Leitch
Starring: Charlize Theron and James McAvoy

I was feeling quite optimistic going to see this movie, after my run of stellar movies in the last few weeks, and what with this being another war (albeit a different 'colder' one) given it's stylish looks in trailers, there was plenty to be optimistic about, unfortunately this is the first film in a while that left me feeling disappointed.

Story

In cold-war era Berlin, a female operative is sent into Eastern Berlin to find a fellow operative gone rogue and to find a list containing the names of all the operatives in MI:6, along the way she has to deal with rogue agents and the communist regime.

Verdict

Let me first say from the start that this is by no means a bad film, it's not a particularly good film either and given its stellar cast this movie had every opportunity to be brilliant, alas it was not to be.

The main problem was its pacing and scripting, a good 60-75% of the film meanders around different plot points with little to no connectivity, at one point in the film, the plot essential MacGuffin, the list, went unmentioned and unsearched for a good half hour, while the protagonist, played by Charlize Theron, and the rogue agent she was searching for, James McAvoy, get side-tracked doing various things, oh and I saw the third act twist coming from a mile off which is never good while building intrigue in a movie.

It also feels like a waltz we've all danced before too, the Cold War setting is ironically, extremely cold, teamed with Theron's extremely by the numbers straight-faced action girl fails to carry the bulk of the weight. We've all seen Russians getting killed during the Cold War a million times between films, TV shows and video games and while I can see I might be hypocritical after singing the praises of a WWII film last week, that did things differently, this just feels like every Cold War story we've ever seen.

It's not all bad however, McAvoy is great in his role as an unhinged operative deeply immersed in the underground Berlin scene to the point of almost losing his mind is a treat, dominating every scene he's in, as he has a tendency too, some of the later action scenes are almost exhilarating, burdened only by somewhat unbelievably resilient henchmen, one of whom took three stabbings and two shootings to keep down and lastly, the music provided by Tyler Bates who oversaw the Guardians of the Galaxy Vol 2 soundtrack on top form with more select choices from the time period, he seems to have found a nice little niche.

In summary, while not being a great film, it has its moments and while I wouldn't recommend it, it's certainly better than a certain Sony Animations film currently doing the rounds. But if you miss it you haven't missed much.

The Hitman's Bodyguard (Originally published September 1st, 2017)
Directed by Patrick Hughes
Starring: Ryan Reynolds, Samuel L Jackson, Gary Oldman and Salma Hayek

After Deadpool last year, Ryan Reynolds is a bankable comedy actor, not as if he wasn't before but a string of bad choices prior to this it was difficult to bank on a Reynolds performance.

This movie sees him team up with movie veteran Samuel L Jackson, in an action comedy romp across most of the UK and surprisingly, The Netherlands, the perennial peaceful country, which is nice juxtaposition.

Story

The world's greatest hitman Darius Kincaid (Jackson) is called as a witness in the trial of a Belarusian dictator. He is assigned a bodyguard (Reynolds) whose career has fallen from its dizzying heights after losing a client.

The two must learn to co-inside as they avoid the dictator's henchmen, who have killed every witness called thus far and get to Amsterdam to the trail.

Verdict

My first thought after leaving this film was that it was more fun than it had any right to be. Sure its setup was so cliché that it wore cliché as a sporty trilby, but it's kept afloat by two things, the chemistry between Jackson and Reynolds and some utterly bonkers and well-choreographed action scenes.

Speaking of Reynolds and Jackson, it's them that people see this movie for really and for their part they make the cliché script work with red-hot chemistry. Reynolds isn't quite 'full Deadpool' here but he's good for cutting wit and a rib-tickling action scene outside a waffle shop in Amsterdam. There's also a love story side plot with Reynolds character, although this mainly falls into the background. As for Jackson, he doesn't really play anything more than 'a Samuel L Jackson character' you know the one, he uses the word 'motherfucker' like most people use commas. While it isn't exactly ground-breaking, it's still entertaining to see Mr Jackson do his thing, and after all these years he's understandably perfected his act, he also looks like he's enjoying himself too, which is nice.

Elsewhere in the cast, we have a turn from Salma Hayek as Kincaid's violent, foulmouthed wife, she and Jackson have one of the movies best scenes, as he tells the story of how they met, in a bar in El Salvador. There's also a villainous turn from one Gary Oldman, who shows just how good a villain he can be, his screen time is short, but effective, making a hateable villain in roughly three scenes is a steep task but with someone with Oldman's pedigree in the role, it's no surprise he makes it work. There's also a blink-and-you'll-miss-it appearance from Richard E. Grant, as a coked-up lawyer, truly the role he was born to play, it was very strange to hear him swear, in that mildly posh accent.

In conclusion, think of this movie as a glazed doughnut, it isn't haute cuisine, but it's nice while it lasts, and too much of it can give you diabetes.

Kingsman: The Golden Circle (Originally published September 26th, 2017)
Directed by Matthew Vaughn
Starring: Taron Egerton, Colin Firth, Julianne Moore and Mark Strong

So the first Kingsman movie was a very nice surprise, a fast and fun take on the spy genre with slick action scenes and likeable characters, especially it's everyman hero, Eggsy. Well, Eggsy and the gang return in this sequel, does it hold up? Well, let's see...

Story

A year after the conclusion of the first film, the Kingsman are attacked and all but destroyed by the Mysterious Golden Circle organisation, led by the sociopathic drug lord Poppy Adams (Julianne More).

Following the destruction of Kingsman property, Eggsy (Taron Egerton) and Merlin (Mark Strong) head stateside and discover their American cousins The Statesmen, and the feared dead agent Galahad (Colin Firth). Together they work together to stop Poppy and the virus she has released in contaminated drugs, threatening millions Worldwide.

Verdict

When the first Kingsman film came out, it was a breath of chaotic, fresh air. From the same team that brought us the Kick-Ass films, this was a new take on the old spy formula, however, Austin Powers this was not, feature strong language and over-the-top action sequences it was a creative barrel of fun.

Fast forward two years and here we have the sequel, not as creative yet still lots of fun. The action scenes seem to have been refined this time out with the film starting almost immediately with a physics defying car chase involving a souped-up London cab. It's fast, it's visceral and it jumps straight off the screen, grabbing your attention like an angry, drunk man at a bus station.

Unlike an angry, drunk man however, the film has likeability in spades, in particular main character Eggsy, is just as likeable as he was last time out, in fact, more so, as the edges have been smoothed out from last time out, he's actually given a love story with the princess from the end of the first film, which is a nice side development which occasionally intertwines with the main plot. The returning players from last time out all bring their usual gifts to the film, Colin Firth (who I take no shame in spoiling as he's openly featured in the trailer) shows his charisma and charm and even some vulnerable moments and Mark Strong is well... strong in the part of Merlin, reliable as ever as an actor, he's even given a few moments to shine, which is nice.

Elsewhere, the newcomers are a mixed bag, Channing Tatum is unremarkable in the film, bringing little to proceedings besides a preposterous Southern accent and a scene in his underwear, which I think must be added to all Channing Tatum films by law. Then there's Jeff Bridges as 'Champ' the leader of the Statesmen and like Mark Strong, Bridges is a reliable hand to carry a character, Halle Berry provides a highlight on the American side of things, bringing life to the 'brainy support character' archetype. Rounding out the Statesmen is Pedro Pascal, an actor I have no knowledge of, but did impress in his action scenes and character moments, hope to see more of him in the future.

There's one more stand-out, and while it isn't a spoiler (he's listed on the film's wiki and IMDB page, and also on the credits in trailers) it may come as a surprise to many that he's in it so feel free to skip the following paragraph.

Cameos are almost a staple in films now, and this person's appearance here stretches the boundaries of the word 'cameo' as he has a substantial part and more than a few scenes. This person is pop royalty Elton John. Elton doesn't have many acting credits to his name, so it was a surprise to see him pop up in a film with this amount of exposure, it was an even bigger surprise when he provided me with one of the movie's biggest laughs. He can't be said to be doing anything more than 'hamming it up' but good lord, it was funny. Playing a foul-mouthed fictional version of himself, Elton not only gets some funny dialogue moments, he also gets involved with some action scenes, one in particular including platform shoes, a flowery outfit straight from his 80's collection and several goons. Nothing that will make the Academy take note, but nevertheless entertaining and bizarre turn.

In conclusion, this film isn't as original or creative as the original, nor does it bring anything particularly new to the table, but while it lasts it's an unapologetic barrel of fun, which can only really be summed up with the logical idea of; if you liked the first one you'll like this too, so if you did like the first one, go see it, if you didn't don't. See? Proper consumer advice, don't say I don't help...

Black Sabbath: The End of the End (Originally published October 4th, 2017)
Directed by: Dick Carruthers
Starring: Ozzy Osbourne, Tommy Iommi and Geezer Butler

I was at Black Sabbath's last ever gig. Beating out terrible weather and even worse public transport, which lead to us needed to get a black cab from Birmingham to Walsall, at great expense, but I digress.

It was a hell of a way to spend two hours though I tell you that. Singing along to Sabbath's greatest hits and trying to decode whatever the hell Ozzy was saying between songs, something that extends to the interview sections of this film.

Story

Not so much a story in this one to be honest, footage of the band's final ever show is interlaced with interviews with the band after the concert and footage of a studio session that took place after the concert.

Verdict

As much as this movie is about celebrating Sabbath's music and legacy, it has a surprising amount of heart. Throughout the movie the members of the band talk about each other with incredible admiration, especially when talking about Tony's battle with lymphoma, and about his incredible ability to come up with catchy riffs.

It's amazing that after nearly 50 years and the multiple fallings-out they talk so admiringly about each other, Ozzy for example was full of praise for Geezer Butler's lyrics, at least that's what I think he was saying, he could have been complimenting the carpet for all I know, I'm joking of course, although he is getting harder and harder to understand, I can only imagine what he sounded like when he was drinking, oh wait, I could just watch the Osbourne's.

The film takes an emotionally turn most of the way in, when it touches on Tony Iommi's battle with cancer part way through the recording of their latest album, the members of the band talk frankly about his struggle and his resolve to keep working through his chemo, in particular the admiration in Geezer Butler's face for his friend.

Having been through all that Iommi's playing is still incredible, and Ozzy sounds like he did on the records 40+ years ago, unfortunately they are missing Bill Ward, the drummer, however the guy they have filling in, Tommy Clufetos is just as good if not better in some ways.

In conclusion, it was amazing to have been there live, and it was great to relive that night and it's worth watching for long-time fans, or just fans of heavy metal/rock not just for the concert clips but the insightful interviews, and backstage clips, if you're into it pre-order the Blu-ray and enjoy yourself.

IT (Originally published October 5th, 2017)
Directed by Andy Muschietti
Starring: Bill Skarsgard, Jaeden Lieberher, Sophia Ellis and Finn Wolfhard

I'm not all that big on horror movies to be perfectly honest, movies don't scare me, they never really have, sure they can startle and make me jump a few times, but most movies don't have the right elements of horror to actually scare me, I am however, a big fan of the works of Stephen King, not because they scare me but because they're so well written that I'm invested and from time to time send a shiver down my spine.

Did It scare me? No. Did I enjoy it? Very much so, yes.

Story

One stormy night, a young boy with a paper boat encounters Pennywise the Dancing Clown, an incarnation of the demonic entity It.

Following this a group of unpopular youngsters pursue the demented clown, fighting their own fears along the way.

Verdict

The main bit of praise I can give this film is it's characterisation, each of the child characters has their own struggles and problems, which really makes you empathise with them, sure a lot of them fall into archetypes, but it's the way those archetypes are then carried off and built upon and for the most part their all used incredibly well, in no particular order these are the main characters: The grieving brother with a speech impediment, the tomboyish girl, the loudmouth, the Jew, the hypochondriac, the fat one and let's not forget, the Black one. That probably doesn't sound like praise but what they do to carry these characters, each had a specific fear, and each had their own problems.

They're also being terrorised by a group of bullies, led by the sadistic Henry Bowers, whose sanity gradually deteriorates throughout the run time, which unites the group as one, against Pennywise and Henry.

Now let's turn our attention to the actors bringing this to the screen, starting with Bill Skarsgård, who portrays Pennywise, incredibly well it must be said, his creepiness factor is through the roof, the smile, the voice, all of it is chilling. It must also be said that all of the children are incredibly promising, especially Jaeden Lieberher who portrays Bill Denbrough, the brother of Pennywise's first on-screen victim Georgie and Sophia Lillis who plays Beverley Marsh, a sexually abused tomboy accused of promiscuousness at school, who shows herself to be incredibly brave and an asset to the group, I think these two young actors have a bright future.

Another great part of the film is it's direction, specifically the opening scene with Georgie and the boat in which we're introduced to Pennywise, the way it's shot with the weather and use of shadows is incredible, and another scene which I don't wish to spoil (it includes a creative use of hair and blood) is another standout.

In conclusion, this is a movie defies genres, yes it's a horror movie, but it also has the hallmarks of a coming of age drama, in the style of Stand By Me as well as a few comedic moments, if like me, you're not a big fan of horror, give it a go anyway, you might be impressed.

Chapter Three: November/December 2017

<u>Thor: Ragnarok</u> (Originally published November 2nd, 2017)
Directed by Taika Waititi
Starring: Chris Hemsworth, Tom Hiddleston, Cate Blanchett and Mark Ruffalo

I must admit to a bit of superhero fatigue at this point, there never seems to be a point where there isn't a new superhero movie out. This is after all the third Marvel Cinematic Universe offering this year alone, combined with DC's efforts this year, it adds up to a whole lot of superheroes. You can have too much of a good thing after all.

The first two Thor movies are probably two of my least favourite MCU movies, both were nothing special and the second one was aggressively dull. However the trailers for this seemed to indicate a change in tone for the God of Thunder, did it work?

Story

Thor is haunted by visions of the fall of Asgard. He is however kept prisoner on a planet ruled by an eccentric leader and forced to do battle with his fellow Avenger, Hulk.

Together with Hulk, and his untrustworthy brother Loki, Thor must stop his sister, the Goddess of Death, Hela, from destroying Asgard for good.

Verdict

One thing is clear from Thor's very first scene, this is not the same Thor from The Dark World. He's lighter, more sarcastic and irreverent. The cynic in me thinks that Marvel has looked at the success of Guardians of the Galaxy's lighter, more comedic tone and decided to run with it with Thor.

The comparison with Guardians doesn't end with the comedy, it's space setting and visual design sometimes invokes thoughts of Guardians too. This movies comedy is a little hit and miss at times, at its worst it seems forced and hackneyed, but at its best makes Thor a more approachable, and likeable, character. Of course there was comedic moments in the first two, not on the scale of this though.

Make no mistake, Thor: Ragnarok is a very good movie for its genre, it's visually stunning and its tone remains consistent, to me it's a great deal better than its two predecessors.

I think a lot of the improvements can be credited to a change of director, and a new vision. The movie's director, Taika Waititi, who himself features in this movie as a humorous side character, brilliantly crafts inventive and lively action set pieces, as well as actual living, breathing worlds, the planet Sakaar looks and feels like a thriving planet and is extremely visually interesting. The direction of the climactic battle on Asgard is also breath-taking.

The cast assembled is one of immense talent also, we of course have the returning favourites: Chris Hemsworth, Tom Hiddleston and Mark Ruffalo, who as always capture their characters brilliantly, Hiddleston's Loki has always been a stand-out character from right back in Phase One and his character development in this movie helps to make him a complete character, as opposed to a complete 'villain'. Something must also be said about the chemistry between Ruffalo and Hemsworth on screen, their interactions jump right off the screen as their characters come together so well, a good example of which is seen in scenes on Sakaar.

As for the newcomers, we had two brand new antagonists, firstly Jeff Goldblum as The Grand Master on Sakaar. This was typical Goldblum fare, an eccentric and colourful character that fits him right down to the ground, it seems like he had tremendous fun in this part, his character doesn't turn out to be massively significant to the story as a whole, especially in the later stages, but he helps flesh out the world while he's there.

Then, as the film's 'big bad' we have a turn from Cate Blanchett as Hela, Thor and Loki's previously unseen sister, and the Goddess of Death. It's nice in a Marvel movie, which are often criticised for having weak villains, to see a powerful villain who are not only a threat to the heroes but are perhaps stronger, making the heroes need to think to defeat them in the climactic battle. Blanchett's performance is strong and domineering, occasionally wandering into hammy territory, but if anything, this works with the films tone, especially sharing villain duties with the equally hammy Goldblum.

In conclusion, Marvel's strong streak continues with this visually impressive and warm movie, which helps move the whole plot of the MCU a step towards its eventual endgame, Infinity War.

Raging Bull (Originally published November 8th, 2017)

Directed by: Martin Scorsese
Starring: Robert DeNiro, Joe Pesci, Cathy Moriarty and Nicholas Colasanto

A few months ago, I mentioned I was going to start review classic movies as well as current cinematic releases, well it's taken me a while but here we go.

Martin Scorsese is a filmmaker of great renown, in fact that may be an understatement, he's practically Hollywood royalty. With a string of classics as long as your arm on his CV he is quite rightly regarded as one of the greatest filmmakers of all time.

His partnership with Robert DeNiro is also a highly regarded one and has heralded such acclaimed movies as *Taxi Driver (1976)* and *Goodfellas (1990)*. This is seen as a seminal Scorsese work, even being described as his 'magnum opus'. With that said, let's take a look.

Story

Jake LaMotta is a hard-hitting middleweight boxer, known for being a bully both in and out of the ring. Jake navigates the hardships in the ring and in his troubled home life with the help of his younger brother and manager Joey, but his life is only ever one fight away from unravelling completely...

Verdict

It's been a long time since I've seen a movie as visually stunning as Raging Bull, shot entirely in black-and-white, each frame looks and feels like an artwork in its own right. Some of Scorsese's shot choices are utterly breath-taking, especially in the boxing sequences, this artistic filming style coupled with the film's incredible score makes for a visually and audibly stunning experience.

The choice to make the movie black-and-white is an inspired one I feel, firstly given the time period in which the film is based (early 40's to late 60's) it helps build a realistic feel of the time, and practically, the prosthetic DeNiro is wearing on his nose would have been markedly more noticeable in colour, it's noticeable in black-and-white but doesn't compromise the look as much, it could have been extremely distracting in colour.

The acting then, well, as expected from a Scorsese film, it's marvellous. It's incredible disheartening to see Robert DeNiro in a string of second-rate comedies in modern times when you see what he was capable of. Portraying Jake as likeable one minute and brutal and uncompromising next, a scene later in the film showing the character at his lowest ebb is where the performance reaches its peak for me, with all Jake's pent-up emotion released in own frustrating and nerve-shatteringly moving scene.

Supporting DeNiro was the equally talented Joe Pesci. Seasoned Scorsese viewers will know just how mighty Pesci can be, but to a wider audience, he's criminally underrated (his role in the Home Alone movies as one of the burglars being probably his most mainstream role) he is mighty here. As the younger of the LaMotta brothers he is mocked and beaten by his brother, giving him his own hair-trigger temper, but beneath that lays a softness that isn't evidenced in his brother, Joey has the vulnerability that makes him a more complete person, not to mention considerably more well-rounded than his brother.

It is not without its quibbles however, the main one being it really could have been 10 minutes shorter and not lost anything. It has a common movie problem of building to a satisfying conclusion only to carry on for another 15-20 minutes. Some scenes aren't what you would call 'filler' but would have made the film generally more focused if they were cut.

Do not go into this movie expecting Rocky, it is not a tale of triumphing over the odds, it's a gritty tale of life. It's unflinching, gritty and bittersweet, a film that presents the idea that not all stories have a happy ending. The highs are high, and the lows are devastatingly low, and for that reason, it gets a hearty recommendation, this really is a must-see for film fans.

Justice League (Originally published December 23rd, 2017)
Directed by Zack Snyder (except not really)
Starring: Ben Affleck, Henry Cavill, Gal Godot, Ezra Miller and Jason Momoa

I think I've put this off long enough.

So, to recap, this follows the 2016 movie Batman v Superman: Dawn of Justice, a film I thought was okay but incredibly flawed and had the most divisive reception for any film I can remember and Wonder Woman, a movie I thoroughly enjoyed. Will Justice League be another divisive entry into the DC Extended Universe? Or a gem of a superhero movie?

Story

Superman is dead and a threat from beyond the realms of time and space threatens to tear Earth apart. Bruce Wayne recruits new heroes to stop the oncoming onslaught from Steppenwolf and his minions, along the way they must learn to work together to stand a chance.

Verdict

I find myself with an overwhelming case of Deja-vu. You see, after BvS landed in cinemas it left me somewhat perplexed. I had enjoyed parts of the movie and not enjoyed other parts, par for the course in most movies really, I found myself feeling the same about Justice League.

I do think it has been judged too harshly from some quarters and as a whole it was an enjoyable movie, albeit one that didn't know what tone it wanted to have at times, much like BvS but the performances from the new characters were very enjoyable, specifically Jason Momoa and Ezra Miller who played Aquaman and Flash, respectively.

For all its positives though it still falls somewhat short of the mark on a few fronts, it doesn't help that DC are effectively playing catch-up with Marvel over five years too late, the benchmark set by which is unfairly used as a measuring stick. I don't think it would benefit DC to play catch up with the MCU, not only because it would end up fielding more criticism for doing so and really their characters should be able to stand up on their own without comparison. When your character roster includes Superman and Batman, you shouldn't be trying to play catch up with anyone, focusing instead on making the best possible movies you can.

The villain of the piece is another one who suffers from an inconsistent tone. Steppenwolf is established at the start of the movie as an all-powerful destroyer from beyond the stars, yet in the underwhelming final confrontation he goes down seemingly without challenge, I know he's probably a warm-up for bigger and better things to come but the final few scenes really let him down.

It bears the fingerprints of executive meddling too, but I've resolved to not talk about behind-the scenes troubles as really, they shouldn't matter to the final product, there is a few glaring tone issues which might result from changing directors so close to the end of production.

Aside from the performances I've mentioned there's other performances of note, Gal Godot looks as comfortable as ever as Wonder Woman, Jeremy Irons manages to pull off a sarcastic Alfred pretty well. It's such a shame that Ben Affleck looks as though he's on autopilot for most of the movie. Watching promotional interviews prior to release, Ben looked like a broken man, crushed under the weight of unwarranted criticism, his despondency is visible in times on screen as he coasts through his scenes, he's in no way bad, just that it looks like he's been drained of all enthusiasm between movies.

In conclusion then, Justice League is a bit of an odd duck. Enjoyable in places and extremely flawed in others, if you're invested in the series then it's definitely worth your time, I'd hold out for a potential Director's Cut Blu-Ray though, if one is forthcoming. Don't let its mixed reviews put you off however, it really is one that you have to see and make an opinion of for yourselves.

Star Wars: The Last Jedi (Originally published December 29th, 2017)
Directed by: Rian Johnson
Starring: Daisy Ridley, John Boyega, Mark Hamill and Carrie Fisher

For the past three years, I've been to the cinema at midnight, on a cold December evening to see the new Star Wars film. I go with the same friend every year, it's become a little pre-Christmas tradition for us, we spend months pawing over every trailer and screenshot until the fateful day where we sit in a cinema, with hundreds of other sad individuals just like us, so we can see it as soon as possible.

In 2015, it was The Force Awakens, it felt like a true return to a pinnacle Star Wars hasn't reached since, arguably, The Empire Strikes Back, in short, it made me so happy to be a Star Wars fan. Then, the following year, the first spin-off arrived, Rogue One, which was something completely different, yet added something to the overarching series.

Both times I came out of the cinema enthralled and starry eyed, eager to see it again, this year however, I left the cinema with more questions, and wanting to see it again to make sure I got everything, still wanting to see it again, must be good right? In fact, I'll go so far as to say, it's been the one where I've most wanted a second viewing. so let's see what I gleamed from two showings of the latest offering shall we?

Story

Straight after the events of Force Awakens, Rey must persuade Jedi Master Luke Skywalker to train her, and help the Resistance defeat the sinister First Order. Meanwhile, the influence of the First Order grows by the day and the Resistance must struggle to survive.

Verdict

Oh, boy, this is a fun movie to try and review without spoilers.

The Last Jedi isn't the follow-up to The Force Awakens I expected. A lot of things I saw happening went in a completely different direction, some for the better and some for the worse.

The first thing I can say is it's an incredibly long film, around 2hrs 45mins I'd say, if not pushing 3 hours, it is however, filled to the brim with events and ideas that sometime struggle to contain themselves neatly within the narrative, also there are some problems with inconsistencies that often comes with a bulky run-time such as this.

At times it feels like Rian Johnson had a completely different vision for the series than JJ Abrams, which would be okay normally, but since JJ is directing Episode 9 now, it'll be interesting to see where he takes the story. The reason I say this is the tone taken by Johnson is different in feel to Abrams' whereas Abrams favours a clean, almost colourful aesthetic, Johnson favours a darker, grittier one, with an abundance of the colour red.

This, in itself, is not a bad thing, and The Last Jedi is not a bad film. In fact it's a very good film, it is in fact, a very different film, therein lies the reason for the fan backlash in some quarters. Fans of series like Star Wars get invested in the series to a point where they make up their own narratives, when these narratives aren't played out on screen, they lash out.

This happens wherever there is fandom, it is unavoidable. There is surely a corner of the internet that despises the Disney Star Wars films, like there is one that despises new Star Trek and new Doctor Who, the list goes on.

Objectively, as a film and as a Star Wars film, The Last Jedi is very good, there are a few moments that stand out as some of the best Star Wars has to offer, it's space battles for instance are top notch. Equally there are some things I don't like about the film, things I won't detail because of spoilers but there one in particular one thing that almost took me out of the movie completely. Something that objectively might make sense the more you think about it but still doesn't fit in with what the movie teaches us.

It may help if I do a spoiler-y post soon to help properly explain my grievances, but please don't go away from this thinking I disliked TLJ, because I didn't, I found it's narrative (for the most part) enthralling and it's new and returning characters engaging, I don't agree with the sectors of fans who have ridiculed the movie, I'm sure if you looked hard enough you'd find someone who doesn't like the most critically acclaimed of movies.

My advice is, ignore what you may hear, as always go in to these objectively, oh and take plenty of snacks because it's a long one.

Chapter Four: Other Writing of 2017

How Many Sequels Do We Need? (Originally published June 6th, 2017)

I've long said that there is no one in Hollywood as artistically bankrupt as Michael Bay. Churning out inconsequential sequel after inconsequential sequel adding about as much to Hollywood as a fart does to a funeral.

The Transformers films are the worst. I go to the cinema quite often, so as a result just recently I've been 'treated' multiple times to the trailer for the next execrable explosion and stereotype extravaganza, and it seems to my immense surprise that absolutely zero has changed over five films.

How many magical McGuffins can one universe possibly have? I say this because it seems in every Transformers film there's an artefact that a certain Transformer wants that's been here for 'thousands of years' and lo and behold there's one in this too, according to the trailer, as well as a stereotypical black character who spends the trailer saying stereotypically black things, oh and also, Optimus Prime is evil now, which is something every bad screenwriter does when they're out of ideas.

There's now talk of a Transformers shared universe too, well it makes sense, everyone else is having one, and I'll be damned if we don't give Michael Bay another billion dollars to go on his money pile at his mansion made of gold.

It really annoys me that cinema goers will throw millions, if not billions, of dollars at the latest unimaginative sequel yet new properties with promise and imagination are left to scrape the bottom of the box office with nothing to show for it except a few good reviews. For example, Suicide Squad despite being the cinematic equivalent of herpes made $745.6 million dollars against a $175 million budget. Both of the last two wretched Transformers movie made over a billion dollars. Conversely, Moonlight, this past years Best Picture Oscar winner mind you, only managed to make $65 million, there's something very wrong there.

I'm not completely against sequels, despite what the previous five paragraphs tell you, I just think a sequel should have a reason to exist other than needing another money pit to swim in. I like some sort of story progression. Take the Marvel Cinematic Universe, true not all films are sequels to each other but it's been building a story arc for ten years, and doing so very well, granted there are some duds in there, Iron Man 2 and both Thor movies spring to mind, but as a general rule, it's done a great job in building stakes up to a huge conclusion, it has a reason to be a shared universe, after all there's more Marvel super heroes than you can shake a stick at, not all of whom deserve a movie, I'm not holding out fora Squirrel Girl movie anytime soon, but it has the material.

I'd like to end on another example of Hollywood circling the drain. I was recently dragged to the cinema by my better half to see The Boss Baby, an experience I found only slightly better than having nails jammed in my eyes (my other half liked it, because she has the taste of a seven-year old) yet imagine my dismay when I saw on Twitter DreamWorks announcing a sequel. While I will be avoiding it like the plague, so it won't affect me, why does it need to exist? The 'story' for lack of a better term, left no jumping off point for a sequel, and while it's popular with kids, so is eating dirt and I can't see that getting a shared universe anytime soon.

The Great Doctor Debate (Originally published June 10th, 2017)

I'll be the first to tell you that I'm a bit obsessed with Doctor Who. I have well over 100 DVDs of it, Classic and NuWho, not to mention knowing slightly too much about it, seriously I'm like a living Doctor Who Encyclopaedia.

What with the latest series currently lighting up airwaves and gaining much (deserved) acclaim, I thought I'd add my hat in the ring as to my hopes for the new inhabitant of the TARDIS and the future AND rank the Doctors by my opinion worst to best! I'm spoiling you with two columns in one!

The Bookie's Favourites:

Phoebe Waller-Grace: I was hooked on Waller-Grace's sitcom Fleabag, it was a refreshing change to see a female sex-obsessive in a sitcom for a change, and for what it's worth, she is very charming and charismatic, with just the right sprinkling of kookiness, I would only like to see a female cast if it isn't a stunt however, I'd love to see a female Doctor, but not for a female Doctors sake.

Kris Marshall: The bloke from the BT ads as the Doctor, who'd have guessed? Apparently borne of wanting a David Tennant-esque Doctor again (which strikes me as a step backwards) he does have his own merits, I can't say personally that I've seen a lot of what he's been in, but I used to like My Family, and I hadn't watched anything of Tennant or Smith's prior to their casting so who knows?

Richard Ayoade: Now we're talking! Seriously, though how does this concept not intrigue you? The IT Crowd star would fit in great as an awkward yet smart Doctor, using brains rather than Braun, not to mention his own creative endeavours, he could add to the show behind the scenes too, which would be nice. Also, he'd be the first missed-race Doctor, which is also nice.

Tilda Swinton: She's somewhat dropped off in betting odds now, but I think Ms Swinton would be the best choice of the bunch. Possessing a great range of acting talent not to mention a certain air of authority that's very rare in actresses, she'd be able to balance The Doctor's funnier and dramatic sides in equal measure, however, her ever increasing schedule makes her casting highly unlikely.

My Dream Doctors (My Sometimes-Ridiculous Suggestions)

Benedict Cumberbatch: A serious suggestion to start us off. Benedict Cumberbatch is an actor of astounding talent, who I think would have made a great Doctor, HOWEVER, now he's played Sherlock, it would rule out him ever been cast for me, the characters are often similar enough as it is without having the same actor, however, him playing The Master would be a different kettle of fish...

Tim Minchin: Weird and Clever. Two words that could describe both The Doctor and Tim Minchin. Seriously though he's got the sort of image that would make an eccentric Doctor, and the charisma to back it up, the biggest drawback being his inexperience in acting. Sure, he has credits under his belt, but it'd be a risk, not the first time they've cast someone with inexperience though.

Sean Pertwee: Specifically, I'd like to see Sean step into the Third Doctor's shoes, so we can include that incarnation in any future multiple Doctor specials (You can also could Reece Shearsmith as the Second Doctor). Sean not only looks like his dad (Eerily so) he has the chops too; I have no doubt it's make a great treat to see the 'Man of Action' Doctor karate chop his way through a 60th anniversary special.

Paul McGann: The fact Paul McGann hasn't had a series of his own is an absolute travesty. As a listener to the Big Finish audio dramas, I can tell you that assuredly. His work in Big Finish can often dwarf a lot of the TV Series, especially Lucie Miller/To the Death (Go and buy them, they're great). I'm not proposing he regenerate back into McGann, just that he get a standalone series of his own, I'm sure if he did, he'd rocket up people's favourites list.

The Ranking:

I've thought long and hard about the criteria for this list, as previously mentioned I am a Big Finish listener, and the Doctors who would grace the bottom of the TV Doctor's list would jump up the list pretty quick if Big Finish was brought into account, Colin Baker being a great example of that. But for clarity, I'm going to rank based only on TV performances, to put them all on a level playing field. Also remember this is a list of my FAVOURITE Doctors, not the best. Okay? Here we go...

13: Colin Baker (Sixth Doctor, 1984-1986)

Poor Colin Baker, not only did he get shafted by the costume department, that coat lives in my nightmares, but by this time, the series wasn't exactly top of BBC's priorities list, this resulted in a lack of support and a lack of budget, which in turn lead to poor stories and poor ratings. The BBC were so fed up of Doctor Who by this point they put the show on an 18-month hiatus in the middle of Colin's run.

Had I included Big Finish stories, Colin would be much further up the list, he's proven himself extremely capable with the right scripts and support, but his TV stories were never really above decent (Except Vengeance on Varos, that one is very good).

Recommended Story: Vengeance on Varos

12: Peter Davison (Fifth Doctor, 1981-1984)

The second doctor in that I feel sorry for, doesn't really look good does it? Given the unenviable task of following Tom Baker in the TARDIS, Peter Davison always came across as someone very capable, yet also somewhat bland. He had good stories don't get me wrong, Caves of Androzani frequently ranks among the best of all time, but he never felt as though he put his own stamp on the character.

Recommended Story: The Caves of Androzani

11: Paul McGann (Eighth Doctor, 1996)

Make that three in a row that have my sympathy. Given one episode in the mid-90's to sell a series to an American audience who only really knew Tom Baker in the role, and given a mediocre script, McGann couldn't resurrect the series for long as he was one and done. Until 2013 that is, where he reminded us what we all missed.

Having said that, I've seen what American producers had planned for their Doctor Who, in retrospect I'm glad we didn't get that series.

Recommended Story: The Night of the Doctor

10: Sylvester McCoy (Seventh Doctor, 1986-1988, 1996)

It could be argued that McCoy played two different doctors, he changed his portrayal so drastically. Going from a clowning figure in his earliest appearances he transformed into a manipulative, darker incarnation and he did so well, the final classic series seemed to be bringing the whole thing back to its halcyon days in terms of quality, then the plug was pulled and that was all she wrote.

Recommended Story: Remembrance of the Daleks

9: John Hurt (War Doctor, 2013)

All it took was one episode for John Hurt to win the hearts of Whovians worldwide, such was the strength of his performance. Exploring a previously unexplored version of The Doctor, the one from The Time War, Hurt played a jaded, battle-scarred version of the Time Lord, one who didn't even call himself The Doctor, unfortunately John Hurt passed away in January of this year, leaving a legacy as a magnificent character actor, and with this performance, always a Doctor.

Recommended Story: The Day of the Doctor

8: William Hartnell (First Doctor 1963-1966, 1973)

William Hartnell's importance cannot be understated. Without his guidance and ability, I wouldn't be sitting here nearly 54 years after he started playing The Doctor. In short, he made Doctor Who's popularity, he set the stage for all his successors. Bringing with him an air of authority, he could be grumpy old man one minute and compassionate loving Grandfather the next, his speech in The Dalek Invasion of Earth is still referred to these days, and for good reason, that's as good a testament as ever for William Hartnell.

Recommended Story: The Dalek Invasion of Earth

7: Christopher Ecclestone (2005)

I really wish I could put him higher. I wish I lived in a universe where he made three series as The Doctor. It's no exaggeration to say that without Christopher Ecclestone, the revival of Doctor Who could have been another Crossroads. He could be comedic and still carry the regret of the war he'd just struggled through, he was wary of things, and boy could he soliloquy, Ecclestone was 'Fantastic' (see what I did there?) but with a lack of adventures, he can't go any higher for me.

Recommended Story: The Empty Child/The Doctor Dances

6: Patrick Troughton: (1966-1969, 1983, 1985)

'The Cosmic Hobo' was the successful experiment that would eventually become Regeneration, he set the bar. It's a real shame that a big chunk of his adventures are 'missing' because those lost episodes were said to be real classics, even given what we have available, it's hard to argue how good he was.

Recommended Story: The Tomb of the Cybermen

5: Jon Pertwee (Third Doctor, 1969-1974, 1983)

The closes The Doctor ever came to James Bond, a real debonair man of action who spent most of his tenure trapped on Earth. Which sounds insane now, but it worked, as he got to work with Brigadier Allister Lethbridge-Stewart, an all-time great Who character, I've always had a soft spot for Pertwee, and after recently revisiting a few episodes, I still enjoy them as much as I ever did.

Recommended Story: The Time Warrior

4: Tom Baker (Fourth Doctor, 1974-1981)

It took much uhmm-ing and ahh-ing deciding whether to put Tom fourth or third, on one hand he was one of the most popular and most watch (not to mention acclaimed) Doctors and on the other, I have much more vivid memories of later Doctors, that's not to say I don't absolutely love some of his stories, my favourite isn't Genesis of the Daleks though, although that is great, there's so much selection. But with popularity comes hype, and nostalgia, and I'm sorry to report some of his stories aren't as good as you remember, but when he was good, he was great.

Recommended Story: The Invasion of Time

3: David Tennant (Tenth Doctor (2005-2010, 2013)

Ooh, controversy time. Many Whovians my age will swear blind that David Tennant is the best of all time, and if that's they're opinion great, and while I love MOST of his stuff, I do say that his Doctor was a bit too human. There was a lot of companion romance in Tennant's era, which shouldn't happen, The Doctor is an Alien for Christ's sake, that's like kissing your dog. I also think he's a victim of overhype much like Tom Baker, some of his stories aren't as good on a re-watch as they are at the time. Having said that, he does have my favourite Doctor monologue, the 'It's Not Fair' one from The End of Time.

Recommended Story: The Stolen Earth/Journey's End

2: Peter Capaldi (Twelfth Doctor, 2013-2017)

I remember being very excited when Capaldi was announced as the next Doctor back in 2013, a very highly rated and respected actor taking the TARDIS was tantalising. I'm pleased to say he surpassed my expectations. There may have been sub-par stories in Capaldi's era, but there's one constant, Capaldi's performance. He looks like a guy living his dream and enjoying his job which is great to watch, he brings a very experienced look and a genuine charm to the character, and it's a real shame that this series, which I think has been the best in many years, is his last.

Recommended Story: Listen

1: Matt Smith (Eleventh Doctor, 2010-2013)

Words cannot describe how much I love Matt Smith's doctor. When Tennant was around, I was a fan, when Smith came along, I was a devotee, from the moment he slurped fish fingers and custard to his moving final speech, I lapped up everything he did. He was the perfect mix of relatable enough to be human yet enough eccentric to be alien. I was genuinely crushed when he left, and I still love going back and watching his series over and over again, I really hope we see him back for a special one day.

Recommended Story: Vincent and The Doctor

And the you have it, my hand is played, I could have done two separate write-up's, but I was feeling generous, and if I didn't do it now, I'd forget. Here's to many more years of adventures in the TARDIS!

On a Positive Note... (Originally published June 22nd, 2017)

A few weeks ago, I took to this site to slate sequels and Hollywood's reliance on them, since then I've realised that the entire piece was much more one sided than I'd desired. So I thought I'd follow up now with a positive piece about sequels, for better or worse they have their place in Hollywood, and media as a whole.

The Marvel Cinematic Universe

I touched on these in the last topic, holding them up as a positive example there too, as I do here, as currently Marvel are leagues ahead of their closest competition DC, yes they struggle on the villain front, but you can't deny they're vision of telling a wide story arc over nearly 10 years of movies, not to mention introducing new heroes into popular culture. For example the Guardians of the Galaxy, I'm sure many people's lives (including mine) are brighter for knowing of the Guardians' existence.

Star Wars (Excluding Prequels)

The recent crop of Star Wars movies have reignited the phenomenon that is Star Wars, spanning from a trio of classic films in the late 70s/early 80s we now live in the second (arguably third) Star Wars boom. Whereas I don't include Episodes I-III in this heading (there will be a write up about them in the future) the spirit of Star Wars as a story has been focused on one bloodline for seven movies over 40 years, with a spin-off universe to come, Star Wars hasn't been better since the Empire Strikes Back heyday, and I love it for it.

Star Trek (Not All)

The second entrant with a qualifier, this may be the only example I know where its sequel is arguably the first 'good' film. Wrath of Khan is a classic that I still enjoy today, and that continued over the next two movies, seeing one good story arc from beginning to end in what should have been a nice conclusion, and then Shatner directed one and well, this is supposed to be positive, so I'll stay clear.

AND THEN, after ten movies, six with the original crew, four with New Generation, the Star Trek universe was rebooted and re-cast, all under the watchful eye of JJ Abrams. With Chris Pine and Zachery Quinto taking over the iconic Kirk and Spock roles, the two flourished in bringing these characters to a whole new world of fans, with a sequel that for me challenged Wrath of Khan (Into Darkness) and an extremely fun third movie in the reboot, I'd hate for them to stretch this franchise into the death it encountered last time out.

Rise/Dawn of the Planet of the Apes

I'm a latecomer to the *Apes* hype. Having only watched *Rise* and *Dawn* a few months ago, but boy am I glad that I did. Telling a tight, engaging story of man's cruelty and experimentation as well as characterising Apes of all things, *Rise* set the playing field for a wider story that *Dawn* carried on, hopefully *War* will wrap the story up in as grand a fashion as the last two have been presented in.

Rocky (All except V)

Right, last one with a qualifier I promise, but *Rocky* isn't just a good story on screen, it's a heart-warmer off it too. Representing Sylvester Stallone's last throw of the dice really, it took him from destitution to superstardom. The first two *Rocky* films are the two classics, based off the classic underdog story in a boxing ring as small-time boxer Rocky Balboa gets a once in a lifetime opportunity to fight for the World Heavyweight title, and miraculously goes the distance with the champ, and number 2 being the inevitable rematch, seeing Rocky come out of top.

The following sequels might not be classics as their predecessors, but I still have a bit of a soft spot for 3 and 4, and a real place in my heart for number 6 (*Rocky Balboa*). 5 being the only one that I actively don't like, it's great to me that a story like Rocky's can be revisited years later from a different angle (*Creed*) and still make for compelling viewing, I would have also included the *Rambo* movies here too, but as much as I like them, I'm not willing to call any of its sequels 'good' in the same way I can't call *The Hangover Part II* 'good' I like it, but I know it isn't good.

The Dark Knight Trilogy

I have saved the best 'til last. What I would hold up as a true peak of comic book movies, The Dark Knight trilogy.

More or less, it was exactly what Batman needed after the career killer that was *Batman & Robin*. An excellent filmmaker with a fresh twist to put on the Caped Crusader. The first movie in the series, *Batman Begins,* sees Bruce Wayne's gruelling journey towards becoming Batman. *The Dark Knight* hits a peak not seen in comic book movies before, by re-introducing Batman's mortal enemy The Joker, played by the magnificent Heath Ledger, but you don't need me to tell you how good this movie is when every critic and it's dog already has, just be sure that it is really, really, really good. Before *the Dark Knight Rises* brings Nolan's Batman story to an end with another charismatic villain performance and the usual stellar supporting cast. Truly a great series.

So there, something positive to read, lest you all call me a misery guts, check back this weekend as I risk my sanity listing all my problems with the Star Wars prequels, which could go on for some time.

Star Wars Prequels: A Rant (Originally published June 24th, 2017)

So, Star Wars is going through somewhat of a resurgence recently. The Force Awakens made enough money to make Bill Gates blush, and Rogue One added another boatload of cash to the official Disney money-pile.

Don't get me wrong, we've been reaping the rewards, Force Awakens was a more than worthy entry into the main series and Rogue One told a pivotal story in the Star Wars universe, but it could have been worse, it could have been MUCH worse.

Cast your mind back to 1999, I was only 4 in 1999 so I'll excuse myself from the reminiscing as I was almost certainly drawing on a wall in crayon at the time. But most of the world were going hopping mad over a new Star Wars film, sounds familiar doesn't it?

Truth be told, Force Awakens is the first Star Wars movie I saw in cinemas, having watched all previous six episodes on DVD after their cinema run, and I consider myself lucky that my first Star Wars cinema experience was the midnight showing of Force Awakens, as I loved every second of it, but imagine for a second being at a midnight showing of The Phantom Menace, I imagine that once the excitement dissipated, it was replaced by disappointment, or in some cases, despair.

You understand of course that Phantom Menace isn't completely without merit, it's just that the negatives outweigh the positives.

I know that there are plenty of people on the internet ready to spew bile on command about the prequels so mine will probably get lost in the shuffle, but still I hope to add so amusing and valid points about this period, I am more offended by the wasted opportunities that the prequels represent as opposed to the movies themselves, drab as they could be. I shall go through point by point and list my quibbles with the prequels, and if any shred of sanity and dignity remains, I shall name some positives.

Killing Off Darth Maul

One potent criticism of the prequels is that there wasn't an overarching villain as there was in the originals, and the thing is, they had one right there, Darth Maul looks incredibly cool, his fighting style was great to watch, the fight between him, Obi-Wan and Qui-Gon being to me one of the best moments the prequels turned up.

That being said, why was the decision made to take a villain, who could have easily carried a few more films, and kill him off in the first film of a new trilogy, he could have even been a key figure in Anakin's journey to the Dark Side, imagine in his final test of allegiance towards Darth Sidious, he is charged with fighting and killing Darth Maul, don't tell me you haven't dreamed of that fight, we all have, and it would make sense, the Sith operate the 'Rule of Two' meaning one master and one apprentice, therefore Sidious would need to get rid of Maul if he wanted Vader, think of the whole story including Maul, and things look immediately brighter.

Racial Stereotypes

Look, I am not an easily offended man, but even I must admit that something is off here. Firstly, the Trade Federation representatives are blatant Japanese stereotypes, it's not even hidden really, the accents the design with slanted eyes, and I'm not going to be an idiot and say George Lucas is racist, that would be absurd, he's married to a black (or African-American if you prefer) woman to start with, so if he was racist I'd imagine there'd be a lot of awkward meals at Skywalker Ranch.

Then there's Watto, I think I've seen propaganda that portrays a less stereotypical Jewish character

No he's probably just misguided, otherwise he wouldn't ask Ahmed Best to voice Jar Jar Binks in an in-your-face faux Jamaican accent. I've just checked, Ahmed Best is from New York City, meaning that the accent was in no way natural, neither was anything about that character, but we'll get to him.

So Much CGI

I'm an actor you know. Well, I'm an actor in local stage productions, nothing on this scale, but I can't imagine having to act to a guy covered in ping-pong balls, or just to a blue screen, in some places here it shows too, some transactions are so jarring that it just makes them look so forced (no pun intended).

Whereas in the originals a nice mix of cutting-edge effects and models and puppets were used, and to great effect, in the prequels, more or less everything is CGI, there was not one real clone, no clone costumes were ever made, because they were all CGI. Which strikes me as overkill, I would have made the battle scenes have much more impact if real people were in the suits rather than a combination of pixels fighting each other.

The Direction

Empire Strikes Back is widely considered the best Star Wars film. It was also the first Star Wars film to not be entirely directed and written by George Lucas, and just look at the results, when writing with someone else Lucas contributed and the movie was great, the same goes for Return of the Jedi (although the Ewoks have Georges' fingerprints all over them).

Come prequels time, it was all Lucas and boy did it show. George was never a strong director as good as A New Hope is, there are cast members who criticise his directing style and going back now you realise that the dialogue isn't as strong as Empire or Jedi, and that returns here, some dialogue is the prequels makes me wonder if George has ever heard human interaction.

It all goes to show that even the best creative minds need help and in George's case what he really needs is an editor.

The Acting

Let me just say, that Ewan McGregor really did his best with what he was given, and was at times, great in the part. Hayden Christensen however, really wasn't. I don't completely blame Hayden, sometimes an actor needs a good director to bring a performance out of them, and as previously discussed, George Lucas isn't that. He's proven to be at least decent in films after this, but God he is so wooden in these films, it's like watching a fence with a face drawn on it. Especially in the romance scenes, to say Hayden Christensen and Natalie Portman had chemistry is like saying Michael Bay makes good movies. They don't and he doesn't.

Elsewhere performances range from decent to grating. Christopher Lee does his best with what he's given, even in his eighties he still wields a sword (or lightsabre in this case) with such grace. On the other side of the scale whoever was voicing General Grievous must have been actively trying to be grating, and that's without mentioning Boss Nass...

Jar Jar Binks

Jar Jar Binks could slide down a flagpole right to the end and I'd still want to cave in his CGI skull with a baseball bat. I don't think there has been a more aggressively annoying character, every 'quirky' speech pattern makes me want to put a hot poker down my ears and quite frankly the rise of the Emperor was directly his fault, seeing as he cast the vote to grant the chancellor emergency powers. So from this we can gain that Jar Jar Binks is directly responsible for all that is evil in the universe and I wish he'd have stayed underwater.

Boring Story for 75% of the Trilogy

Most of the trilogy comes from a trade disagreement. That doesn't sound very much like Star Wars does it? Watching bureaucrats bitch at each other in outer space is not what I want to see, if I wanted to see strange looking space people talking nonsense in a crowded room, I'd watch Prime Minister's Question Time.

All the Missed Opportunities

Let me now list some good things from the Prequels:

- Darth Maul
- Pod Racing
- Battle of Geneosis
- Some of Mace Windu and Count Dukoo
- Anakin's descent in Episode III
- The Lightsabre duel between Darth Vader and Obi-Wan.

A films series that is completely bad can just be put down as bad and forgotten. But something like the prequels who had flashes of almost brilliance to be so utterly banal and boring is the worst thing. What really disappoints me is that had the prequels been handled by another director with George watching from afar, Lucas' reputation would still be intact. Whereas now due to the prequels he's often the victim of ridicule, some of it fair, some of it not, after all, he gave us Star Wars in the first place, let that be his legacy.

Please remember that this is just my silly opinion that is often played for laughs, if you disagree, wonderful, the world would be a bleak place if we all agreed with each other, feel free to Tweet me or whatever for an intelligent discussion, until then, May the Force Be with You.

How Obnoxious Do Characters Have to be Before We Dislike Them? (Originally published June 27th, 2017)

Quite recently, I picked up Uncharted: The Nathan Drake Collection for PS4. I had played Uncharted before, but not really stuck to it, my ineptitude in any game with guns in won out, but this time I've stuck with it, I'm about 75% through the first game and I'm enjoying it, I feel the shooting becomes a bit repetitive and I'd rather be doing more climbing and puzzles, but still an enjoyable game.

Something else that strikes me, is how much of an insufferable twat Nathan Drake is, he's portrayed as this unstoppable hero, but with each smug quip I feel more and more inclined to be wanting to shoot him than the bad guys, who coincidentally, I haven't been told what they've done to deserve shooting at, but they aren't white so that's justification enough in video game world I suppose.

I'm not suggesting Nathan Drake is a racist character by the way, to suggest such a thing would be absurd, especially when he's shooting English guys by his third game, so I better be quiet before the smug tosser comes after me too. He'd probably talk me to death, make me endure his asinine sarcastic quips until I beg for the sweet release of death.

Not that I'd mind so much if I didn't have to occupy the bloody guy for 10 hours plus, each line of dialogue drives through me like a stake through a vampire, yet people really do seem to like him, can't say I understand, maybe it's the fact that his games are fun, so are Batman's games, but I wouldn't want to have a pint with him either, well I would, but not because of his personality, I'd want to share a drink with him because he's Batman, the only drink I'd want to share with Nathan Drake is cyanide.

Maybe I'm taking things too seriously, who knows? Maybe I'm the only wrong one and he's actually a tragic figure who came from nothing? Or perhaps he comes from a background of privilege and uses that to become an archaeologist so he can travel the world smashing priceless ancient artefacts like a certain Miss Croft? Here was me thinking an archaeologist was supposed to maintain tombs, rather than raid them...

Maybe it's because he's American? I'm not saying all Americans are annoying by the way, just that their heroes tend to be cocksure, arrogant white guys with haircuts made out of Lego, take for instance the character Nathan Drake is mostly inspired by ('inspired by' in this case meaning 'ripped off from') Indiana Jones, yes Indy is cool, but from what I remember he's an insufferable yahoo too. I liked his dad better, but then again, his dad is played by Sean Connery, who makes anything cool.

Having said that, take Sean Connery's best-known character, James Bond, sure he's portrayed as being suave and cool, but if we scratch below the surface, we find that he's an arrogant, womanising (and possibly alcoholic in some movie) twat-bag. Is there any 'cool' character in media who is actually a good person? Or just pertaining to the standards of 'coolness'? What is coolness? The only coolness I want Nathan Drake to be associated with is liquid Nitrogen.

Doctor Who Series 10 Review (Spoiler Free-ish) (Originally published July 6th, 2017)

Well, this past Saturday saw the end of another series of the long-running BBC drama, and if I may play my hand early, this might be one of, if not the, best series since Doctor Who was rebooted, join me now as I look back episode by episode over this past series.

Episode 1 - The Pilot

So, right from the start, this episode's job was to introduce Bill into the universe of Doctor Who, a job I'd say it did admirably. Right from the start of the series, Bill seems most like the audience surrogate than any companion I can remember, asking the questions that you'd have thought would have been asked a million times by now.

At the time I had a feeling that Bill was somewhat too workshopped and focus grouped to the point where I was worried it might work against her, with her being not only black, but also gay and adopted, it ran the risk of rubbing people up the wrong way, not that it bothered me, I'm all for representing all areas, I just thought it might stretch the character a bit thin to carry all three, luckily though Bill is incredibly likable, and pulls it off brilliantly.

Establishing Bill's sexuality earlier and passing it off as no big deal was probably the right way to go, it wasn't played for laughs it was introduced, it was established and moved on from as if it was just normal, which is a step in the right direction and shows extreme restraint from Moffat, he also worked incredibly hard to get us invested in Bill and Heather's relationship in a short amount of time, the story and conclusion of it hinged on us buying into it, which luckily it was pulled off very tastefully and the conclusion definitely pulled at my heartstrings, it also planted a seed for later in the series, but more on that later.

My biggest quibble from this episode was the Dalek appearance, it was completely unneeded, and just felt like an appendence for appearances sake, the episode and the series as a whole didn't need it, which is a breath of fresh air, seeing as the Daleks are usually the failsafe fall-back for the show. But apart from that very solid start.

Episode 2 - Smile

Bill's first trip in the TARDIS certainly couldn't be called boring. Landing on a planet built for human colonies by robots who communicate through emoji. I can't say that I didn't cringe when I first saw the robots, but I'll be damned if I didn't end up liking them by the end of the episode. They turned out to be a great framing device around the idea of robots understanding human emotion.

A lot of NuWho's 'future' episodes don't establish the foundations that this episode had, they always feel unbalanced, this however was brilliantly paced right to its conclusion and the fact that we got a resolution that meant the robots and humans could live side by side meant a lot to the humans as characters, a running theme of this series is humanity's flaws, their greed or their wrath, something that viewed through the eyes of The Doctor is strange, as he's never really understood humans and this doesn't help, but here he swung in saved the day and the humans got their new colony. Bish, bash, bosh.

Episode 3 - Thin Ice

A creature under the Thames and less enlightened times. That's probably the best way to describe this episode, it was a nice touch to include Bill asking whether she'd be alright in the past ('I'm not exactly white' I think were her exact words) and I don't remember Martha saying this (although having said that, I think she said something similar in The Shakespeare Code) again Bill is fitting her role as audience surrogate brilliantly.

The story felt very Dickensian in tone, with the rich baron-type exploiting people and things for financial gain and downtrodden vagrant children. Speaking of the baron-type I don't think Doctor Who has established such an instantly detestable character as Lord Sutcliffe, who in one fell swoop shows racism and contempt for his fellow humans and gets a smack in the chops for his troubles from the normally non-violent Doctor. I also like how he established that Lord Sutcliffe could only be human, as aliens would never be as bigoted, which makes you think really.

This episode reminds me in some ways of The Beast Below, only I prefer this one, they both concern trapped creature exploited by humans for their own gains, and The Doctor works to free the creature, a nice little story here, nothing ground-breaking and the kids can be annoying but that's just kids I suppose.

Episode 4 - Knock Knock

David Suchet in Doctor Who? Yes please. David Suchet as a mysterious creepy landlord? All the fucks yes! Honestly this could be one of the best guest spots the series has seen in some time, he slips into the series effortlessly, playing a devious yet at the same time tragic character, driven by an ill 'daughter' that makes him let cockroach-like creatures take over the house, consuming its inhabitants.

The exchanges between Bill and her friends are quite welcome here, it's nice to see into a companions personal life from time to time, not to the extent we saw Clara's life away from the Doctor, but enough is established about Bill to drive her character forward, there's a somewhat awkward moment between Bill and a male housemate, but this is resolved quickly and moved on from, so we're keeping the tone up here.

The ending twist really helped the story too, as The Landlord's story unravelled and we saw the reason behind his motives, it brought great closure to the character, also we got a happy ending where everyone survived which is rare in The Doctor's world, so that was nice, there's some nice moments in this episode but it doesn't measure up as a high point in the series, it's still good, just overshadowed by later episodes.

Episode 5 - Oxygen

I read prior to this episode that this episode's aim was to make space 'scary' again, and well, it certainly achieved that. In recent times space has been somewhat sterilised, and this is an effort to give it the terror it deserves.

It's another episode that focuses on mankind's greed, which may turn people off somewhat, but this episode deserves a watch for the claustrophobic atmosphere and the ideas presented, the idea of having to buy oxygen in space is terrifying enough without the thought of turning into a space zombie on your mind. Essentially people are being killed because it's more expensive to keep them alive with oxygen, so of course The Doctor does something smart and makes it so it's more expensive to kill them, thus saving those still alive.

Now, for that ending twist, I'm trying to keep things spoiler free for those waiting for a DVD release, but I can't go without mentioning this as it'd limit what I can say about future episodes. The end of the episode sees the Doctor going blind as a result of spending too much time in space without a helmet, a near ingenious way of keeping the series free, and pursuing new ideas.

Episode 6 - Extremis

The opening chapter in a rare three-parter, Extremis lays the groundwork for the upcoming story arc surrounding The Monks, a race of decaying-corpse like creatures, who want to save the world, in return for total control. The Doctor is recruited by The Pope himself to translate a text known as 'Veritas' that makes whoever reads it commit suicide.

Elsewhere in the plot, in the past, The Doctor is given the task of executing Missy for her multiple crimes, the running time is spent cutting back to see if the Doctor went through with it, he didn't of course, which isn't really a spoiler because isn't that obvious? Instead locking her in the vault that has been the mystery box from episode one, a bit of an anti-climax, but Missy is always great so what they hey.

The Doctor working around being blind in this episode really is a treat, using his sonic sunglasses to help him, but ultimately, he can't go far because he can't read the text to translate it. Also, Nardole comes into his own as a character here, with some great dialogue, and you see how important he's become to The Doctor, especially in trying times.

The ending is another twist, in a series becoming as fond of a twist as a rollercoaster designer, which leads us nicely into the next chapter of this story and gives us an explanation of how the story can continue, I won't spoil, go watch it yourself.

Episode 7 - The Pyramid at the End of the World

So, The Monks land a giant pyramid in the middle of a tense military zone, bringing their warning on impending destruction with them, insisting that they only help if they are 'loved' and under no other motivation, meanwhile a computer mistake in a lab in Yorkshire produces a substance that can reduce humans to mulch, the threat of ultimate destruction at an all-time high brings the humans to beg the Monks.

The way The Doctor works out what will kill the human race is mind-boggling in his usually way, there truly isn't a room he stands in where he is anything less than the smartest person there, there was a nice divide in this episode too, between The Doctor, who wants to avoid the Monks at all costs, and the world's military powers going to beg them for help.

As the middle part of a larger story it was always going to leave dangling threads, leading into the conclusion, but the way it leads in is entirely unexpected, catastrophe is averted, but the monks are still asked to save one person, out of love, they do and that leads us into next week...

Episode 8 - The Lie of the Land

The Monks rule the world, and no one remembers it being any different. The Monks have whitewashed history so only they are seen as benevolent saviours, all while ruling with an iron fist in their mysterious pyramid.

Once again, we're sent back into Bill's past too, as we learn more about her mother, and the importance she'll have to the world, as well as Bill having the importance of restoring the norm.

Honestly, this was probably the weakest episode of the series, and as a result the ending to The Monks Trilogy falls rather flat, it's a twist on the 'all you need is love' ending we've seen many times before, Bill basically using her memories of her mother to defeat The Monks and then they just sort of leave, while by no means terrible, the series certainly has stronger entries.

Episode 9 - Empress of Mars

Of the 'classic' monsters, The Ice Warriors haven't had the proper welcome back the rest have, sure, we saw them in 'Cold War' during Matt Smith's run, but no full-scale return, luckily Mark Gatiss is here with his clearly classic Who inspired story with The Ice Warriors in full force.

Gatiss is unmistakably a great writer, but his Who contributions have been somewhat hit-and-miss, this however is a hit, as far as reintroducing a classic monster in a big way, I'm surprised it's taken 12 years to bring the Ice Warriors back in full force, as they seem to be such interesting characters, not necessarily 'bad guys' as such, in fact they've helped The Doctor in the past, and here they occupy that same grey area, being awoken from their cryo-sleep by some space-travelling Victorians.

Capaldi is stellar here, as is usual, as well as great guest spot from Ferdinand Kingsley, who plays arrogant soldier Catchlove, another easily hateable character established quickly and dealt with in a satisfactory way.

The ending is also very nicely done, rather than fighting the aliens The Doctor resolves to helping them, in this instance, helping them take their place in the universe, with the help of a fan-pleasing cameo from a certain alien (Spoilers. Shhh.)

Episode 10 - The Eaters of Light

In the same way that it took 12 years for The Ice Warriors to make their full return, it took the same amount of time for a writer who wrote for classic Who to return for NuWho. Rona Munro, who penned the last classic story, Survival, is our scribe here, telling a tale of the lost Ninth Roman Legion and a gang of Scottish children fighting them off.

There's a theme between Munro's two episodes of children fighting something much bigger than themselves, here a gang try and fight a legion of the planet's best warriors, as well as a creature that 'eats light'.

The creature design on the monster is incredible here, and the story successfully makes it threatening to not only the locals but the TARDIS crew too, the whole story feels like a labour of love from the writer which makes it all the better to watch.

It's downfall, however, is it's placement, between Empress of Mars and the Earth-shattering finale, it runs the risk of being forgotten to time, which is a shame, because it's an interesting little story, and it's based in some fact, AND a historical, which many classic Who fans want more of, so enjoy it.

Episode 11 - World Enough and Time

This is the episode I've watched over and over since it aired, it left my jaw slack for days afterwards, and could well be one of my favourite Who episodes ever after a few more watches, it is that good.

The TARDIS crew land on a spaceship reversing away from a black hole, a ship that once was empty, but now has thousands of unwanted passengers...

So this episode saw the return of two major figures The Mondasian Cybermen, not seen for over 50 years and John Simm's Master. Neither of these are spoilers as it was given away in promotional material, so please don't send me abuse.

I described this two-part story as 'Earth-shattering' and that's exactly what it is, it's an episode where the Doctor and his friends are in more danger than seems possible to recover from, back them into a corner and tears the Doctor's hearts out. I cannot put into words just how great it is, it's the sort of episode I'd use to show people what Doctor Who is all about.

Episode 12 - The Doctor Falls

This is it. The grand finale to an explosive series, and what a finale. Carrying on directly from last week's episode, both masters are working on a diabolical plan that it seems even The Doctor can't stop.

In what seemed like an impossible move, it carries the quality of its first part into this one and brought the series to a resounding conclusion in what is probably the greatest finale the show has ever had, it's focused, it's heart-breaking and intense. It's also incredibly difficult to do it justice without spoiling it all.

The conclusion to the series wander into tear-jerking towards the end, but in a bittersweet way, all characters get their pay-off and The Doctor is left with the pieces and refusing to regenerate, when he's met by a big surprise to lead us into Christmas...

So that's it, all 12 episodes ran through, I can't wait to hear the identity of the new Doctor and I already miss watching the show, Christmas will be bittersweet, as we say goodbye to a truly great Doctor, and a controversial, but great writer too.

My Top 10 Movies of 2017 (Originally published December 31st, 2017)

It's that time of year again! People are making merry and drinking their own bodyweight in alcohol and critics are making their annual arbitrary Top 10 of the year list, a practice I'm now going to add to.

A few housekeeping notes before we start, only movies I have seen (obviously) make the list, I have no doubt Blade Runner 2049 was great but it wasn't on in cinema when I wanted to see it so I can't judge it. Also, all but the top 3 are really interchangeable in any order. With all that said, on with the list!

Honourable Mentions:

Two Marvel movies miss out on my top 10 but could have easily made the list if not for a few outstanding efforts and slight superhero fatigue, those two being: Thor - Ragnarok and Spider-Man: Homecoming. I thoroughly enjoyed both movies, but they miss out.

10. Murder on the Orient Express

This year, I craved different movies, I saw movies of all shapes and sizes and this is one I had been anticipating since its first trailer due to its stark visual aesthetic (and excellent moustache, natch) and it delivered a classic narrative and jaw-dropping cinematography, one to look out for when the Blu-Ray hits shelves.

9. Star Wars: The Last Jedi

I know a review of this movie hasn't yet appeared on this site, this is due to me wanting to see it again before making a more informed critical decision, however, the fact that I've been itching to see it again must say something of its quality. It was bold and new for Star Wars with twists and turns and some truly memorable scenes and moments. I look forward to re-watching again and again.

8. The Lego Batman Movie

I know what you're thinking. "How can this grown man rank a movie aimed at kids, a Lego movie no less, above movies more aimed at his demographic?" That's an oddly specific question, but here is the answer. Lego Batman is sheer unadulterated joy. Every frame bursts with energy and love, and it has some of the sharpest superhero parodies you'll ever see, I adore this movie, kids' movie or not.

7. It

In my quest to broaden my cinematic horizons I went into this unsure of what I would think, I'm not a fan of horror films you see, generally they don't interest me. This looked different however, and it's based off a Stephen King novel (King is one of my favourite authors) I came out of the movie utterly enthralled with this movie, it's direction, it's character and plot delivered in spades to make one of the most memorable cinematic experiences this year.

6. Baby Driver

Full disclosure, I almost didn't include this in light of recent events, it didn't seem right to praise it given the apparent discretions of a prominent cast member. That being said; it wouldn't be fair on the rest of the cast and creative to dismiss it from my list due to one specific member of the cast's misdemeanours.

Baby Driver was a movie that truly surprised me, I'd heard good reports in the first week of its release but expected a better than average by-the-numbers action flick, how wrong I was. About five minutes in, I made a realisation: "This is really bloody fun." As the movie carried on, it never stopped being engaging, or fun, which earns it two big thumbs up from me.

5. Wonder Woman

Wonder Woman offered something different than any other Superhero film this year. A strong, female lead for one (seriously, how has it taken Marvel over a decade to make a female-led movie?) peerless action and an extremely strong performance from lead actress Gal Gadot, I look forward to seeing more Wonder Woman in the future.

4. Guardians of the Galaxy Vol. 2

Despite my current Superhero fatigue, there certainly has been some stand out movie in the genre this year. This for me stand out as the best though. Three years on from the surprise hit of the first movie, James Gunn and his roving galactic gang of colourful characters return for another highly energetic romp. I rate this higher than the first instalment however, for its character development, stronger villain and excellent direction. With Vol 3 confirmed for future release, I don't see this gravy train slowing down any-time soon.

3. War for the Planet of the Apes

Wrapping up the best trilogy in recent memory, War delivered yet more of what Dawn and Rise gave us in the past. How many movies do you know of that can make great characters out of computer-generated apes? This also featured the masterful direction of Matt Reeves and a breath-taking motion-capture performance from the master of mo-cap, Andy Serkis. One of these days, the Academy really should recognise the sheer power of his performances in motion capture, as this movie is a masterclass in acting, motion-capture or not.

2. Logan

The absolute pinnacle of comic-book movies. There's an elite group of comic-book movies that transcend the Superhero mould and become something truly special. The Dark Knight is one and this is another. So different to any other comic book movie before or after it, Logan packs a powerful punch that leaves you absolutely speechless. It is beyond superlatives, as is its leading man, Hugh Jackman who for nearly two decades has made Wolverine an iconic on-screen character. If this is his last turn as the mutant, he couldn't have left at a higher point.

1. Dunkirk

Here it is, my movie of 2017. When I saw this back in August, I knew it would really take some beating and nothing has, not only is it my favourite movie of this year, it may be one of my all-time favourites. What Christopher Nolan has achieved with very little dialogue and with a World War II movie no less is utterly incredible. Its direction is flawless, its acting is masterful, and its cinematography is breathtaking, words really cannot truly describe this utter gem of a movie, now it's out on Blu-Ray and I implore you to watch it, it is a true cinematic masterpiece.

Chapter Five: January/February 2018

The Greatest Showman (Originally published January 2nd, 2018)
Directed by Michael Gracey
Starring: Hugh Jackman, Zac Efron, Michelle Williams, Rebecca Ferguson and Zendaya

You know me, I'm a sucker for a good musical. So a new musical film with music from the guys who did La La Land and starring Hugh Jackman? Count me in.

For the uninitiated, this is the musical biopic of P.T. Barnum famous Showman and circus extraordinaire, I suspect it's a highly romanticised version of events, as most biopics are but that hardly matters if the film is up to scratch, without further ado, roll up, roll up and see this review (sorry, couldn't resist.)

Story

P.T. Barnum is a down on his luck, recently unemployed shipping clerk, who dreams big. He risks all he has to put smiles on faces and deliver the best show, to do this he assembles a ragtag bunch of misfits and makes them stars. But will he learn when a risk is too much?

Verdict

The first striking thing about this movie is its startling choreography. From the opening song and dance to the end credits, it looks absolutely stunning as these big dance routines take place on screen.

To that end, there's the music, which is one of the most hyped things about the movie, when it delivers, it delivers big time, there's a fair few corkers in there. From the opening song ('The Greatest Show') to its incredibly well-sung final song ('From Now On') and in the middle a big, powerful anthem for all those who've been downtrodden in their lives ('This Is Me'). I feel there's definitely an Oscar winning song in there somewhere.

As stated near the start of this piece, I get the feeling that this is a somewhat watered-down version of events, as it zips along at a very fast speed, giving the positive of never lagging pace-wise, and a negative of potentially neglecting developing characters. For the most part it strikes a happy middle ground, but there are a few anaemic character moments that feel slightly false.

Amazingly, this is Michael Gracey's (the director) first feature film, which seems even more amazing when you watch the film and see how effortlessly he directs the film, from the big group circus scenes, to the intimate scenes later in the movie, it bears the hallmarks of a director of significantly more experience.

The cast also slips effortlessly into their characters, Hugh Jackman is characteristically brilliant in his portrayal of Barnum, from the lows of unemployment to the dizzying heights of his successes, while also carrying his load of intricately choreographed song-and-dance routines. Other stand-outs from the cast include Zac Efron, who has come a long way from his High School Musical days, fellow Disney alumni Zendaya also impresses, making that twice this year she has impressed me on screen (the other time being Spider-Man: Homecoming) and last, but not least Keala Settle who plays Letty Lutz, the bearded lady, who has a particularly impressive singing voice and acting range.

In short, this is a very enjoyable piece of musical Hollywood. It doesn't quite reach the dizzying heights of La La Land, but it's stand-out choreography and memorable soundtrack makes it a very enjoyable experience.

Bright (Originally published January 4th, 2018)
Directed by David Ayer
Starring: Will Smith, Joel Edgerton, Noomi Rapace and Lucy Fry

I, like everyone else, had seen the reviews of Bright after it came out and resigned myself to not touching it with a ten-foot bargepole. However, fate intervened, as I stayed over at a friend's, I said how I wanted something to review while I was there, and suggested we watch a film, when will I ever learn to keep my big mouth shut?

Story

In a world where fantasy creatures' live side-by-side with humans in a modern New York setting, an outcast orc cop teams up with a veteran cop, they're framed after getting involved with a magical MacGuffin and end up being pursued by both the Police force and a Hispanic gang.

Verdict

You see that story summation? You're lucky I got that much as for 90% of the run-time I had no idea what was going on or why I should care. The plot moves faster than a jet plane, bringing up vital plot points without establishing them and then talking about them as if we knew what the hell they were talking about.

This is a movie with more holes than Swiss cheese, and cheese at least has the advantage of tasting nice. It starts off with some of the most heavy-handed metaphors you'll ever see committed to screen, you see, in this world orcs are marginalised and treat as outcasts to the point where members of the police force are blatantly prejudiced against them. Jeez, I wonder what that could represent.

At the start it's established that our human lead (played by Will Smith, who might as well have had buffering symbols spinning in his eyes) was shot by an orc during what I assume is a stake-out, it's really badly explained, basically one minute they're talking about burritos and the next Will Smith's character finds himself shot.

Then after about 30 minutes of fairly dull 'I don't trust my partner' scenes the plot takes a right turn at bonkers boulevard and introduces out of nowhere that a band of vigilante elves are using magic wands, and this is important for some poorly explained reason. From there Will Smith is blackmailed seemingly a hundred times to frame his orc partner, again for poorly explained reasons.

While I could harp on all day about its plot deficiencies, of which there are many, that's not the only place it falls short, the direction is sub-par for a start. Every scene is so poorly lit you can barely see what's going on, not that you'd want to because the creature design is so god-awful, every scene set outside seems to have a weird filter on that makes it even MORE difficult to see and the visual design is as pleasing to look at as Susan Boyle in a swimsuit.

I understand that not every movie has to be an Oscar-worthy character drama, but at least give your viewers a plot that they can understand, or at least vaguely follow, this movie is just one long insult to its audience's intelligence.

I remember a time when Will Smith was nominated for Oscars, and it wasn't that long ago. Here he sleepwalks through his cookie-cutter character and incredibly uninventive dialogue, I can't say I blame him, even with the terrible material he is still insanely charismatic, doesn't make this film any better to watch though. He spends the whole film phoning it in with the rest of the cast who don't so much play 'characters' as they do stock stereotypes. All the black characters talk like 90's rappers, all the Latinos might as well punctuate each sentence with 'ese' or 'homes' for how stereotypical their dialogue is and all the characters with moustaches are all dicks, because aren't they always.

It may surprise you (or not) to learn that this movie was directed by the same visionary behind Suicide Squad, and if Will Smith had any sense, he'd block the guys number to prevent any further damage to his career.

In brief, this is a terribly shot, terribly scripted and terribly acted movie that zips along at the speed of light, probably hoping we don't notice how awful it is. Well, I did notice movie, and you are truly awful.

Molly's Game (Originally published January 5th, 2018)
Directed by Aaron Sorkin
Starring: Jessica Chastain, Idris Elba, Kevin Costner and Michael Cera

I had high hopes going into this movie, it had a strong cast and was written and directed by Aaron Sorkin, who wrote such films as: A Few Good Men, Moneyball and The Social Network, so it had some pedigree to aspire to, however, promise does not always equal results.

Story

Former Olympic-level skier Molly Bloom, finds herself running poker games for the super-rich in Los Angeles and quickly discovers how much money there is to be made in running poker games, however it all catches up to her when she is indicted in a mob case, as a few of her ex-customers weren't as innocent as they seemed.

Verdict

Molly's Game is a hard film to review. I say that because technically it is a very well-made movie, but practically, it's slow, over-long and unfocused. Not good qualities to have when you have the talent on board your project.

The story is interesting enough, it doesn't focus on the interesting parts however and when it does, it stretches the scene until it's no longer interesting. It's a movie that's almost two and a half hours long which really should have only been one and a half hours, one and three-quarters tops.

The film also assumes that the viewer has a working knowledge of poker, as it throws all the poker terminology it can at you in a relatively short space of time. I've never played the game, and I imagine a fair few others would say the same so that went over my head, and as a poker heavy film, it makes it difficult to get into.

The start of the film occupies itself with telling an anecdote which is only tangentially related to the rest of the film, there's also an undercurrent plot of 'daddy troubles' which comes across as forced, which the screenwriter balances by trying to make the father character as much of an arse as possible, only to be forgiven immediately during one emotional scene late in the film, it just doesn't ring true.

Acting wise everything's fine really, Idris Elba is the highlight as Molly's lawyer, Jessica Chastain didn't impress as much however, she's a decent enough actress but doesn't have the magnetism to carry a film on her own, elsewhere there's Michael Cera who's rather mis-cast, I never can buy him as a bad guy, he has too much of an innocent face, as strange as that sounds.

As I say, films like this that are functional enough to not be offensively bad, yet still manages to bore me at time of viewing, it doesn't make for great material as there isn't enough to pick apart, except for it being slow and the same can be said of Gone With The Wind and that's well-regarded.

In brief, if you like a slower-paced movie with decent enough performances then knock yourself out, I just think it could have been much better.

Three Billboards Outside Ebbing, Missouri (Originally published January 23rd, 2018)
Directed by: Martin McDonagh
Starring: Frances McDormand, Woody Harrelson, Sam Rockwell and Abbie Cornish

This was a movie where the more I heard about the movie, the more I wanted to see it. A murder mystery plot with pitch black humour is right up my alley, what I didn't expect was it to affect me in quite the way it did.

Story

A grieving mother (Frances McDormand), fed up with the perceived lack of police activity hires three billboards just outside of her quiet hometown, Ebbing, Missouri. The town quickly turns against her in support of the popular Police chief, Chief Willoughby (Woody Harrelson).

Verdict

This movie literally left me speechless, I can't remember the last time that happened when I enjoyed a movie so much it genuinely left me gobsmacked, as the credits rolled, I sat there, in silence, jaw slack, this is why I love movies so much.

Let's start with the seemingly obvious, the cast in this are absolutely incredible, not only are the performances terrific, it's also masterfully written as a character piece. Frances McDormand leads the cast, as Mildred Hayes, a mother whose daughter was raped and murdered close to her house, in a complex and masterful performance she channels a mother on the verge of breakdown and a borderline sociopath bent on revenge. As much as we sympathise with Mildred, she's not always easy to like, that just stands as testament to the performance and writing that both sides of the character can be balanced and not seem like a stretch, from scene to scene she can turn the character on a dime so believably it's insane.

Elsewhere in the cast is another pair of layered performances of two characters with such devastating arcs, one of which actually made me shed a tear, unapologetically I might add. First let's talk about Woody Harrelson, a seasoned vet of cinema at this point, if you think you've seen all he has to offer, think again. His character, Chief Willoughby is an anomaly of cinema, when the films sets out it's plot, you expect the usual tyrannical local police chief, only for the movie to subvert those expectations and gives you a sympathetic and thoroughly human character, with flaws and troubles, then an extra twist is added, which in many ways, turns Willoughby into the more traditional protagonist role, it's so difficult to talk about this movie and it's complex twists and turns in a non-spoiler way, but I'm going to stick to it, as it's a film you really need to experience to enjoy fully.

Finally, Sam Rockwell is the third in a trifecta of masterful performances. Portraying the somewhat unstable police officer Jason Dixon, yet again the writing subverts all usual cinematic conventions to deliver a character of such variety that trying to predict what he'll do next is near impossible, it could be argued that Jason has the most satisfying arc of the three main characters, as satisfaction for these characters isn't something that happens frequently in this movie.

Just as I was writing this, the Oscar nominations were announced and as suspected this movie has a fair few nominations, I genuinely think it'll be a travesty if Frances McDormand isn't honoured with the Best Actress gong, I've never seen a performance that begs for the distinction without wandering into 'Oscar-bait' territory (Looking at you, Anne Hathaway in Les Mis. Both Harrelson and

Rockwell are nominated for Best Supporting Actor too, God help whoever has to make that choice.

It isn't just the acting where this movie excels however, as it's helmed by Martin McDonagh (an Academy Award winner in his own right) he's also responsible for the incredible script, the show of a multi-talented filmmaker. Some of his direction choices call back to Westerns, both classic and modern, image wise I'd say it feels most like No Country for Old Men, if a little less intense at times. As a script it brilliantly balances some heavy emotionally driven drama and pitch-black humour without feeling like it's overworking itself, it's also brilliantly paced, you barely notice the two hours go by, the narrative does such a great job in pulling you in early, and doesn't let go until the final frame, it takes you on an emotional rollercoaster that it takes a few hours to recover from, even then it'll stay with you for days on end, there's no higher praise than that really.

In conclusion, this is a cinematic masterpiece, and I speak no hyperbole there. In a few years it'll be seen as a true Hollywood classic. It is, however, an incredibly emotionally heavy movie, don't let that put you off though, it's a ride that you simply must take yourself.

Darkest Hour (Originally published February 6th, 2018)
Directed by: Joe Wright
Starring: Gary Oldman, Kristin Scott Thomas, Lily James and Ben Mendelsohn

Winston Churchill seems, just recently anyway, to be enjoying a resurgence. In that he has been portrayed in one movie or another several times over the past year. I see the appeal of course, with Britain in such a dire state now, many people would rather look back on a time when it seemed we were achieving something, even if that time was during a war.

Of course, Churchill is not the hero he is very often portrayed as, he himself is responsible for the deaths of millions of Indians in what many would consider a genocide, not that any movie would ever tell you this for fear of backlash from the nationalist right, who see Churchill as a hero of the highest order, despite copious evidence to the contrary.

Anyway, once more we go back to the mine of the Second World War in search of a great movie.

Story

It is a time of great unrest in Britain, the threat of a German invasion is becoming more and more realistic, and Prime Minister Neville Chamberlain shoulders the blame for Britain falling behind in the war. This leads to the appointment of Winston Churchill, a politician with many detractors within his own party. Not long after his appointment, the British Army is in a seemingly inescapable quandary and the pressure is on Winston to save the war effort.

Verdict

Over 70 years after WWII ended, it is still seen as a narrative goldmine by moviemakers, as barely a month seems to go by before we slip back into the familiarity of the Second World War. Not that I'm complaining, my favourite film of 2017 was a WWII focused film, so there is definitely room to impress.

Speaking of Dunkirk, this movie can almost be a companion piece to that movie. It's set during the crisis at Dunkirk and large chunks of the film are dedicated to saving those trapped on Dunkirk, so in that respect it's interesting to see this as a telling of the same story but from a different perspective.

Apart from that though, I'm sad to say Darkest Hour didn't thrill me in anywhere near the same regard as Dunkirk. It's another one of those films that's difficult to review, as it's perfectly functional as a film, even on the cusp of being something truly great, but doesn't seem to ultimately satisfy when it comes down to it.

A lot of this could be the familiarity of its setting, the opposite side of the coin to what I said a few paragraphs ago, some of it I feel is that it's a story we seem to have heard a thousand times and as a result isn't nearly as tense as it tries to be.

Of course, even a film we all know the conclusion to can be a tense experience if the movie does enough to draw you in to the drama unfolding on screen, but this, more often than not, doesn't. The plot meanders a fair bit during the middle portion of the film and then delivers an entirely predictable and tired conclusion.

One of the movies saving graces, however, is Gary Oldman. Oldman is a tenured veteran of Hollywood, capable of carrying a movie on his performance alone, while I didn't think the movie was 'carried' by Oldman as it did have its highlights, but the plaudits for Oldman are entirely deserved. If you allow yourself to the entirely engrossed in what's going on on-screen then you could forget that it is Gary Oldman you're watching and could be forgiven for thinking it was a documentary featuring the actual Churchill.

Elsewhere, performances are functional but seem to be massively overshadowed by Oldman's mighty performance, I found a few more highlights were Ben Mendelsohn as King George VI and Ronald Pickup as Neville Chamberlain. Again it's difficult to pile praise upon them when they have to share the screen with Oldman's performance, but had he not been there, I feel they would have received higher praise.

In conclusion, Darkest Hour is a perfectly acceptable, if not entirely thrilling, showcase for the talents of Gary Oldman, it achieves what its sets out to do but doesn't do anything more than that.

The Room (Originally published February 16th, 2018)
'Directed' by: Tommy Wiseau

Starring: Tommy Wiseau, Greg Sestero, Juliette Danielle and Phillip Haldiman

There are many different kinds of bad films, there are your objectionably bad like the Transformers films, which are bad because they're terrible plotted and clichéd but still made with some level of professionalism (as much as I hate to use that word anywhere around Michael Bay) and then there are the films which are so apocalyptically bad, that they somehow come back round to being good, and a perfect example of this is The Room.

For those not in the know, The Room is a 2003 'drama' film written by, directed by and starring Tommy Wiseau, an alien who came to Earth an unspecified number of years ago and has been living among us, trying to grasp the basics of language ever since. Upon its release it was met with widespread revulsion until, like most bad movies, it found new life as a 'cult' film, showing to audiences dressed as characters and armed with American footballs and plastic spoons (don't ask).

So, is The Room a misunderstood gem, or a big pile of dog mess that you've accidentally stood in?

Story

Johnny is a banker in San Francisco engaged to be married to a sociopath named Lisa, who has fallen out of love with him and is sleeping with Johnny's best friend Mark. That is literally the entire story.

Verdict

Oh boy, oh boy, oh boy. Where to start? I watched this movie at university as part of a module, I literally wrote four pages of notes on this wretched pile of wonderfulness.

Let's begin with Wiseau, I would never knock anyone for trying to learn a language and at least trying, especially English which is difficult at the best of times but I'm pretty sure Wiseau just hadn't learnt English, he sure as hell doesn't seem like he can speak it, and what's worse is, he wrote this movie!

The dialogue is the worst use of the English language I've ever seen, t doesn't even feel like it was written in English, it feels more like it was written in a different language and then fed through Google Translate, so everything is just a bit off. Here's an example of some stellar Wiseau dialogue, picture the scene, Johnny was expecting a promotion at work, he didn't get it, here's how the conversation with Lisa went down:

LISA: "Did you get it?"

JOHNNY: "Nah."

LISA: "You didn't get it did you?"

HE LITERALLY JUST TOLD YOU.

There's no end to the terrible dialogue either, it starts terrible and only gets worse. There's a scene about halfway through where Lisa's mother reveals she has breast cancer, and she tells her as if she's telling her she's just adopted a puppy or something. What's worse is the fact that this supposedly vital plot thread is never brought up again, instead we focus on the worst love triangle in movie history.

He also has a real problem with repetition too, as some lines are said over and over again multiple times throughout the movie. Some examples are: "Oh Hi, (insert character here), I don't want to talk about it, and I don't love him anymore. For Christ's sake don't invent a drinking game based on this movie, hospitals would be flooded with people needing liver transplants.

As much as the whole cancer reveal scene is terrible, it's not even the worst scene in the movie, there's a scene in a flower shop that seems to have been edited in the wrong order, a rooftop scene where a character is hounded for drug money that makes no sense and has no effect on the story whatsoever and last and least, a scene where characters seem to be dressed up for a wedding followed by a scene where they're not at a wedding and the wedding hasn't happened.

Every scene has a really awkward beginning and end too, for some reason we have to see each character enter and leave a room at the end of every scene, you know how in other movies a scene will cut after the relevant dialogue finishes? Here, that doesn't happen, instead, the conversation finishes, they'll walk awkwardly and silently to the door and leave, whereupon two new people enter the room and start the next scene. Had Wiseau even seen a film before this?

Then there's the acting. Oh, the acting. Tommy Wiseau deserves a special kind of award for just how terrible he is at delivering lines of dialogue, he stresses the wrong word in every sentence, laughs really awkwardly in every line of dialogue. He's so fantastically inept at everything that it makes him the best thing in the movie, every line is so unintentionally hilarious that they've all gone on to have new life as internet memes.

It's not just Wiseau who deserves ridicule though, everyone seems to act like they're part of a painful GCSE Drama piece. No more evidence is needed of this than the character of Denny.

Ah, yes, Denny, let's study him for a while. We're introduced to this whirlwind of a character in the first scene, where he insinuates that he wants to watch Johnny and Lisa have sex. Ew. It's then stated that he is in fact at school and Johnny is paying his tuition. Double Ew. Then he's threatened by a drug dealer type guy with a gun, he seems to shake this off fairly well though as he's back magically appearing in doorways in the very next scene, where he declares his love for Lisa, in a hilarious scene where he asks if he can kiss her. Following this he tells Johnny that he's in love with Lisa, Johnny is incredibly nonchalant about this and that pretty much all the important things Denny does in this movie, and I use the word 'important' very, VERY loosely.

All the characters are ridiculous though, and none of them are in the slightest bit consistent, in fact, I'd wager that Tommy Wiseau thinks consistency is a country in the Balkan peninsula as it's non-existent here. It's so inconsistent that one character changes faces in one scene. You read that right. An actor playing a character was replaced halfway through the movie. Brilliant.

In conclusion, The Room is everything you ever heard it was. Inept, unintentionally hilarious and oh so stupid. Having said that, I do encourage everyone who reads this to watch it, find a local cult screening buy it on DVD but just watch it I guarantee you'll have never seen anything like it. Or will ever want to. Here's an extra bit of fun, let's all share our favourite quotes from The Room in the comments, I'll start us off.

"I can't tell you, it's confidential. Anyway, how's your sex life?"

Coco (Originally published February 17th, 2018)
Directed by: Lee Unkrich
Starring: Anthony Gonzales, Gael Garcia Bernal and Benjamin Bratt

Pixar have a pretty great average when it comes to films. They came out swinging in 1995 with Toy Story, a film that defined many people's (including my) childhoods. From then on, they've rarely had a flop, the closest to less-than-stellar they've been is with the Cars franchise, and even that stands above most animated films.

So will their new Day of the Dead inspired film carry on their stellar reputation?

Story

A young musician, living in a family who have long since banned all music, discovers that he is the descendant of the most famous singer in the country, this leads to him running away from his family and journeying to the Land of the Dead to seek out his great-great grandfather.

Verdict

If nothing else, Disney/Pixar know how to animate. Every frame of this film is like a work of art, bursting with life and colour, that's before we get around to addressing the film itself.

As a Pixar film, it hits all the write notes, easy to follow plot (which doesn't always mean a weak plot), strong characters, emotional moments and memorable songs.

Most Pixar films are known for having easy-to-follow plots, being primarily aimed at children, this is to be expected, usually however it builds in extra twists and turns to keep the adults entertained too, Coco is just the same, it's a tale of forbidden dreams, something covered in movies frequently, it lives and dies on the strength of reasoning behind the forbidden nature of the dream. At times it's hard to sympathise with the lengths Miguel's family go to forbid music, which leaves all your sympathy to lie with Miguel, I can't imagine this was their intention as the family is not framed as a villains, merely misguided.

Apart from that the film is stellar, beautifully animated and expertly voiced, I can't let a few nit-picks get in the way of how good the movie actually is. Pixar films have a knack of creating characters you make a connection with, this film is no exception, they even manage to make the 'dead' characters feel like living characters in a bigger world, which is some achievement.

The film is voiced by an array of Latino talent (predominantly Mexican-American) who give this world it's living feel, especially impressive are Anthony Gonzalez and Gael Garcia Bernal who voice

Miguel and Hector respectively, they are the emotional heart of the film, the subplot of Hector being forgotten is especially heart-wrenching especially when linked with the living world counterpart of his daughter, the aged Coco, who the film gets its name from.

In conclusion, Disney/Pixar have served up another animated classic that will be looked upon fondly for years to come, keeping intact it's stellar record, it succeeds in building a world teeming with life, despite the fact it's inhabited by the dead.

Black Panther (Originally published February 20th, 2018)
Directed by Ryan Coogler
Starring: Chadwick Boseman, Michael B Jordan, Lupita N'yongo and Daniel Kaluuya

A few months back, I said I was suffering from 'superhero fatigue' after a mental 2017 for comic book movies. Yet, Marvel manage to draw me in every time no matter how many times I say I was going to 'take a break'.

I wasn't overly hyped for Black Panther in recent months, as only a dabbler in comic books (I do keep meaning to get back into them but like many things, I don't get around to it.) So apart from his appearance in Civil War, I'm not all that knowledgeable on the King of Wakanda. Sure, I was impressed with his appearance in Civil War, but didn't know at that point whether he could carry his own movie.

It came round to around February time, and the critics were lauding it, I make a point of not letting other critics influence my own opinion so don't seek out reviews of my own accord, these were pushed in my face on Twitter, normally, such an explosion of critical acclaim means one of two things: 1. Critics have been heavily bought over by exclusive screenings with rewards for good reviews or 2. The film is actually, genuinely good. In this cynical world it's sometimes hard to tell, but let's see what our first full-length trip to Wakanda ended up bringing us.

Story

Following the death of his father in Captain America: Civil War, T'Challa (Chadwick Boseman) must return to Wakanda to prove his worth as a king, and as a Black Panther. His reign doesn't start smoothly however as Ulysses Klaue (Andy Serkis) resurfaces, with a deadly team in tow, including someone with a particular interest in the throne of Wakanda...

Verdict

Every-time I go see a Marvel movie, there's a small part of me that want it to dip in quality so I can justify maybe not watching the next one, yet quite recently, I haven't been able to say that, Guardians Vol 2 succeeded in building on the success of the first film and Thor: Ragnarok succeeded in being a MUCH better film than the first two Thor films and Black Panther succeeds on building a new world that is much more interesting than most of what we've seen in quite some time.

Let's get the obvious out of the way first. This is a film deeply entrenched in African culture and visuals. This has caught some slack, disappointingly it seems for all the wrong reasons. I for one, think it's incredibly refreshing to see a film entrenched in African culture and predominantly black, for so long we've been used to seeing Hollywood so whitewashed that this can come as somewhat of a culture shock. But is, in every way possible, a step in the right direction for equality in film, because it shows that not only do you not need a predominantly white cast to make money, but that you can make possibly even more money by casting outside of the usual whitewashing, and I look forward to what it brings, as I was incredibly interested in the world they built.

Anyhow, enough of the soapbox, how was the film? Good, really good, actually. The film seems to come from a place of genuine love, the world built is teeming in passion and life, not only how the landscape looks but the characters too, how much it genuinely borrows from African culture I couldn't say but it makes me interested to find out more.

What of the characters then? Well Chadwick Boseman is a particularly great choice in casting, he seems genuinely incredibly talented and like he's loving being part of this world but the cast boasted incredibly fleshed out and interesting characters, the movie is fit to bursting with interesting characters, that's one of the few nit-picks I have, the film has all sorts of interesting characters, almost too much as it turns out as they vie for screen time when the most interesting aspect of the story, T'Challa and Killmonger, is unfolding.

All this of course can be built upon in the sequel and I'm sure there will be a sequel, especially after is incredibly successful opening weekend.

Killmonger might also be the best Marvel movie villain we've had so far, someone with actual goals and in a warped way, justification. He is my favourite type of villain in that he's completely justified in being angry and in his broader villain-y, he's just going about it in a way that portrays him as the villain of the piece. Also, Michael B Jordan is a great casting choice, he's an outstanding talent.

In summery then, Black Panther isn't something I can discuss at length without spoiling it's plot and characters, but I can say that the critical consensus was correct, this is a spectacular movie, rich in detail and made with genuine love, if like me you are suffering with 'superhero fatigue' this will go some way to curing it.

The Shape of Water (Originally published February 27th, 2018)
Directed by Guillermo Del Toro
Starring: Sally Hawkins, Michael Shannon, Richard Jenkins and Doug Jones

Something in the past I have been guilty of believing is that Guillermo Del Toro is a 'style over substance' Director. I realise that these are not mutually exclusive, a film can be both incredibly stylish and have substance certainly, but I have felt in the past that Del Toro had picked spectacular visuals over storytelling.

This isn't always true of course Pan's Labyrinth, for instance, is beautiful visually and narratively speaking but some of his other movies such as the Hellboy films and Pacific Rim, very much feel like they subscribe to the 'style over substance' tag. Not that it makes them bad movies, Pacific Rim was enjoyable if a bit generic for a Del Toro film, and I quite enjoy the first Hellboy film.

So to modern times, does The Shape of Water impress as much as the hype tells us?

Story

A lonely, mute woman working in a government facility falls in love with a mysterious aquatic creature, but she soon finds that both her life and the creatures are in danger.

Verdict

That story synopsis is perhaps one of the most difficult I've ever had to write. Not because I didn't understand the story, but because to say too much would give the game away and this is a movie that deserves to be experienced on a cinema screen.

As usual, let's deal with some negatives first. The biggest problem I had (although it did subside as the movie went on) was Octavia Spencer's character Zelda, she felt a little too stereotypical for my liking, especially in some early dialogue. She does come into her own as the film wears on, but for a short while she's almost a caricature of a southern African American woman. I had to dig quite deep for that nit-pick, oh and there's a subplot to do with Russians, because this is based during the Cold War, so Russians must be involved somewhere, it's a law, I think.

With those petty niggles out of the way let's get to the heart of the review, shall we? This movie is stunning, absolutely stunning, yes, Del Toro's usual style is present in all its bombastic ways, but instead of overshadowing the story, it really builds an incredible world, an often-dark world, full of shady characters but a beautiful one.

Everything from the design of the sets to the way it's shot jumps off the screen in another astounding way, Del Toro recently claimed the BAFTA for Best Director, and it is well deserved. A truly great director doesn't just point a camera at actors, he immerses you in new and interesting worlds, takes you on a roller coaster with characters that you grow to like, the fact that they can do so in an arty way is just a bonus really.

What of the characters then? Well, for the most part the people you're supposed to empathise with are well-rounded and sympathetic and the guy you're supposed to dislike is a complete and utter bastard. Sally Hawkins is the lead player here, what she has here is a character that many wouldn't look twice at, she only speaks in a very brief dream sequence and for the rest she uses sign language. Making her character mute is a very interesting choice, a lesser writer may have just made her deaf, and have her use the same language, I can't think of any other movies I've seen with a mute character so it's nice to change it up, even nicer to put that character front and centre.

Rounding out a stellar supporting cast is Richard Jenkins, Octavia Spencer and Michael Shannon. The role of the Amphibian Man is played by long Time Del Toro collaborator Doug Jones, as well. The Amphibian Man is another particular case that I'd rank with the likes of Gollum and Caesar of CGI used incredibly well. The creature looks and acts alive, which is a feat in itself with these things, as computer imagery often ends up being the butt of many a joke, but here you can tell love and attention went into it from the conception stage to the final product.

The plot isn't exactly massively original, the themes of forbidden love and such dating back almost as long as cinema has been around, but the little twists and character developments keep it fresh enough to not feel like it's something we've already watched, which is a feeling I get often with films now.

In conclusion, this is a film that comes with a wealth of acclaim, so my confirming this won't come as a great shock, I don't think it's the best film I've seen this year, but I still loved every second of it, and would urge anyone to head down to the cinema to experience it, if possible, it's a film I can see not transferring well to home media, even though it will still be great the effect it has watching it in a cinema immerses you deeply in its watery charms.

Chapter Six: April-June 2018

Isle of Dogs (April 5th, 2018)
Directed by Wes Anderson
Starring: Koyu Rankin, Bryan Cranston, Edward Norton and Bill Murray

Stop-motion animation is now a rarely used form of animation in Hollywood. There was a time where it was the go-to, most probably because it was the only way technology allowed. Nowadays it's more of a niche thing, Aardman still use it in their trademark plasticine animations and Wes Anderson is fast becoming a practitioner in the art form.

Following on from the 2009 stop-motion film Fantastic Mr Fox, which boasts a similar art style to this film, is Anderson's newest cinematic effort, Isle of Dogs.

Story

In a dystopian future in the Japanese archipelago, a strand of dog flu threatens to enter the human disease pool. The mayor, who is from a dynasty famed for its hatred of dogs, exiles all canines from the city to a nearby trash dump, Trash Island.

As the dogs settle into their life of fighting each other and eating trash, the Mayor's ward, Atari, arrives looking for his beloved dog Spots, starting an odyssey across the island accompanied by various dogs, who all help track down the beloved pet.

Verdict

Wes Anderson is known as a director with an artistic eye. All of his movies are extremely nice to look at, but are also generally complex and don't rely on their looks to carry the film, this is no exception, it's beautifully crafted landscapes and characters look as though they took actual love, and attention to detail to create, as well as the dogs and humans themselves, all crafted in visually unique ways to distinguish them from each other.

The story will likely strike a chord amongst the dog-lovers, as a boy searching for his lost pet is likely to do, it doesn't rely on this angle to characterise Atari though, a lot of effort went in to give him purpose and a backstory up to that point, to really drive home his struggles.

One drawback of the movie is it drags a bit in the middle section of the film, once it's cast and their goals have been established it meanders a fair bit, I feel like an animated film should endeavour to keep a fast pace, as too much static scenes are likely to lose their audience, it wasn't a deal-breaker but it sets a nice pace at the start and once again as it enters the third act, but brings itself down in the middle on occasion.

A massive point in its favour however is its star-studded voice cast, led by Bryan Cranston as Chief as well as turns from such heavyweights as Bill Murray, Jeff Goldblum and Scarlett Johansson as well as Japanese talent like: Koyu Rankin (Atari), Kunichi Nomura (Mayor Kobayashi) and Akira Takayama (Major Domo).

One thing I really liked was how the Japanese feel wasn't intruded upon in dialogue, Japanese characters converse in Japanese, and only when there is a translator character present is it translated, I like this as it gives the feeling that we are watching a living world, despite the fact it makes some of the dialogue redundant to non-Japanese speakers, it feels like we're watching actual conversations, which add to the world very nicely.

Speaking of the Japanese feel, I couldn't judge on how accurate its portrayal was, seeing as I've never been to Japan and know very little about its symbolism and culture, it did seem to the outside eye that it was accurate however, it may not be incredibly accurate, but that is a mystery to me. Something tells me that Wes Anderson isn't the kind of director to assimilate a culture and feel just for the sake of it, and no doubt it was brought to life by people knowledgeable in Japanese culture.

Stark visual aesthetic and underused Japanese imagery aside, how does Isle of Dogs hold up as a movie, very well actually, it's dialogue is well written and it's story and characters very engaging, it's use of music is also laudable, it does not often use a big soundtrack but when it drops a song in, it has purpose and fits into its structure very well.

In a world of cut-and-paste filmmaking, it's nice to come across something that looks unique like this, it simply doesn't look like any other animated movie you'll see, it's charming and engaging and thoroughly worth your time, despite it dragging in the middle it offers a rare cinematic experience that will be hard to duplicate.

A Quiet Place (Originally published April 13th, 2018)
Directed by: John Krasinski
Starring: John Krasinski, Emily Blunt, Millicent Simmonds and Noah Jupe

Last year, in my It review, I mentioned that I wasn't quite into horror. That isn't quite true. I can get into horror, so long as the set-up and execution (pun not intended) isn't incredibly lazy. Unfortunately most horror movies are like this, and you know what I mean, music swells up to a crescendo, thing jumps out as if we weren't expecting it. Or in the advanced lesson, music swells, nothing happens, then something jumps out.

However, like any other film, I like films with good ideas in its head and applying said good ideas in a competent way, that said, let's look at A Quiet Place.

Story

In a post-apocalyptic world overrun by blind monsters who hunt by sound a family must scrape together to survive on their own while making as little noise as possible.

Verdict

I was intrigued enough by A Quiet Place's premise to go and watch it without having heard of it prior to booking my ticket. Sure the set up for quietness as a tactic of avoiding stuff has been used before, I remember a film called Don't Breathe in the last few years, but what in this world is entirely original? Having never seen Don't Breathe, this is entirely new to me at least.

The execution of the silence is very-well executed, thankfully, seeing how the film relies on it, it's use as atmosphere leaves a thick feeling of tension over the scenes, building to when that silence is eventually broken, you feel as tense as they do in that situation as their breath becomes fast and panicked, the return of the silence sits on you like a sheet of whale blubber.

This angle isn't the film's only good idea however, the characters are another master stroke, there are only four constant characters in the entire narrative, which gives the story a small focus while holding larger implications, there are hints at the widespread devastation but we only see this small corner of the world, which gives us investment in the survival of these characters. As an addition, one of the characters is deaf, which gives another interesting angle on events as that becomes more relevant as the story goes on.

At the start of the film, Emily's Blunt's character is pregnant, adding another dimension to proceedings as the difficulties of childbirth, especially one which needs to be silent is brought into focus, this all builds to an incredibly smart scene where all the factors come together as a tense and thrilling set-piece.

Acting wise, it's a solid effort from its leads. BAFTA winner Emily Blunt leads the cast as the pregnant mother trying to get by in an increasingly strange world, Blunt has shown herself as a talented actress multiple time and this is no difference. She is joined by John Krasinski, who also wrote and directed the film, I can't say I'm too aware of Krasinski's work, but I was impressed here, both by his directing and acting, there were some truly beautiful shots in some scenes and his characters emotive motivation are incredibly believable. Blunt and Krasinski share incredible chemistry on screen; possibly helped by the fact that they are husband and wife off-screen.

Even the child actors in this film are stand-outs. Playing the films previously mentioned deaf character is deaf actor Millicent Simmonds who simply did not need dialogue to come across as complex and conflicted. Noah Jupe plays her brother in a weak link in the film, not in any way because of Noah, but his character feels like the one with the least development, he does have his moments but often seems like an afterthought.

It is not by any means a perfect film, there is an over-reliance on jump scares at times, this is disappointing as it does such a good job building a nice tension, also, and this may seem petty, but I think it spends too much time towards the end of the film showing us the monster, I've always thought in these films that what we think of is scarier than what we're shown, and intrigue is instantly lost by showing us the monster, it is however, a very well designed and interesting monster. Blimey that was petty.

Also, it's a very short film, it clocks in at 90 minutes, but this is hardly a bad thing as it uses all it's good ideas and is paced well enough to show them all off without overstaying it's welcome.

Overall, this is a cut above usual horror fare, anchored by a talented cast and an intriguing premise, highly recommended for a different horror experience.

Love, Simon (Originally published April 19th, 2018)
Directed by Greg Berlanti
Starring: Nick Robinson, Josh Duhamel and Jennifer Garner

In this more politically correct age, there is a lot of call for minority representation in film. As a general rule I encourage this, of course it can get too far and cross the line into being preachy and pretentious. Casting minorities for the sake of it is just as derivative as deliberately not casting them, not to say that certain stories don't require certain ethnicities but that is beside the point.

Love, Simon then. For the longest time in cinema LGBT issues have been skirted around or made into overblown statements so I was looking forward to this and hoping it would be a step in the right direction.

Story

Simon Splice is a regular American high school student. Except he's hiding one big secret: he is gay. When he discovers a mystery student post on the school site, he begins corresponding with this kindred spirit, all the while trying to juggle his own struggles, while figuring out who the mysterious 'Blue' is.

Verdict

One positive straight out of the gate is the way the theme is handled. The set-up and execution is similar to many high school movies, the lead is a young, attractive male with young, attractive friends but the fact he is gay is established from the outset and real effort is made to make his sexuality as normalised as possible.

There are a few missteps, the slightly cartoonish other gay student could have been more toned-down, although he does get his moments of character development, the slightly clueless vice-principal also strays into cringe territory.

At the centre of this movie is a set of well-developed characters. Simon (played by Nick Robinson) is an extremely sympathetic character, he makes mistakes during the film, for sure, but this mistakes just make him more human, and more believable as a character. Then there's his friends: Leah, Abbie and Nick (played by Katherine Langford, Alexandra Shipp and Jorge Lendeborg Jr. respectively) add an extra dimension to Simon, somehow, forming a support blanket around him, all the while oblivious to his secret. They are slightly stereotypical, admittedly, Nick is the sporty one, Abbie is from a broken home and Leah is in love with the oblivious Simon. Fairly standard stuff, really although not lingered on too much as to make it seem as if it's their only character traits.

There's also a very multi-layered performance by Logan Miller as Martin, who you will spend 90% of the film wanting to punch in the face, if you're anything like me, which was the aim for his character, I hope, otherwise that just shows that I need anger management.

The message of the film is one that is well-delivered, if you're familiar with the teen movie setup familiar but the themes and characters refreshing in part and textbook at other times. Still it's well handled and the build as to who 'Blue' was must have been successful, as I was on the edge of my seat, wanting to know who it was by the end, begging for an answer and not an ambiguous ending.

The ending itself feels like a triumph, an extremely uplifting full stop to a story that takes you in a rollercoaster ride of emotions in its tightly scripted characters and plot points, it takes a cliché setting and does something new with genuinely likeable characters. Highly recommend if you're looking for a feel-good movie with a big heart and a worthy message.

Avengers: Infinity War (Originally published May 17th, 2018)
Directed by: Joe and Anthony Russo
Starring: Robert Downey Jr, Chris Evans, Mark Ruffalo, Tom Holland and Josh Brolin (et al)

Blimey, this is a big one. (That's what she said)

So, here we are, ten years of ups and downs have led us directly to this film right here: Avengers: Infinity War.

If you've been reading my posts lately, you'll know that I've been reliving the first two phases of the Marvel Cinematic Universe (why not go check them out if you haven't already) and it was sort of leading up to this. My original plan was to have done both phases' retrospectives BEFORE Infinity War's release, and this to follow soon after, unfortunately life, and a few well-timed university deadlines, put an end to those plans, so here it is now. Better late than never I suppose.

Story

After years of anticipation, Thanos finally puts his plan to collect all the Infinity Stones into action. Along the way he faces resistance from heroes of all sizes.

Verdict

Well... this is going to be tough.

Leaving the cinema after the first viewing of this film (for there have been multiple viewings) I was genuinely speechless, Every minute of the two-and-a-half-hours I'd just watched was replaying in my head, every moment, every turning point and every battle, and that tells you more than any words ever will.

As stated, this was the culmination of a decade's work for Marvel, something that was work-shopped and planned meticulously, probably down to the last second. So, they had a lot of weight on their shoulders to knock it out of the park after this much anticipation. Well, mission accomplished Marvel.

A good starting point in going over the film is Thanos. It's strange to think that the first time we saw Thanos was six years ago, when the MCU stretched before us like an empty motorway, we had no clue as to the twists and turns to come. For all criticism levelled at Marvel for weak villains, they really pulled through right at the end to give us a villain for the ages.

Thanos is the best type of villain, in that he genuinely believes what he's doing is for the greater good, and in a warped way his reasons for what he does are true, he just goes about them in a way which makes him the villain. His motivations are clear-cut, he doesn't have a complex master-plan, everything is clear for him and he truly believes in his cause, making him an enthralling watch, every time he graces the screen, there is a feeling of magnetism, putting the audience on tenterhooks in anticipation of what he'll do next, and furthermore, everything he does has a reason, he's clinical and driven, you know what his aims are with little to no grandstanding.

One of my main concerns for this film, and all films like it is, is how they share out the screen-time. With all the heroes in the mix, it would have been easy for characters to be fighting for screen-time, happily though, that isn't the case here. The story is split into segments in different places, putting certain heroes in certain places, creating smaller pockets of teams who can easily share the screen together, that isn't to say the movie is thin on the ground in the epic battle department, because it certainly isn't.

One of the movies greatest strengths is its extraordinary battle and fight sequences. Again, a lesser writing would have piled action into one section where it is over-flowing with meaningless action and thin on the ground elsewhere, but here, they are spread evenly through the movie, allowing the story time to breathe in-between. For a film with a two-and-a-half-hour run-time, the action to story ratio is perfectly balanced, it is not all epic fights, but moments of character development too, smaller stories running underneath the main narrative that give different characters different motivations in the fight with Thanos. They exhibit a spark and polish that can only be the product of directors at the top of their game.

It is likely that there hasn't been an assembled cast with more talent than in this film. Starring the likes of Robert Downey Jr, Chris Evans, Benedict Cumberbatch, Chris Pratt and Tom Holland, to go over every performance would make this review the length of a novel s I'm going to pick out a few people I felt stood out.

Firstly, there's Tom Holland. With each passing film, I feel he comes into his own more and more as Spider-Man, this film was probably where he ascended to the title of my favourite incarnation of the character. He's charming, fun and yet, so serious when needed, it's like someone created the perfect Peter Parker in a laboratory, and Tom Holland is the result.

Then there's Chris Pratt and the Guardians, there was a risk that the tone of the Guardians would clash with the general tone of the other Avengers, this was helped by the Avengers they chose to partner with the Guardians in their particular struggle, but the character of Star-Lord in particular sees some great character moments in this film. I said in my Phase Two retrospective that Chris Pratt and Robert Downey Jr seem to be competing for the 'most charismatic man in the MCU' and we see further evidence of this here.

Finally, and to sum up several people at once, Benedict Cumberbatch was by much, much more interesting here than in his own film, and shows why he is a perfect fit for Doctor Strange. Chadwick Boseman was once again fantastic as the Black Panther, it hasn't been long since we last saw T'Challa, but it's always a pleasure to see him. Elsewhere there's stellar performances from: Robert Downey Jr, Dave Bautista, Chris Evans, Pom Klementieff, Mark Ruffalo and, of course, Josh Brolin as Thanos himself.

It is incredibly difficult to review a film such as Infinity War, as nothing I can say in the grand scheme of things would ever matter, it's made more money than most filmmaker's will ever dream of and it's adored by the fan-base on a never-before-seen scale. Yet on the other hand, it's very liberating, knowing that nothing I could ever say would affect anyone in the slightest (not that it would anyway). All that being said I am so happy that I enjoyed this film as much as I did, it's everything we could ever expect from a film of its scale and then-some, and more importantly, it's made watching every Marvel film leading up to it totally, totally worth it.

Deadpool 2 (Originally published May 27th, 2018)
Directed by: David Leitch
Starring: Ryan Reynolds, Josh Brolin, Julian Dennison and Zazie Beets

I think we all knew what to expect from this. I don't think anyone expected, or wanted, Pride and Prejudice from this film, no we wanted more of what we got last time: hilarity, vengeance and a whole lot of nasty language.

Story

After the events of the first movie, Wade settles into his new life as an Olympic champion, with Miss World on his arm, when an evil billionaire threatens to steal Christmas from the orphans, Wade must take up the Deadpool mantle to once again spread great vengeance, violence, but more than anything else... love.

Verdict

In case you didn't work this out, that story outline was sarcasm, I did it because I refuse to approach this film strait-laced and more seriously than the main character. That isn't the criticism it sounds like, I don't want Deadpool to take anything seriously, and I would like to wager few people going to watch do either.

Ryan Reynolds slips back into the red jumpsuit with great aplomb, just as he did two years ago in his first outing, and he hasn't grown or matured a single bit. All the characters you know and love from the first-time round are back, although not as much as I'd have liked, I'll admit, Blind Al in particular is still a treat, as is Weasel even if the person playing him is of questionable moral standing.

The greatest shame is the misuse of the two X-Men we saw in the first film, Colossus and Negasonic Teenage War-Head, more so for the former as she felt like a break-out character in Deadpool that wasn't capitalised on here, she's given new wrinkles to her character and her and Deadpool's banter game is still strong but it feels like a missed opportunity.

Josh Brolin enters himself into another Marvel property here as Cable, a time travelling mercenary with a metal arm, almost like a character designed by a small boy with colouring books, trying to make-up a character that's so cool in his own head. However, fourth-wall breaking fun-ster Cable is not, and the clashes with Deadpool are as inevitable as they are entertaining, with two of the fights the two have in particular standing out as high points for the movie. Brolin really deserves a lot of credit for juggling roles in this and Avengers and not making them seem identical, and besides his voice being recognisable, I think there are ample differences in his portrayals, which is no small feat in itself.

As for the rest of the cast, it's a wide and varied one, stuffed to the gills with in-jokes and references as this movie is, it doesn't skimp on its casting, the new characters add a certain scale to this that was missing before due to the first films smaller budget, here it lets it's hair down with who and what it can include.

Direction-wise, we've had a change of personnel but not of style, Rob Leitch helmed this sequel after Tim Miller dropped out due to 'creative differences' and given Leitch's love for the stylised (his past works including the John Wick movies and Atomic Blonde) it's surprising to see his restraint on the style front, Deadpool is no John Wick, therefore to frame the film as such would be ridiculous, so I commend Leitch for this.

Given the films R-rating, it's no surprise that the blood, guts and language return for this inspired sequel, in fact I'd even say that the action is better shot and choreographed than the first and is certainly more consistent, the first film was a toe in the water to test it, this film is a running bomb into the deep end.

The only real test of comedy is whether it makes you laugh, and I'm pleased to report that the laughs are another thing that survive the trip to sequel-town, even though they don't seem to have moved anywhere, meaning fourth-wall breaks and inside jokes are the order of the day, I do seem to recall laughing a lot during the film but sometimes the reference or line didn't quite hit, sometimes because it was clunky and sometimes because of its unrefined nature, it feels as though the script was a simple loose document ignored liberally for some improv, whereas this can work out fine on occasion, to roll with it too much risks losing a certain structure. Deadpool walls the fine line a few times during the movie but generally hits the mark, its most refined joke is the opening titles, which may seem familiar to some movie-goers.

In conclusion, those who liked the first helping of Deadpool and wanted more, this is the movie for you, it's scope larger and its budget fatter than before, it is not likely to win over those who didn't enjoy Deadpool's first outing though, but I get the feeling that he wouldn't care all that much. It's dumb fun and sometimes, there's nothing wrong with dumb fun.

Solo: A Star Wars Story (Originally published May 27th, 2018)
Directed by Ron Howard
Starring: Alden Ehrenreich, Woody Harrelson, Emilia Clarke and Donald Glover

I remember having to wait years between Star Wars films, ten years between Revenge of the Sith and The Force Awakens in particular, now we get them ever year, like a sci-fi Christmas, except this one has come just 6 months after the last one.

In this film we jump back in the timeline once more to discover the origins of the roguish Han Solo, and how he met his most famous allies. How does it measure up to previous movies? Well, read on to find out.

Story

Desperate to live the life of an outer-space outlaw, Han Solo breaks free of his life of servitude to join a gang of space smugglers, while trying to figure out a way to get back to rescue his lost love Qi'ra.

Verdict

I feel as though Solo was on the back foot from the word go among release. Star Wars fans are a difficult bunch, as evidenced by the split reaction to the excellent Last Jedi, and even I felt less enthusiasm this time round, and I left the cinema like I wasn't disappointed, not too enthralled either though.

One issue I have with spin-offs is, some feel more unnecessary than most films, but what stands out in the Star Wars universe is that there's so many gaps to plug in the canon that making spin-offs seems like a great idea. Rogue One felt like a story we needed to see, of how the rebels ended up with the Death Star plans, and hearing Han Solo's journey to the confident rogue we saw first in A New Hope seemed like a great idea.

To get negativity out of the way first, the pace can drag from time to time, it's not as long as a The Last Jedi, but doesn't feel like it, it certainly felt like it could use more editing to cut out the filler and focus a bit more. Also, and this is a trivial one even by my standards, the lighting can get incredibly dark in some scenes. To the point where it gets difficult to see what's going on, I get that the parts of space we're being shown aren't supposed to be well-lit and happy places but there's no excuse for putting artistry above your audience's enjoyment, that's just pretentious.

On a more positive light, Alden Ehrenreich and Donald Glover were an absolute treat, Glover especially slips into the slick capes of Lando effortlessly, playing the character exactly how you'd expect a young Billy Dee Williams would have played it and Ehrenreich is effectively charming and loveable, didn't feel like he stole the show as Solo, but he had some seriously big shoes to fill, he doesn't feel like he eclipses Harrison Ford, but not stuck in his shadow either, didn't feel like we explored everything he had to offer. Woody Harrelson was characteristically excellent in his role as smuggler and role model Tobias Beckett.

There was a glaring weak spot in the cast, and that is Emilia Clarke. In Game of Thrones she gets away with her robotic delivery because of her character, here she seemed stiff and awkward, her monotonous delivery not helping matters. She also had no chemistry with Ehrenreich's Han Solo, which is a problem given that she played his love interest. Clarke has her strengths, but they weren't on show here (and that wasn't a double entendre).

Another problem I had in the cast department was the lack of a distinguishable villain, Paul Bettany is arguably the big bad, but we rarely get to see his character, so the final fight seems lifeless and lacking stakes. The scenes he was in were wasted too, he chewed scenery like most villains but as for his motivations. They were non-existent, besides just being a 'bad guy' we expect better.

The direction was competent, in places even incredibly impressive, a few action scenes standing out in particular as winners, but it was very much a film handed between directors, with Ron Howard taking the reins from Phil Lord and Christopher Miller, and it's a good job Ron Howard is experienced enough to make the movie work, even excel in some points.

In conclusion, it's fun to be in this universe for another few hours and it fills gaps in canon (with one event in particular becoming fulfilled on screen) but it does feel as though it's becoming less special with each visit, it's overall a competent and even fun experience but it does drag in places, wouldn't blame you if you skipped it, but it does have some element of fun.

Jurassic World: Fallen Kingdom (Originally published June 7th, 2018)
Directed by: J. A. Bayona
Starring: Chris Pratt, Bryce Dallas Howard, Rafe Spall and Justice Smith

I'll be the first to admit that I'm not all that enamoured with the Jurassic Park/World franchise. I like the first one and its still genuinely stunning animatronics work, and pioneering CGI effects, I wasn't so much a fan of the second and third instalments, I found that the quality dipped significantly with each film. However, I recently returned to the series to see if the first Jurassic World caught my attention, and it must have done, because I subsequently booked to see its sequel, covered here.

Story

Four years after the events of Jurassic World, Claire Dealing (Bryce Dallas Howard) and Owen Grady (Chris Pratt) are recruited by a representative of one of the original founders of Jurassic Park to mount a rescue mission to save the dinosaurs who remain on the island from a catastrophic volcanic eruption, only to later realise that the dinosaurs are being sold on for nefarious means.

Verdict

Fallen Kingdom is not above wallowing in the odd cliché in it's run-time, and at its worse feels like it's running through a checklist of cinematic cliché, but for all that, it really isn't a bad movie.

I think the worst criticism I can give is that its plot is entirely predictable, most of the reason for this is its plot points were given away in the trailers, to a somewhat suspect degree, as you'll realise when you watch. Its twists and turns can be seen a mile off by anyone with any foresight, and the villain's reason for being so cruel is so flimsy it's laughable.

Through all this though, I couldn't bring myself to hate it, it delivers on its promise of dinosaur action and takes an unexpected, yet quite welcome, turn down Gothic Horror Boulevard in the third act that adds some colour to its cheeks. The excitement is phased out quite nicely as to not feel rushed yet doesn't seem to drag either.

Characters contrivances aside, the plot feels somewhat like a Frankenstein's monster of elements from previous films; from The Lost World, we have the greedy businessman trying to profit from the dinosaurs and from Jurassic World we have the genetic mixing of dinosaurs, which I suppose is more of a running theme dating back to the original as opposed to ripped from the previous film, but it does feel like more of a re-tread of the last film in parts.

As mentioned a few paragraphs ago, the film takes a Gothic horror turn towards the final portion of the film, and it certainly delivers the jolt of energy the film needed, as suddenly there was a tense atmosphere, of desperately trying to escape a hyper-evolved being, it's incredibly effective and very well directed too, there are some really incredibly impressive shots to be found in the final third, all of which added nicely to the series' visual flair.

Speaking of visuals, the design on the dinosaurs is as polished as ever, especially in the close-up work with the T-Rex and the Indoraptor (the new big genetically-created Dino) for a series that pioneered visual design it's nice to see that it's still carrying the flag, so to speak, in that regard.

The main reason I enjoyed the first Jurassic World film was for Chris Pratt's performance as Owen Grady, the ex-navy officer turned animal behaviourist. Pratt is an unquestionably charismatic performer and I find his ability to carry a film stunning, and with better material comes a better performance and he nailed the role in the first Jurassic World movie that made me eager to see more this time around.

Unfortunately, I don't really like the character development he and Claire go through between films, the couple splitting up between films cliché is another that the film gladly slips into, and I never personally bought their chemistry as a couple the first time around, not to discredit either performer, I just didn't feel a spark between them. I do prefer Claire's character this time round, as she feels more rounded than before.

One final gripe I had is one I also had in the previous film; I found the child character incredibly irritating. Now, I'm not a fan of child actors, or children in general to be quite honest, it's very rare I ever feel like a child actor has added anything to a film and here she just serves as a screaming mouth on legs, this must be a thing with Colin Trevorrow's writing as I found the kids in the last movie annoying too, and they weren't so much characters as plot devices, as is also the case here.

To sum up this sequel, it's a fun few hours of dinosaur related thrills, marred occasionally by cliched characters and a predictable plot, seek it out if you enjoyed the last one, but I wouldn't blame you if you waited for the Blu Ray release, but you could certainly do a lot worse, Jurassic Park III for example...

Hereditary (Originally published June 22nd, 2018)
Directed by Ari Aster
Starring: Toni Collette, Alex Wolff, Milly Shapiro and Ann Dowd

Well, you certainly couldn't avoid the hype for this movie recently. Marketed with the tag: "This generation's The Exorcist" which always makes me wary. Surely if the movie can stand up on its own merits it wouldn't need to be compared to a movie that's over 40 years old? Come to think of it, a lot of things about its marketing push makes me suspicious, usually when a film is hyped this much it's a sign that the studio doesn't have much faith in the product, as well as its somewhat misleading trailers it threw up a lot of red flags.

So, was I justified to be suspicious, or is this truly a film that will live for generations?

Story

Following the death of her mother, Annie Graham (Toni Colette) starts to notice strange occurrences, and changes in her children and the world around her, as she digs through the mystery surrounding her mother's life and death.

Verdict

For those of you who've been reading my reviews for any length of time will remember me stating that I wasn't all that fond of horror films, but as time has gone on, I've gained an appreciation for horror films that think outside the box and have some level of creativity, which is why it just kills me to say that Hereditary may have ended any goodwill I have towards horror movies.

With my stall firmly set out, I'll start with my positive takeaways from the movie. Toni Colette was a firm stand-out, even with the often-questionable material given to her, she delivers a superb, emotional performance. Also, the effect of showing events of the film in the dollhouses was a nice touch, although pushing it towards the end.

Now, down to the nitty gritty of things, and I'm not going to dance around the subject, I really disliked this movie. It's been a while since I've purely disliked a film, it almost feels refreshing.

I think my biggest gripe is how the movie thinks it's so much smarter than it actually is, presented as a pretentious chin-stroker while simultaneously indulging such obvious horror tropes, it makes it look worse than it is, make no mistake it's all very well put together and acted but it seems so in love with itself that it forgets to have a compelling narrative.

There's a point in the film, roughly halfway through where it seemed like it may be building to something interesting, only to completely lose its focus and fall back on the aforementioned clichés, it wouldn't be so bad if the film didn't seem so pleased with itself at every turn.

As I said, it's competently laid out, and starts to build an interesting tension, which just makes it even more disappointing when it suddenly becomes just another generic horror movie, with no teeth to do anything interesting or boundary pushing. For instance, it tends to fall back on gross-out imagery, now, I have no problem with blood and gore, I'm intelligent enough to make the distinction between fiction and reality, but here it feels so forced and unearned, like it felt it just needed to show us horrible things to be a horror movie, rather than showing us it for any logical reason.

It also commits the cardinal sin of horror intrigue, by explaining the threat, not only that but making the threat so piss-weak it takes you out of the rest of the film. My rule of thumb is always that what's in your head will always end up being scarier than what is presented to you, I had the same problem but on a lesser scale with A Quiet Place, and it's magnified here, because A Quiet Place had interesting characters, setting and threat, this film has none of those things.

The best thing that can be said about Hereditary is, it's just another horror film, it's not the ground-breaking experience it thinks it is, it's a cookie-cutter plot with cliched characters, so pretentious that it didn't realise that all its ideas have been done before and better, not helped by a media profile that would make Stalin blush.

In brief, Hereditary is only "this generations The Exorcist" only in the fact that it too was overhyped and overrated. There are much better uses of your time.

Chapter Seven: July/August 2018

Tag (Originally published July 6th, 2018)
Directed by Jeff Tomsic
Starring: Ed Helms, Jake Johnson, Annabelle Wallis and Hannibal Buress

This movie grabbed my attention simply by the premise, and I absolutely understand why it's six blokes in this game, as women in movies tend to be much more sensible, something which is actually referred to in this film.

It's also been a while since I reviewed a comedy, and I felt I needed a laugh after the Hereditary debacle, and the cast and set-up did enough to draw me in so here we go.

Story

A group of six friends have been playing the same game of tag for nearly thirty years, but one of the party has never been tagged in all that time, and the remaining friends see an ideal opportunity to finally get him, his wedding.

Verdict

This is another one of those films that is difficult to review, as it isn't bad enough to be derided as a terrible movie, yet I didn't love it enough to call it great either. However, there are things about it worth talking about, so I'm going to give it a good old college try.

First off, the cast deserve a special mention, at first glance you'll see just how much talent there is on display (Jon Hamm, Jeremy Renner, Ed Helms et al) but chemistry is not built on paper, and I'm pleased to report that their chemistry is strong enough to make the movie enjoyable while it's there. The performances of Hannibal Buress and Jeremy Renner were my particular favourites, it gave a rare chance for Renner to show off his comic chops and he fits his character perfectly.

On the flip side of this however, despite strong performances and chemistry, the characters are often tissue-thin and shallow archetypes and thus, I didn't feel invested in their characters, therefore it can't leave too much of an impression on my memory. For example there's the stereotypical stoner character and the token black guy, even if he does show flashes of a more interesting character, which isn't capitalised on nearly enough. Not to mention Ed Helms playing the 'doctor who's not an actual doctor' that he played in The Hangover movies (he's a dentist in The Hangover and a Vet in this one), I was half expecting the jokes to be lifted from those films.

This isn't the kind of film where one would usually scrutinise direction, but there are stand-out moment's direction-wise. Mostly the slow-motion scenes from the perspective of Jeremy Renner's character, which for me are the biggest hits of the movie and show frankly psychotic attention of detail, something that is a running theme as the film speeds towards its climax.

Within said climax lays my biggest critique of this film. Without giving spoilers (as is my protocol) the film takes a dark turn in the final third, which doesn't feel deserved nor necessary, the change in tone is frankly jarring, and felt like the screenwriter's had a moment of writer's block and needed a suitable conclusion, so pulled this out of the hat, and it was a very, very unnatural turn, and the fact that there are two of these dark turns feels even more jarring, almost to the point of being uncomfortable, in fact they feel like they're trying to see what they can get away with.

In conclusion, if you can look past the incredibly jarring final twists, there's a light, entertaining movie in here, nothing that will stick in the memory, but enjoyable while it's there. In short, forgettable, but enjoyable.

Everybody's Talking About Jamie (Originally published July 6th, 2018)
Directed by Jonathan Butterell
Starring: John McCrea, Josie Walker, Tamsin Carroll and Phil Nichol

Being into musicals as I am, it always excites me when one is broadcast live to cinemas, as I don't get many chances to go down to London and take in a show. This particular one is one that I liked the sound of from the start, so for it to be broadcast live is a real treat.

I went into this one as blind as I could, avoiding the cast recording once I knew it was being broadcast, so I saw the songs in context first. I also avoided all other reviews to remain as objective as possible, so with that said, here's what I thought.

Story

16-year-old Jamie New has a dream; to be the most fabulous drag queen Sheffield has ever seen. But there are roadblocks in his way. Ignorance, bigotry and opposition faces him as he fights, along with his ever-supportive mother to be accepted for who he is.

Verdict

As previously stated, I had deliberately exposed myself to as little information as possible about this show, in some ways a bit of a risk, what if I had let myself in for an over-hyped sugary show? Gladly though, I eat all of my doubts with a giant slice of humble pie.

Everybody's Talking About Jamie is a modern-day masterpiece. I don't say this lightly, there are many shows vying for attention on the West End, and even more choice in cinemas, but this stands out as a shining diamond of modern-day struggle and triumph.

Championing individuality and equality is something musical theatre excels at, perhaps more than film, and we've seen winning show in that mould before (Billy Elliot, Hairspray to a lesser degree) but this brings about a very modern struggle and one that, unfortunately, happens on our doorsteps to this day.

Another thing I must praise the show highly for is its cast, not only in its performances, which are universally brilliant, but in its diversity, all aspects of multicultural British life is on show here, and it's refreshing and beautiful to see.

Of all the great performances, I could go on forever heaping praise on different people, but for now I'll focus on two particular people who I think deserve specific praise. Firstly is Jamie himself, played by John McCrea, who looked as though he was born for this part, embodying Jamie's sarcastic camp personality in every scene, his character work is the truly stand-out aspect of his performance. Secondly there's Jamie's mother, Margaret, played by Josie Walker, whose voice is both perfectly suited to musical theatre and to die for. She also has some stand-out character moments, mostly in the connection with Jamie, which is incredibly believable as a mother-son dynamic, it really makes their interactions pop off the stage.

I also think praise is deserved for the score also, with music by Dan Gillespie Sells of the rock band The Feeling, stepping into musical theatre was a brave step, but a step that paid off spectacularly, paired with the lyrics of Tom MacRae (who according to my research is also a musical theatre debutante) make for a memorable score, featuring songs that will stick in your head, and some which may stick in your heart. I think the fact that both men had never written a musical before deserves special praise given the strength of the score, which sounds like it's come from seasoned pros.

Tom MacRae is also the brains behind the book of the musical, which is a script that changes from heartfelt emotionally charged scenes to whip-sharp witty comedy and manages to balance both and not feel top heavy or inconsistent. Jamie's journey is conveyed incredibly well from scene to scene, it could have leaned too much on either the emotion or comedy and felt like a lesser script, luckily it find a happy middle-ground and keeps a workable pace as to not lose the audience's attention, the sign of a true pro, which MacRae is, being a veteran TV writer, however stage writing is a different beast completely, and a more seamless transition from screen to stage writing would be difficult to find.

Every aspect of the show all works together like cogs in an efficient clock, the school-age character are believable and gave me pangs of nostalgia from my school-days, the tone of the score suits every occasion, from upbeat pop opening number to heartfelt ballads from Jamie's heartbroken mother, it all fits together so well and the tone never feels inconsistent, it earns every single emotional moment, and balances it with levity, it's a difficult juggling act that could have ended horribly, but in the end the juggling acts turned out spectacularly.

If I had any quibbles, it would be that the school-kids seem a bit TOO lifelike, almost to the point of stereotype, but the thing about that is, stereotype is usually based on reality, if you're around my age, I guarantee that you'll recognise at least one of the school characters. Any criticism, however, is insignificant in the shadow of the show's successes.

If the previous 800+ words haven't convinced you enough, I cannot recommend this show highly enough. See the encore showing at cinemas or make a trip down to London and experience it yourself, you will not regret it.

The Incredibles II (Originally published July 25th, 2018)
Directed by: Brad Bird
Starring: Craig T. Nelson, Holly Hunter, Sarah Vowell and Samuel L. Jackson

So, fourteen years have passed since the Parr family graced our screens, one I remember fondly from my own childhood, and one I still find incredibly enjoyable to watch now. So, in revisiting this IP there's the obvious trepidation about revisiting a long-dormant franchise, will it be a worthy addition to the canon? Or a cobbled together cash grab aimed at the nostalgia crowd? Well, these fears are assuaged somewhat seeing as this is a Pixar project, and Pixar has an extraordinary hit-and-miss ratio.

All the fan favourites return for this follow-up, as well as director Brad Bird. So has their absence made our hearts grow fonder?

Story

Immediately following the events of the first film, the Parr family are approached by Winston Deavor, a wealthy businessman interested re-legalising 'Supers'. He offers a position to improve the public perception of Supers to Elastagirl, who unravels a plot by the nefarious 'Screen-slaver' who takes control of people via screens, leaving Helen to fight this new threat, and Bob fighting a completely different threat... domestic life.

Verdict

There was a fear I had, around eight years ago, when Toy Story 3 was released, that it might have been impossible to recapture the magic of all those years ago, to a completely new audience as well as the old one. Luckily enough, the film delivered and was a more than worthy follow-up to the first two, so after this I have confidence in Pixar, perhaps more than most studios to deliver in films, long-dormant follow-up or otherwise.

Having said this, can I honestly say that Incredibles 2 is better than the first? No, but is it a worthy follow-up? Absolutely, the same charm and lovable characters are still there, doing what they do best, and what this film does best is showing us the characters we know from a different angle, especially Elastagirl and Mr Incredible, in maybe a sign of the times, this is very much Elastagirl's film, while Mr Incredible is cast in a more supporting role. Not that this is a bad thing, she more than carries the load of the movie and while the 'domesticated man' angle can be a little cliched, you can't help but like Mr Incredible more, as he genuinely seems to do what he thinks is best, right or wrongly.

Another new wrinkle added to this film that was missing from the first film somewhat, and that's the development of Jack Jack (the baby of the family, whose powers begin to develop in this film) which, to me, offer some of the movie's funnier moments, in particular a 'fight' between Jack Jack and a raccoon, where his powers seem to come at random, because of course a baby would have no control of these powers. For most of the film, I didn't think Jack Jack was used enough, until the final third where he becomes an important part of the equation in a great pay-off to the preceding events, so bravo for turning my criticism around there, Pixar.

I think the biggest mark I have against the film is that the villain isn't as strong as the first time around, their motivations aren't as well-defined as Syndrome's were in the first Incredibles, however, this isn't as big a mark against it as it seems as Syndrome is a genuinely interesting and believable (not to mention somewhat sympathetic) villain, which given the ever-changing landscape of superhero-movies aren't always consistent to say the least. Screen-slaver has some good moments but doesn't seem to click when the pieces fall into place, her motivations don't always match her plot, she doesn't have the same justified reasons as Syndrome and that works against her.

Overall, Incredibles II is a very enjoyable movie, and a welcome return to characters we fell in love with all those years ago (shout out to Edna Mode, who also made her triumphant return in this movie) it's not as much a solid-gold classic as the original, but it is a more than worthy follow-up to it, and another solid hit for Pixar whose hit-rate continues to astound. If you loved the original, you will not be disappointed with this sequel.

Hotel Artemis (Originally published July 25th, 2018)
Directed by Drew Pearce
Starring: Jodie Foster, Sterling K. Brown, Sofia Boutella and Jeff Goldblum

After a few big-budget films in the last few weeks, I thought I needed a bit of a change of pace. I came across the trailer for this while surfing YouTube for videos about films (I don't get out much) and thought the premise was cool enough, even if it was somewhat reminiscent of the hotel from John Wick expanded into a full movie, a thought that never seemed to leave me throughout the run-time.

Besides that, it boasts a talented cast, and stylish looking direction, so I thought it was worth a go.

Story

Set in a dystopian future, and during the worst riot in Los Angeles' history, a bank heist goes horribly wrong, and Sherman (Sterling K. Brown) takes his mortally-wounded brother to the secretive Hotel Artemis, a specialist members-only hospital for criminals, ran by a nurse with a murky past (Jodie Foster) as the events of the night devolve into chaos.

Verdict

Hotel Artemis has slipped under the radar somewhat, buried under a tidal wave of big studio releases, and when a film has the acting return of Jodie Foster, that's bizarre. Granted it isn't a big, glitzy production, it's a more stylised and lower-budget fare with a good idea, good ideas don't always buy success as unfortunate as that is.

As I said in the very first paragraph, this premise may seem familiar to fans of John Wick, albeit more expanded and under different parameters. I don't want to dwell on that too much as the hotel in John Wick was one part of a much bigger beast, whereas this hinges on that premise for its entire run-time, that has the potential to run thin after a while, so the success of the film hinged on the strength of its characters and how they interlink.

Thankfully there are strong characters for the film to base itself around, The Nurse character has the most potential given how little is established about her and the film is smart in how it gradually feeds her backstory to the audience and how she links to other characters and the more you learn, the more you connect with her, what she's been through and why she is where she is, and it's a real treat to see Jodie Foster back on our screens and her casting is a perfect one, she brings gravity and humanity to a character who can sometimes seem cold and aloof.

Another actor who impressed me here was Dave Bautista, who to me, improves in every film he's in, Drax was one of my favourite things about Guardians Vol 2 and I think he has a lot more to offer than bland muscle-man, and while his character here does sometimes devolve into a generic 'muscle' character, there are flashes of something more in his portrayal, that he is more than just a muscle-man, and I think we need to see more of that from him.

Whilst I enjoyed Hotel Artemis, it's not above descending into generic violence, despite its more interesting parts, I think some of the choices are to the detriment of the film, specifically Zachary Quinto's character often seems like a cheap way of raising the tension, when there's enough tense scenarios in the film to build around and it seems like it was looking for a reason for more stylistically choreographed violence, again, not always a bad thing as its direction is very easy on the eye and incredibly stylish, but often feels unneeded.

Put all these parts together and it makes Hotel Artemis an enjoyable, if somewhat disposable, experience. Its short running time (94 minutes) helps its case as well, as it keeps a swift pace and tells it's contained story efficiently, had it been longer it would have felt bloated and padded, as it is, it's just the right run time.

In conclusion, Hotel Artemis is a fun action-thriller that stretches its thin premise just the right amount with likeable character that engage with, it's nothing that stands out as special in today's market, but definitely worth a look.

Mission: Impossible - Fallout (Originally published August 3rd, 2018)
Directed by Christopher McQuarrie
Starring: Tom Cruise, Henry Cavill, Ving Rhames and Simon Pegg

I must admit that I'm a new passenger on the Mission: Impossible party bus. You see, I've never had a great love of Tom Cruise and I'm very rarely in the mood for an action film, and I'd somewhat naively categorised them as simple, brainless action films, by the time I'd watched Ghost Protocol, I was quite happy to admit that I was very, very wrong about the series.

Now, the media profile for this film was huge, and my review comes three weeks after everybody showered it with praise, with some even calling it one of the best action films of all time, and after the high benchmark left by the previous two films, this is high praise indeed.

Story

After the events of Rogue Nation, members of the Syndicate hatch a plot to steal plutonium from the Russians to cause untold destruction and Ethan Hunt is sent to stop them, however, him and his team are hamstrung by a CIA operative, sent to oversee the mission. leading to intrigue, twists and turns.

Verdict

Sometimes, writing story synopsis without spoiling big plot points is very difficult, and a film series like Mission: Impossible, with its many twists and turns, pose one hell of a challenge and the above is the best I can try and explain Fallout without giving away its many treasures.

After seeing Ghost Protocol and Rogue Nation in quick succession like I did, I found it difficult to believe that a franchise that's six films in could possibly improve, but alas, it did, somehow raising the stakes from last time out and increasing the epic, yet coherent, set pieces.

One treat of the M:I series is the recurring element of Tom Cruise performing unbelievable stunts, the peak of which for me is the moment in Ghost Protocol where he climbs the outside of a skyscraper in Dubai, and that trend continues here with an incredibly tense high-altitude skydive set piece which is perfectly performed and shot, so bravo there.

Usually, action films are thin-on-the-ground plot-wise and are merely an excuse for the hero to look good and kill a lot of baddies, but this is an area in which Mission: Impossible frequently excels, and I'm also a fan of how each instalment flows into the next, as it feels like this film and Rogue Nation in particular are two parts of one, epic story and the recurring characters all have something to add.

Tom Cruise is really at his best in these films, you really get the impression that he's truly passionate about the series and the characters to continually put his body on the line at the age of 56. A lot of the talk around his stunts are that he's known to perform them himself, and we're told this so often that I think we may have stopped appreciating it. I know his age doesn't really factor into it too much as he's in better shape than me and I'm more than half his age, but it truly is amazing the extents he'll go to too to make an entertaining movie.

Cast-wise the main gang are back, sans Jeremy Renner, whose commitments to Marvel made being in this impossible (pun not intended) and all are at their best. The addition of Henry Cavill is a welcome one indeed, with the opportunity to show he's more than just Superman, he grasped it with both hands, showing his capability in the brutal practical action scenes, and holding his end of the stunts too, his character development is stellar too, if a little bit telegraphed towards the third act, but all in all few complaints can be aimed at the cast. Ving Rhames is perfect as always for Luther, Simon Pegg gives the film some much needed levity and Rebecca Ferguson is mysterious and deadly, just like last time.

Christopher McQuarrie once again talks the director's chair for this instalment, being the first director to return to the franchise after showing some of his potential in Rogue Nation, and I'd call this a triumphant return, everything he got right last time he expands upon, the action is tight and intense, the plot keeps a nice pace, while containing enough twists and turns to keep you guessing, and some of the landscapes are beautifully captured, I'd call this a directorial triumph for Mr McQuarrie as well as praising his efforts on the script.

There are very few negatives I can levy at this film as a whole, given how tight its structure and pacing is, there are a few nit-picks however, the head of the CIA is a bit inconsistent, derailing the team one minute and helping them out the next, with her justifications changing on a whim, but that's really the worst I can say about it as everything else is polished to a mirror-shine, its action set-pieces in particular feel earned and a coherent part of the plot, which is normally where most action films fall down, this film simultaneously never takes its foot of the pedal, yet is spaced out enough to tell an engaging and thoughtful story. This is the pinnacle of action filmmaking; it doesn't get much better.

Ant-Man and the Wasp (Originally published August 4th, 2018)
Directed by Peyton Reed

Starring: Paul Rudd, Evangeline Lilly, Michael Pena and Michael Douglas

It was always going to be difficult to follow the colossal success of Infinity War; it was probably a wise decision to make somewhat of a 'palate cleanser' between Infinity War and next year's Captain Marvel.

The success of 2015's Ant-Man was somewhat of a surprise to the layman, a film based around a somewhat unknown superhero like Ant-Man straight after Age of Ultron (somewhat of a recurring theme here, I see) was a risk, but like Guardians of the Galaxy before it, turned out to be a surprise package with a likeable leading man and entertaining peripheral characters. With Ant-Man established and his absence in Infinity War unexplained leaves a gap for this film to slot in nicely, and tell its own story separate from the larger timeline, with perhaps not as much pressure.

Story

After helping Captain America during Civil War, Scott Lang struck a plea deal and is under house arrest, separated from Hank Pym and Hope, he adjusts from day to day life away from superhero duty, when a message from the quantum realm drags Scott back into action once more.

Verdict

As stated in the opening paragraph of this review, Ant-Man and the Wasp serves as a palate cleanser between two massive releases in the MCU and in that regard it's a particularly entertaining palate cleanser.

I was as surprised as anyone about the quality of the first Ant-Man film, as the character sounds absurd on paper, so my expectations were to see more of the same here and that's exactly what I got, it takes what it established 3 years ago and expands upon them. I also particularly liked how Scott's absence in Infinity War is explained here and tied neatly into the ongoing narrative of the MCU.

One of this film's greatest strengths, and one of the first films also, is Paul Rudd himself, he's so innately likeable that the idea of an Ant-Man doesn't seem quite so absurd, he also shares good chemistry with Evangeline Lily, the 'Wasp' half of 'Ant-Man and the Wasp' team-up. Michael Douglas gets more time to flesh out the character of Hank Pym in this instalment too, while he was certainly a presence last time out, he felt underdeveloped, something that is fixed in this film.

Elsewhere in the cast Michael Pena is a highlight once more as Luis, however, he doesn't get as much chance to monologue as last time, the character feels more contained, yet restricted, which isn't to say he doesn't have highlights as he can always be relied on for some much-needed levity and humour.

Speaking of characters, we come to one of my criticisms about this film, and it revolves around the 'villain' of the film (Ghost). If you break it down, she isn't particularly a 'villain' so to speak as her motivations are quite understandable, and things could have been resolved much easier had the characters just talked, rather than chase each other round the city and fight, granted there wouldn't have been much of a film otherwise, but following two stand-out villains really shines a more negative light on the character. She also doesn't really get the chance to flesh out the character, and parts of her backstory and motivation borrows heavily from other MCU villains, so the chance to make her relatable is lost. The actress playing her though (Hannah John-Kamen) does her best with the material and is one to watch for the future.

While the movie is nowhere near the best of the MCU, it struggles with balance issues and only really serves to bridge a narrative gap between two bigger releases, it's a light and entertaining watch, particularly praise-worthy being the few scenes we get in the quantum realm, they're visually striking and at times, breath-taking.

Unfortunately this aspect of the story takes a back seat for the usual superhero fare (car chases and fights) which is a shame as that's a part of the story that's most emotionally, and creatively, gratifying, seeing as how Hank aims to enter the quantum realm in search of his wife, this gets side-tracked into the plot of Ghost wanting Hank's technology and the plot unfolds from there.

All that being said, if you were entertained by Ant-Man, I'm fairly certain you'll enjoy this too, it's just the filler we needed after the big blowout that was Infinity War and leaves us in a nice place to carry on from in next year's Avenger's sequel. It's nothing mind-blowing and it takes no risks, but it didn't really need too and it's still fun while it lasts.

The Festival (Originally published August 14th, 2018)
Directed by Iain Morris
Starring: Joe Thomas, Hammed Animashaun, Claudia O'Doherty and Emma Rigby

I like The Inbetweeners, it had an underlying smart satire of teenage life, and had cringe-y, gross-out humour that felt like it was earned. It helped the tone along and lent itself well to the jokes.

I'm not, however, a fan of gross-out humour where it feels forced. I'm not going to laugh because someone threw up, unless there's a reason for them too. While this might drop my biggest quibble with The Festival, let's push on, shall we?

Story

After being dumped at his graduation and having a very public breakdown, Nick (Joe Thomas), is persuaded to go to a three-day music festival by his best mate, this begins a weekend of awkwardly avoiding his ex and trying to enjoy himself.

Verdict

I had low expectations going into The Festival. Sure, I liked The Inbetweeners and this is by the same director, Iain Morris, but you see the thing is, he hasn't moved on. Hence why he's using the same cast.

There's nothing wrong with having a niche, but even then, we should expect something to progress. Every story point I could see coming a mile away, on one occasion at the exact moment a character was introduced. Of course I wasn't expecting Shakespeare, but the film telegraphs its plot points so much it might as well have made the character wear boards, saying things like: "I'm the comic relief drug addict" or "I'm going to fall in love at the end."

I'm not going to say there's no fun to be had here, some scenes did make me chuckle a bit, and Joe Thomas is a perfectly likeable main protagonist, but the whole thing is just so shallow. I remember in The Inbetweeners, you grew to sympathise with the four main characters, you invested in their struggles and laughed when they embarrassed themselves. Maybe I shouldn't compare the two so much, but can you blame me when it shares some of the same cast and director? Sure, other properties have done that, but they've at least tried something new with the formula, look at Edgar Wright's Cornetto Trilogy, three films with the same basic formula, but each film has its own identity. It doesn't feel like Simon Pegg is playing the same character in Hot Fuzz as he is in Shaun of the Dead, but in this film, Joe Thomas may as well still be playing Simon.

As I say, I didn't go in with high hopes for The Festival, and while I didn't hate it, I wouldn't recommend it either, the jokes are puerile and sophomoric with no real justification, the characters are one-dimensional, and despite Joe Thomas' best efforts, the main character comes off as selfish and unlikable, right up until his token redemption.

In conclusion, a few laughs to be found but the same can be said of punching your friend in the stomach, and that won't cost you the price of entry, but it won't endear you to your friend and neither will this film.

The Equalizer 2 (Originally published August 24th, 2018)
Directed by: Antoine Fuqua
Starring: Denzel Washington, Pedro Pascal, Ashton Sanders and Bill Pullman

The first Equalizer was a bit of a pleasant surprise. A stylish, well-presented pleasant surprise at that. Reuniting Denzel Washington with Training Day director, Antoine Fuqua it was a stylish take on the well-used vigilante revenge thriller, it was a good example of using a generic premise and giving it a twist to make it seem relevant, even if not entirely original.

A few years on, and Denzel is back for more, is this a sequel of diminishing returns? Or will it use the originals momentum to build on?

Story

Robert McCall has moved on since his reign of vigilante justice, now living in Massachusetts and working as a Lyft driver, and helping out the less fortunate when he can. He is pulled back into the vigilante life after the murder of a friend as a conspiracy unfolds.

Verdict

I watched this film a few days after watching the first, having missed it the first-time round, and as stated in the opening paragraphs, it was a surprise. It's visual-style and direction were, on occasion, breath-taking and it was a breath of fresh air when compared to usual action film fare.

A good sequel to me should expand what was established first time round, so with Robert McCall established as a near-indestructible bad-ass, it would have been inadvisable to not expand the character and horizons, and Fuqua was way ahead of me, as McCall has gone from seeking revenge for a child prostitute to seeking revenge for a former FBI agent.

With that being said, let's get the criticism out of the way. It's too happy to hop the plot around, from scene to scene we go from Robert's house in Massachusetts (the most awkward place to spell) to Washington, and then to Brussels in Belgium, and of course there's the stock footage of planes take off and land. Some of the location-hopping is necessary for the plot but the way it's put together makes each scene seem to hop back and forth, it's off-putting but not a deal-breaker.

However, despite the lack of focus on locations, but I have the feeling I'm going to recommend The Equalizer 2, yes, the plot lacks a bit of focus, and the father-son demographic in the plot is somewhat forced and just seems token, but I really came to like the characters. Denzel is at his best here, his characters actions are much-more justified here, as the character he's seeking revenge for is established as someone he has a long history with, as opposed to avenging a young girl who talks to him about books.

The film is visually-stunning however, opening with a well-choreographed and brutal fight scene on a train and climaxing with an incredible, tense cat-and-mouse chase set against the background of an ongoing storm, and with a sniper watching from a tower, upping the tension as Robert McCall goes about his usual business i.e. nailing people to walls. It also gave the film the reason to use falling rain as a visual pastiche again, as it worked so well the first-time round.

The film also boasts a really well-worked twist towards the end that surprised me with its set-up and execution, so there's another positive to its name. So its plot widened its focus to a much bigger stage, as well as upping the action set-pieces and maintaining its appealing visual direction that made the first one enjoyable.

In conclusion, The Equalizer 2 is a very enjoyable, and stylish, action yarn with a very strong lead performance from the as-usual charismatic Denzel Washington. Sure, it's nothing new in the world of film, but it is a lot of fun while it lasts and a few of the set-pieces will stick with you, so you can't really ask for more. It's not going to win many awards, but that's not the intention, if the intention was to create a well-directed, visually striking action film, then it more than achieves it.

The Happytime Murders (Originally published August 28th, 2018)
Directed by Brian Henson
Starring: Melissa McCarthy, Bill Barretta, Maya Rudolph and Joel McHale

Good God, this film sucks.

Oh, sorry, I should probably give more build-up to that.

The Happytime Murders is the latest film from Brian Henson, the Son of Muppets creator, Jim Henson, and poor Jim is probably not only rolling in his grave but doing a choreographed dance routine.

Story

In a world where puppets and humans live side-by-side and puppets are treated with universal contempt by humans, jaded ex-cop turned puppet private eye Phil Phillips is pulled into a murder mystery when puppets start being murdered in L.A. He's forced to co-exist with his former partner, who caused him to lose his job.

Verdict

As stated at the start of this review, this movie sucks. There's no getting around this. It's a cinematic travesty.

I first learned of this film earlier in the year, and was intrigued by the idea of an adult puppet movie, after all, I have previously been part of a musical called Avenue Q, which got to the idea roughly 15 years before, not only that but it is actually funny, smart and at times, emotional. The Happytime Murders is none of these things.

The best sign of a good comedy is how many times it makes you laugh, and Happytime shows itself to be a misnomer as it didn't make me happy, in fact it didn't make me laugh. Once. For a comedy movie that lasts an hour and a half that's the most damning indictment of all.

This movie does not have 'characters' so to speak, it has stock archetypes. Imagine a stereotypical, grizzled private eye, and that's exactly how the lead character is. Constantly smoking? Check. Exposition-laden grizzled narration? Check. It's like this movie had a checklist of clichés that it wanted to complete within its running time, if that's its intention, it succeeds at that at least.

The human lead is Melissa McCarthy, who is very much a Marmite character, you love her or hate her, personally I have no strong opinion either way, I enjoyed her in Bridesmaids but recently she seems to be becoming the female Adam Sandler, churning out lazy comedy after lazy comedy with little to no development. Here however, she's the closest thing to watchable the movie has. Like Sandler, she has an undeniable chemistry, she just never knows how to apply it in good movies, and this is no different, like everyone else, she has a shallow stock character, but her delivery of the ham-fisted dialogue at least breathes some life into it that is lost when coming from a puppet.

The most damning evidence I can present to this film's awfulness is the fact that I watched it in a cinema that was sparsely populated, and nobody laughed throughout the entire movie, and a comedy that makes no one laugh is like a chocolate teapot, not any use for what it's made for and no-one would thank you for giving it to them.

In short, an adult puppet comedy is a good concept, it's all in the execution. Avenue Q, which as I said is similar in concept, but works due to it being actually funny and clever. The only execution that would work for The Happytime Murders is the guillotine.

Chapter Eight: October-December 2018

BlacKkKlansman (Originally published October 5th, 2018)
Directed by: Spike Lee
Starring: John David Washington, Adam Driver, Laura Harrier and Topher Grace

Undoubtedly one of this year's most important film releases, BlacKkKlansman is the latest film from acclaimed director Spike Lee, known for shining a cinematic light on the plight of being an African American in a discriminatory world (Do the Right Thing and Malcolm X being the best examples in his filmography).

The film generated positive buzz from its premiere at the annual Cannes Film Festival, where it walked away with the Grand Prix award, Spike Lee's first honour from the festival.

The film itself could not be timelier, given the current political, and social, climate in the States right now. It was even released in the US exactly one year to the day of the now infamous Charlottesville 'Unite the Right' rally, where one woman lost her life in a racially charged attack (which we'll revisit later).

So in tumultuous times such as these, will BlacKkKlansman capture timely lightening in a bottle?

Story

In early 1970's Colorado, Ron Stallworth (John David Washington) a young, African-American man becomes the first Black cop in Colorado Springs sets his sights high early, by trying to infiltrate the infamous hate-group, The Ku-Klux Klan, enlisting a white cop to be his face in the organisation as they unravel a conspiracy to launch several attacks.

Verdict

As I said earlier, this film could not be timelier. It is like a cinematic time-capsule, not only being terrifying, but familiar in modern times, if that was Mr Lee's intention, then he comfortably achieved it.

Not only is it a stark reminder of how we haven't learned much in the last 40 years, it's also an extremely engrossing and well-made movie. The story, despite being so unbelievable is based on a true story, some text at the start of the movie assures us that it is based on: "some fo' real, fo' real shit" (his words, not mine).

As much as the story is engrossing from pitch alone, this film is very-much character driven, it hinges on us not only buying into the plot to infiltrate the Klan but to buy into Ron's struggles, along the way learning more about the world and the characters around him.

John David Washington is our lead man, and he seems to have inherited magnetism and charisma from his famous father (Denzel Washington) and he slips into the Ron Stallworth role with ease, making it look easy to recreate this real-life person and making us buy into his struggles and come to like the character, he's stuck between two worlds; the mostly-white and routine police department, and his blossoming relationship with a Black activist, who he was initially sent to investigate but grows close to.

While a double-life plot is nothing new, the stakes are so high on his life and career that it becomes logical, one wrong move either way and his life is under threat from either Black nationalists or white nationalists, it's an important pendulum that has to be kept balance for narrative cohesion, and the eventual time when the mask falls is as sweet as ever for it, him getting one over on the Klan while his relationship with Patrice (the leader of the black student union, with whom he has become involved) comes to a bittersweet end, even in its conclusion it balances the vital narrative pendulum.

Elsewhere in the cast there's the cinematic chameleon Adam Driver in co-lead position as Flip Zimmerman, the white cop who becomes the public face of 'Ron Stallworth' to the Klan. My description of Driver as a chameleon is a deliberate one, as he seems to blend into whatever role he plays with expert skill, he's one of my favourite parts of the new Star Wars films, and threatens to steal the film from Washington here, his character is nuanced, he's a Jewish man which would put him at odds with the Klan's ideals but he both has to conceal his heritage, while not particularly identifying with it either, this is an arc that creeps up in importance, all coming together for the conclusion very nicely.

Topher Grace is also worth a mention for his portrayal of David Duke the 'Grand Wizard' of the KKK, the memories of Spider-Man 3 far behind him, he gives a uniquely disturbing performance, making your skin crawl with his every speech.

Those who read my reviews on a regular basis will know that I keep my reviews as spoiler-free as possible, and while I'm going to stick to that I will mention the incredibly harrowing and moving ending. Tying the narrative quite nicely to modern times, it literally took my breath away with its visceral and unwavering portrayal of genuine hatred.

In conclusion, this is one of this year's strongest offerings so far and a fantastic return to form from Spike Lee, his directorial style is recognisable here, laying on deliberate African-American stereotypes to subvert their usual uses to tear them down, instead building them up all framed with a 'so unbelievable it must be true' plot and you have an effective and incredibly startling piece of cinema.

King of Thieves (Originally published October 6th, 2018)
Directed by James Marsh
Starring: Michael Caine, Jim Broadbent, Tom Courtenay and Charlie Cox

There's something amazing about Michael Caine. Firstly, he's 85 years old and still playing leading roles in movies, which in today's looks-based industry (well, actually the business has always been big on looks, but humour me here) is unprecedented. He also has a strange effect on me, as whenever I see him on a poster, it makes me want to see it, most of it is my admiration for his career and longevity but part of me wants to see if, even this late on, he can still prove himself among the world's best actors.

King of Thieves sees him return to familiar ground, cast as a criminal, something he's been adept at since his younger days, this time around with its eye on a recent real-life crime, The Hatton Garden job, a robbery labelled 'the largest burglary in English legal history' a fairly lofty event for the film to portray, so will Caine, and his fellow cast of veteran screen actors prove themselves once more, or will the movie itself be criminal?

Story

Brian Reader (Michael Caine) is a veteran thief, long since retired from a life of crime, who finds himself dragged back into the underworld following the death of his wife, who kept him on the straight and narrow. Along the way he'll team up once more with his old crew to pull off one last, big job: The Hatton Garden safety deposit.

Verdict

I didn't really know going in what to expect, apart from the fact they'd be a heist at some point, obviously, seeing the pedigree of the cast (as well as Caine, there's reliable hands such as: Jim Broadbent, Michael Gambon and Tom Courtenay.) there was certainly a chance for the film to surprise, unfortunately, for the most part, it fails to make the most of its all-star cast.

The plot, such as it is, is nothing new. A fairly basic framework of an old-school bank heist, just given an extra twist by being committed by criminals in their 60's and 70's, the appeal of seeing these familiar faces on screen isn't enough to carry its tired plot.

There are some nice dialogue beats between the familiar characters in the mix, but it isn't anything we haven't already seen a hundred times or more in films now, in fact, Michael Caine is barely a year off playing a similar bank robber character in Going in Style, granted there are differences in the characters backstory, but it does feel as though we're treading old ground for most of the films run-time.

So, what about that cast then? Well, as reliable and venerated as most of them are, they mostly fail to bring life to their characters, there are times when characters could be best described as sleep-walking through their dialogue, Caine in particular looked indifferent to his performance, others try and lift some scenes, but in vain as most of the script is lifeless and repeat the same beats like clockwork.

The film has a nasty habit in the first act of repeating itself fairly often as the characters distrust for each other grows alongside their suspicion, and the same conversation is pretty much repeated verbatim three times inside half an hour, each time feeling wearier and wearier. We know the characters don't trust each other; it doesn't need to be established constantly in exposition dump after exposition dump.

I've spent a fair time here railing against the film, so it'll come as a surprise that I didn't think it was bad. Uninspired and hackneyed yes, but not bad. It's directed and framed well enough, with some nice touches, such as editing in footage of younger versions of the actors, that come with the territory of having an experienced director (it was directed by James Marsh, who directed the Oscar-winning Theory of Everything) but this is side garnish for a meal that isn't that interesting in the first place.

In conclusion, for a film built on nostalgic recognition and featuring such a respected cast, it really doesn't do much with the tools at hand. Bland, lethargic and predictable, it's an entirely skip-able exercise in mediocrity.

First Man (Originally published October 22nd, 2018)
Directed by: Damien Chazelle
Starring: Ryan Gosling, Claire Foy, Jason Clarke and Kyle Chandler

Ryan Gosling and Damian Chazelle are proving themselves to be somewhat of a Hollywood dream team. After La La Land, their next collaboration was going to be one to watch, and they set their sights big, taking on the story of Neil Armstrong and the very first moon landing. Although to call it a film about the moon landing would be doing it an injustice, as this only makes up a relatively short amount of the films run-time.

The aspiration on show to take on such a well-known pop culture icon is staggering, many would buckle under the weight of expectation, the weight is not only on Gosling's shoulders in portraying such a universally known figure, but in Chazelle's in following a rich and long heritage of space depictions in cinema, especially as we celebrate the 50th anniversary of 2001: A Space Odyssey, Sci-Fi's ultimate blueprint, this comparison may not be entirely fair, however, as mentioned earlier, despite the films marketing campaign suggesting otherwise, the moon landings and sequences in space don't dominate the films proceedings, but I digress, let's dive in.

Story

American icon Neil Armstrong goes from family heartbreak to international acclaim, when his career as a NASA pilot takes him all the way into space, on his way to becoming the first human to walk among the stars.

Verdict

Damian Chazelle is quickly becoming one of Hollywood's most valuable directors, and after this film, it's not hard to see why. His vision for beautiful filmmaking knows no bounds.

Don't let the films posters and trailers tell you otherwise, this isn't a story of a man walking on the moon, it's a love story, first and foremost. A very human love story tinged with grief and unspeakable loss. Neil Armstrong is not the American icon he has become, he is a regular man, dealing with the fall-out from some of life's most unsavoury aspects, and how difficult dealing with emotions can truly be.

Those, like me, who knew little about Armstrong besides his reputation will be stunned at the sheer depth of life he had, both good and bad. It does a great job of humanising a man that many hold as not a regular human, but a hero to be revered, he was not just the first man on the moon, he had a life beyond that, and this film beautifully shows us that side of him, much to its credit.

That word 'beautiful' is a key one that will come up more than once while describing this film. There are many superlatives to be used to describe this, but none as powerful as the word beautiful, it takes a lot for a film to achieve beauty, in not just its visual presentation, but in its performances, Ryan Gosling was the perfect man to show us the human side of Neil Armstrong, his strength is subtlety, he isn't a performer that gives big, energetic performances (not that I don't doubt that he could) instead he gives smaller, nuanced and emotional roles, the tone in which he portrays Armstrong is a perfect match for the films overall restrained tone, it's one of bubbling tension. He doesn't wear his heart on his sleeve, he keeps his passion and emotion just under the surface.

Helping Ryan Gosling massively is his co-lead Claire Foy, who portrays Janet, Neil Armstrong's first wife. In many ways, Foy is the emotional heart of the story, in that she is allowed the sudden outbursts of emotion to try and break her husband's facade of emotional stability, the chemistry crackles and pops off the screen, and their story is a believable one, a couple worked through unbearable odds to keep the flame burning, Claire Foy is the wick that burns the metaphorical flame in this film.

My one main gripe with the film is the portrayal of Buzz Aldrin, who sometimes comes across as a jackass. Maybe this was intended, I cannot attest to Mr Aldrin's character, so maybe it was a researched decision? Either way he comes across as incongruous at times, and extremely selfish at others, this eventually softens however towards the film's conclusion.

Last, but certainly not least, I must give a special mention to the direction and cinematography in this film, as it is nothing short of stunning. The contrast used between the scenes on Earth and the brief sequence on the moon is nothing short of jaw-dropping, the reflections in the astronauts helmets giving a unique perspective of the scale of the venture, giving the feel that they are mere specks in the shadow of their gargantuan achievement, just as the moon casts a shadow over the Earth. The feeling I got from seeing the moon portrayed in this film comes very close to the feeling I got after watching 2001 for the first time, one of sheer awe and amazement. It was, forgive the overuse of this word, beautiful.

I could go one for hours about how the film looks and was filmed, from the numerous scenes in the cockpits of various vehicles and spacecraft to reflections in visors, even to the framing of seemingly regular scenes on Earth. It all goes to show that Damian Chazelle and his crew weren't content with just making their space scenes stand-out, they wanted to make everything look its best, and they certainly did.

In conclusion, it would have been no easy task to just tell the story of the first moon landing with any conviction, and a near impossible one to get us to relate to a figure such as Neil Armstrong, but this movie not only achieved that, it surpassed any and all expectations to become not only a stark, dramatic story of love and loss, but an awe-inspiring achievement in cinematography. You will have to look very hard to find a film that not only looks this good, and surprises dramatically, like First Man does.

Bohemian Rhapsody (November 2nd, 2018)
Directed by Bryan Singer (+ Dexter Fletcher)
Starring: Rami Malek, Lucy Boynton, Gwilym Lee and Ben Hardy

Many moons ago, I recall hearing of a Freddie Mercury biopic entering production. It was set to start Sacha Baron Cohen, and this news was very exciting to me, I am, like many people, a huge Queen fan, I own all of their studio output and have seen the remaining members perform twice with new front-man Adam Lambert. Plus, Baron Cohen is a decent likeness of Freddie Mercury and a known singer, so all the pieces seemed to fit perfectly.

But it wasn't to be, the film spent almost a decade in various stages of development, Cohen left, reportedly after a fall-out with Queen over the films content, Ben Whishaw was pencilled-in as a replacement, then he left too.

Even when filming eventually began, with new lead Rami Malek, the film suffered with production problems. Director Bryan Singer became unreliable, arriving late to set or not arriving at all, leading to his eventual dismissal from the film with it so close to completion (a reported 80% of the film was already finished) so Dexter Fletcher was brought in to finish the product, and finish it he did, bringing the films storied and tumultuous development to a close, despite this, Fletcher does not receive a credit on the film, due to how close it was to completion, a decision handed down by the Directors Guild of America, to which all Hollywood films must comply with.

So, given the roller-coaster ride of its development, is Bohemian Rhapsody an ugly duckling? Or does it defy its rocky start to life, and emerge at the other side a beautiful swan?

Story

Bohemian Rhapsody charts the story of the British band, Queen, and more specifically legendary front-man Freddie Mercury, from their humble roots in London pubs, to the monstrous success of their Live Aid performance. All the while dealing with unsure record executives, the pressures of stardom, and Mercury's ever-growing ego.

Verdict

After viewing early trailers for the film, I started to become worried that this film may re-write some of Mercury's history to make him into something he wasn't. My fear being that the producers, and the band themselves, were scared of scarring Mercury's reputation and acknowledging his flaws. Happily, my fears were unjustified.

Bohemian Rhapsody took me completely by surprise upon watching. It was one of those pleasant surprises that come along once in a while, being that it took a subject a lot of people care deeply about and handled it with such care and dignity, that I felt I had no choice but to smile by the end credits.

Mercury's story is not one with a happy end, this is something we already know. His AIDS-related death in 1991 being one of the world's most high-profile AIDS-related deaths, and while this is acknowledged as the case, it is tactfully addressed without managing to mar the conclusion with inevitability.

The first thing I think should be singled out for praise is the performances. Led by the supremely talented Rami Malek, the film is one that is an all-round success from an acting standpoint. The aforementioned Malek shines as the flawed genius that was Freddie Mercury, wringing each drop of emotion from the heavier scenes, and putting his all into what seems like a complete transformation into Freddie. He is not content with playing Freddie as just the flamboyant frontman, but all aspects of his personality, somehow bringing vulnerability to such an utterly bombastic personality.

There are also great turns in the film from: Lucy Boynton, who plays Freddie's best friend Mary Austin, a rarely discussed but utterly complex character, who had such a devotion to Freddie from an early age, who stuck by him regardless of his sexuality and nursed him into his dying days, Gwilym Lee, who portrays Brian May, Queen's guitarist. Lee does not look like an actor portraying Brian May, he looks like Brian May just stepped out of a time machine, the likeness is uncanny and Allen Leech, who as Paul Prenter, makes your teeth itch from the moment you see him, and his effect on Freddie's life, while devastating, is entirely predictable, yet played so well by Prenter, who Makes hating Paul such an easy task.

From a technical standpoint, it is a visual marvel, especially the final section, a lovingly re-created version of their Live Aid performance, complete with absurdly detailed recreation of the set from the day, its audio mixing and cinematography makes you feel like you are right there in the front row, instead of being sat in a cinema watching, it's an utterly immersive experience and worth the price of admission alone.

It's by no means a perfect film, and I have complaints. The rest of Queen seem to be pushed aside to showcase the day-to-day dramas of Freddie Mercury, which from a pacing and narrative standpoint, is probably a good thing, but the little snap-shots of character we get from them show a dynamic rarely seen, in a way, some of the members of Queen could not be more diametrically opposed, and when this is show it's fascinating. I also feel we don't get to see nearly enough of Freddie's relationship with Jim Hutton, the partner he spent the last years of his life with, granted this sets up a very well-executed payoff towards the end, but I feel their relationship was worth exploring in more detail.

In the long run though, these are but minor quibbles in what is a hugely enjoyable slice of cinema, something that managed to take a figure as well-known as Freddie Mercury and show us more of his life than what we saw on stage. It is unlikely to trouble the Best

Picture category at any major award ceremonies, but I would be very disappointed if Malek were not at least nominated, as his performance is one of this year's most accomplished and may turn out to be a star-making performance. There are also moments technically that rival anything we've seen this year, the sets, audio mixing and costumes being the most notable. It just goes to show the lengths of the films achievements when I mention sound mixing as something that enhances the experience, as this is something usually unacknowledged by most commentators.

In conclusion, this is a biopic with something for everyone, Queen fans will love seeing the inside story and hearing the band's music on the big screen, whereas non-fans will be drawn in by the easily accessible narrative and enjoyable performances. A highly recommended experience, for both a hardened fan and newcomer.

<u>Venom</u> (Originally published November 2nd, 2018)
Directed by Ruben Fleischer
Starring: Tom Hardy, Michelle Williams, Riz Ahmed and Scott Haze

In the wider world of superhero movies, it's safe to say that not much was expected of Venom. Coming after years of toiling in development hell, many thought it would never see the light of day.

This film wasn't even on my radar this year, which is odd for a comic-book film and this was not helped by the films early trailers, which failed to entice my excitement, but with a day to myself and boredom setting in, I thought I'd bite the bullet and go see it, and decide for myself, whether it would be a decision I regretted remained to be seen.

Story

After a lunar mission goes wrong, an alien symbiote is unleashed upon the world, meanwhile journalist Eddie Brock (Tom Hardy) loses everything in an ill-advised sting against the man behind the initial space mission, Carlton Drake (Riz Ahmed), perusing the lead on Drake, Brock bonds with the symbiote Venom, who begins to wreak havoc.

Verdict

After the calamity that was Venom's first on-screen appearance over a decade ago in Spider-Man 3, the jury was well and truly out on his first solo outing, with half of the world hoping the character would be redeemed, and the other half hoping the character would crash and burn, somehow I get the feeling they'll both be disappointed.

It's not that Venom is bad, I didn't think it was anyway, I certainly don't think it warrants its 35 score on Metacritic, but you didn't come to me to hear about other critics, but those of you expecting me to hate Venom will also leave this disappointed.

Venom sits in that incredibly hard to write about category, not nearly threatening to break into the 'good' category but not approaching the bottom of the barrel either, it is thoroughly middle of the road, and that perhaps, is its biggest crime.

It feels like the product of a studio that had next to no faith in it, it pushes no boundaries and doesn't stand out in any way technically. In fact, some of its technical decisions, specifically visually, are more on the 'bad' end of the scale, everything is so murky, in that way that is very off-putting to look at, some of it looks like it has been dipped in pond-water, from a particularly grimy pond.

Acting-wise, it was solid enough. Tom Hardy brought the best he could, even if he wasn't up to his usual standard, he was brought down somewhat by the script (more on that later) and I could say the same for Riz Ahmed and Michelle Williams (who plays Eddie's love interest, Anne) they are very competent actors, given less-than-stellar material.

So, that script then. While occasionally lively and interesting, the script is mostly bland and uninspired, the dialogue in particular is what brings it down, there is enjoyable interactions between Venom and Eddie, but beyond that it's very paint-by-numbers, with a predictable plot and cliché villain that we have seen many, many times before and done better.

There are occasional glimpses within this film, of the film it wanted to be, perhaps the film it was going to be at some early planning stages, as when it edges towards off-the-wall body horror and creepiness, it come alive, but it is dragged back by the formulaic nature forced on it in other parts of the script.

In brief, flashes of what could have been stop this from being completely awful, along with an enjoyable enough lead performance. My expectations were low going in and it at least surpassed those, despite its deep flaws. I would advise caution when approaching the film if you're expecting anything like the MCU, or even the Deadpool movies. It feels like something caught behind the rest of its peers but is not nearly as bad as some outlets make it out to be, give it a watch, then never think about it again, because God knows I won't think about it much again.

A Star is Born (Originally published November 6th, 2018)
Directed by Bradley Cooper
Starring: Bradley Cooper, Lady Gaga, Andrew Dice Clay and Dave Chappelle

I've needed quite a bit of time to process what I think about this film. On one hand I wanted to avoid looking like a massive hypocrite, after everything I've said about remakes/reboots over the years, so this review may seem incongruous.

Secondly, I've done my best to avoid other critiques of this film more than I usually do. My usual rule is to expose myself to next to no hype or criticism before I see this film, even if it's a reviewer I liked, this allows me to retain my own opinions without input from elsewhere, often though, some of my points are shared by other reviewers, but I like to think it lends a certain honesty to my work.

As I write this, it's about three weeks since I saw the film, and I've gone over it in my head ever since, if you're good at reading tones you've probably deduced what I think/thought, but let's go into it a bit more.

Story

A popular country music artist, struggling with alcoholism, discovers and begins a relationship with a younger singer, exposing her to the music world through his concerts, as her career takes off, his personal life descends further into addiction, putting a strain on his personal and professional life.

Verdict

Going into this film, I was a very conflicted man. On one hand, I wanted to really enjoy the film, I never really want to watch a terrible film, even though they make for better reviews, but on the other hand, I had trepidation about its status as a remake, the third remake no less, and that a popular acting talent was moving behind the camera. Coming out, my mind was made up, Bradley Cooper had made the transition spectacularly.

There are a few different ways in which acting talent move behind the camera, there are some who do it for ego-driven reasons (see William Shatner and the disaster that is Star Trek V) and some who do it out of passion (Clint Eastwood and to a lesser extent, Ron Howard) and it is immediately clear in Cooper's first attempt that he is firmly in the latter category. the film's direction and technical ability of storytelling is simply staggering.

There are very few movies that manage to touch me emotionally, being a critic will do that to you, but by this film's climax, I was close to becoming a blubbering wreck. This was half because of the incredible acting on show (more on that later) and the other half was how the story was told, the accomplished direction and the extremely effective cinematography.

It really is astounding how right Bradley Cooper has got it on his very first attempt, but here we are. You would be tempted to quit while you were ahead, but if this start is anything to go by, his presence behind any camera would be welcome. Also, the more I think about this film, the more I realise how brave it was of Cooper to make his directorial debut with a remake of an already well-known property, yet still make it his own.

Admittedly, I have never seen any other version of the film, so I don't have a reference, but I'd be very surprised if the three that came before it came anywhere close to this film, it creates lives for its characters, you get so entranced in their struggles that you forget you're sat watching a cinema screen. The characters are familiar but don't feel overdone, hitting that sweet spot of relate-ability we crave in characters.

One of the films biggest positive is its acting, all the naysayers about the casting of Lady Gaga have been roundly and thoroughly silenced. She is magnificent, her performance showing a level of experience that befits an actress with many more years of experience, it would be easy to dismiss her casting as stunt casting of the highest order, but I can confidently say she was the best person for that character at this time, bringing with her not only the ability to shock us with a nuanced and layered acting performance, but her invaluable musical experience. I would consider her an early favourite for an Oscar and would not be disappointed in the least if she won.

Then there's Bradley Cooper himself, pulling double duty as not only behind the camera, but the star in front of it too, while Cooper has struggled with over-exposure in films over the years, he shows here his true ability to front a film, an earlier comparison with Clint

Eastwood seems apt, as not since Eastwood has someone made starring in, and directing a film look so easy. Of course some of the camera work can be attributed to his Director of Photography and Cinematographer, but his vision cannot be understated, it feels like there's a firm pair of hands steering the narrative at all times.

Then there's the music, as this is a musical as well as a drama, but do not expect you're usual Broadway-style tale of joy, it is a heavy, gritty story, portrayed beautifully in its soundtrack, some of it written by Gaga and Cooper, with outside help mostly from Lukas Nelson, son of famous country outlaw, Willie Nelson. There are many memorable tunes throughout the film, but the most memorable is the films climax song, I'll Never Love Again, which, I'm willing to bet will walk away with an Oscar next February.

I do have minor quibbles, as no film is perfect after all. Bradley Cooper's accent, while fitting for his character, is sometimes indecipherable, even when it isn't supposed to be, and oddly enough, I don't feel enough is established of Ally (Gaga's character) and her father's (played by Andrew Dice Clay) relationship, as there seems to be an interesting dynamic there, which is never really built upon.

Still, if a film's biggest worries are an accent and underdeveloped side-plot, it must be doing okay, and A Star is Born isn't just okay, it is fantastic. Both an interesting experiment in character development, and a moving drama all in one, anchored by spell-binding lead performances and accomplished direction, this is one of this year's best cinematic offerings, and I expect a large swoop of awards seasons come next year.

The Grinch (Originally published November 28th, 2018)
Directed by Scott Mosier and Yarrow Cheney
Starring: Benedict Cumberbatch, Rashida Jones, Kenan Thomson and Cameron Seely

I do love Christmas, and by extension, Christmas films. Miracle on 34th Street and Elf are both favourites, and another personal favourite is the 2000 live-action adaptation of The Grinch, starring Jim Carrey. I understand it's a very divisive film, and can see why, but like anything nostalgic from my childhood, I hold it up on a pedestal. I do avoid watching it nowadays however, as most childhood nostalgia films I revisit just seem to ruin that sense of nostalgia.

So, on to the present-day, and we have a new Grinch adaptation, made by Illumination Entertainment, the brains behind the Despicable Me films, and it is wholly unnecessary and unneeded when viewed from the outside, there is nothing that can be added to this Christmas classic, it can however add to the bank balance of Illumination's CEO, so here we are.

Story

In an adaptation of the Dr Seuss classic, Benedict Cumberbatch voices The Grinch, a curmudgeonly creature with a burning hatred of Christmas. Annoyed by a The Who's persistent optimism, he hatches a plan to steal Christmas.

Verdict

The story of the Grinch is so well known, it feels redundant to even summarise its plot, so imagine how redundant it is to produce an entirely new adaptation of the film, which I'm going to try and not mention so much as it does get wearing to read about its redundancy, especially since every other critic has said the same.

My first, and most overwhelming, criticism is the animation style. It's the same problem I have with any Illumination animation, their animation is far too clinical and lifeless for myself, all of the models have an 'uncanny valley' feel to them of looking dead behind the eyes. Granted, some of the landscapes look quite nice, but all the character models are still as sterilised as ever, offering no unique and discernible emotions beyond bug-eyed confusion, or making loud noises, which as we've learned from the rise of the Minions, Illumination seem to think loud noises constitute character traits. Alas, they do not.

Which may as well bring us on to the cast and characters, for what they are. Firstly, there's Cumberbatch's Grinch, which is probably the best realised thing in the film, if you hadn't known who the voice actor was, you could be forgiven for not guessing it was him, and for what it's worth he carries the film.

Elsewhere, there's the typical 'loud' characters, here manifested as a group of children, I have a very low tolerance for child actors, when they are talented, they can be as good as any other actor, however when kids are cast in family movies, the result is never an enjoyable experience, they're either being so saccharinely sweet or shrieking annoyingly about the latest on screen absurdity. The 2000 version had Taylor Momsen, who was at times irritating, she had believable character traits, she toed the line between sweetness and suspicion. Here, the little girl is far too righteously sweet, more than any child has ever been, her gang of friend's range in irritability, but rest assured they are cookie-cutter characters, not to mention that they're all annoying little berks.

In the end though, The Grinch left me with a smile and a warm feeling inside, which tells me the film was better than I give it credit for, its ending hit a nice sweet spot of warm, Christmas feelings, but it doesn't win points for that as it was basically working off a cheat sheet.

In conclusion, if you can get over the overall redundancy of the film, and its sanitised animation style, then you'll find a passable, if generic, slice of Christmas storytelling. It's a safe bet with kids and those already familiar with Illumination's work, I doubt it'll be one that will stand the test of time, however.

Fantastic Beasts: The Crimes of Grindelwald (Originally published December 4th, 2018)
Directed by David Yates
Starring: Eddie Redmayne, Katherine Waterstone, Jude Law and Johnny Depp

Setting out to make a spin-off series to something as beloved as the Harry Potter franchise is. usually, either real brave, or really stupid.

While the first film was a good first step into this fresh chapter of the Wizarding World, introducing us to a likeable new lead character, as well as interesting support characters and building background intrigue of an as yet unexplored dark period of Wizarding history.

So, how does this follow-up measure up against its high-pedigreed history?

Story

Since we last saw him, Newt Scamander has been banned from international travel by the Ministry of Magic, however, he is dragged unwillingly into the unfolding global battle against Dark Wizard Grindelwald.

Verdict

Well, this film pissed in a lot of people's porridge didn't it?

There isn't much I can really say about the contentious events in this film without giving out spoilers, which is against my principles as a critic, so I will skirt around these issues while addressing them as much as possible.

Whereas this film does not hit the dizzy heights of the main HP series, it is still fun while it lasts, and a lot of fun in parts when it embraces its status as a magical fantasy, the opening scene standing out in particular, as well as the climactic battle, all look visually stunning as it embraces the past's visual grandeur, while forging its own path.

Its biggest issue is it can't help but feel like the 'middle child' of its series, with it being the second of a planned five-film series, it can't really start going anywhere interesting without getting ahead of itself narrative-wise, it spins its wheels through its two-and-a-half hour run-time, picking up narrative points and either dropping them or hastily resolving them, with little feeling of closure.

It is also packed to the gills with exposition, there's a particular scene just before the films climax, where not one but TWO characters vomits up their entire family backstory, complete with flashback scenes, which grinds the narrative to a screeching halt.

The cast is extremely varied and there are peaks and troughs in the performances, the peaks laying in the lead, Eddie Redmayne, a reliable actor if ever there was one, Jude Law, who slips well into the role of Albus Dumbledore, and, surprisingly enough for me, Johnny Depp as the titular series 'big bad' Grindelwald.

I was a voice in the group decrying the casting of Depp as Grindelwald. Not only because of his, let's charitably say, less than stellar, personal record as of late, in fact that is far down the list as to why I was against his casting. The main reasons lie in the fact that Johnny Depp can only ever play Johnny Depp and given how we've already seen Grindelwald's appearance in the main series, Depp bears no resemblance to what we'd seen. But, in the end I was prepared to be proven wrong, and I'll be damned if he didn't surprise me.

That's not to say I think I was completely wrong, he is still playing off his typical 'Johnny Depp' character type, he's just simply inverted it from being a lovable anti-hero, to a cold, remorseless villain, and it works. I would like to see more depth from him in the sequel, but it's nice that he's actually playing a character, rather than just being himself in another wacky costume.

The basis of most of the backlash against the film surrounded the continuity rewriting, and I could write about that, but it would derail the reviews focus, so I'm not going to go into it in too much detail, but suffice to say that if you're invested in the series, then certain events, and appearances might take you out of the film a bit, but if you're a relative newcomer, chances are you won't notice anything.

In conclusion, while the film is uninspired and meandering, it's nice to be back into this familiar universe, and there are some eye-catching moments that will please long-term Potter fans, while infuriating them in later scenes. It does feel like the series could do with a serious shot in the arm in future instalments, as this feels like a slight miss-step
in the series, at only its second hurdle, which gives me the feeling the Rowling could maybe use some screenwriting help. In brief summary, a fun time while it happens, but inconsequential to the longer series narrative.

Creed II (Originally published December 6th, 2018)
Directed by Steven Caple Jr.
Starring: Michael B. Jordan, Sylvester Stallone, Tessa Thomson and Wood Harris

The first Creed was somewhat of a pleasant surprise, not only a spin-off, but a spin-off of a series that outstayed its welcome almost 30 years ago, it had no right to be as good as it was, but there it was. Given the films stellar cast and stellar director, there are few reasons to doubt how intended up being so good. Matching up Ryan Coogler with frequent collaborator Michael B. Jordan, sparks were practically guaranteed to fly.

So, with the franchise well and truly reinvigorated, here we are for the sequel, without Coogler, who instead finds himself in the producer's role, with Steven Caple Jr, a highly rated up-and-comer, occupying the vacant director's chair. So, is Creed II a knock-out? Or does it barely get past the first round?

Story

Three years on from his star-making bout with "Pretty" Ricky Conlan, Adonis Creed (Michael B. Jordan) becomes Heavyweight Champion of the World. Not long after, he is faced with a fearsome challenge, against the son of the man who killed his father.

Verdict

The saying goes (even if it is completely scientifically inaccurate) that: "Lightening doesn't strike twice." But I'll be damned if this film doesn't prove that saying wrong all over again.

Much like its predecessor, Creed II is very much a character drama, focusing on Adonis' burgeoning boxing career, as well as his blossoming relationship with Bianca (Tessa Thomson) the film successfully guides us through a complex mix of emotions, from vengeance to acceptance, all while presenting all its characters with nice arcs, and presenting them all extremely well. Take Viktor Drago, for instance, in appearance, he is nothing but a walking slab of meat who can just about punch and grunt but dig a little deeper and you'll find the reasons behind this brutish facade, all of which is presented to make this Drago less of a 'foreign menace' but more of a sympathetically misguided brute.

Which may as well bring us onto acting, and it goes without saying that Michael B. Jordan is great here, as despite the one blip (a big blip though Fantastic Four was) he is one of Hollywood's most reliable hands, but this film also gives us another chance to see how good an actor Sylvester Stallone can be. It is my theory that Stallone is only ever good when portraying Rocky Balboa, from an acting standpoint, and that may be unfair, but it is a testament to how great he makes Rocky, especially in the two Creed films, he isn't the Italian Stallion now, he's a dried up husk, trying to live his life as best he can, and help Adonis along the way. He's given a nice, yet subtle arc in this film, that succinctly plays off his relationship with Adonis, he makes slipping back into Balboa look as comfortable as slipping back into a comfortable pair of shoes.

The other big champion (pun very much intended) of this film is its cinematography. As in the last film, the fight choreography is crisp and brutal, you can feel every punch land with a bone-crunching thud, and feel every minute tick by, the stand-out being the final fight with Drago, has subtle call-backs to the Drago fight from Rocky IV, without getting bogged down in continuity, there's also an exquisite update of the classic 'training montage' from Rocky IV which tactfully calls back again, without feeling too pleased with itself.

It is by no means a perfect film, it can feel a big formulaic as sequels go, and as with most Rocky/Creed films, it follows the same basic plot structure, but going back to basics worked last time and it works here. I'd say the biggest fault of the movie is it flags somewhat in the middle, dropping a bit of its pacing in the process, but all of this is forgotten by the final act.

With that said, and as much as I enjoyed the film, it should be the last. This feels like the story they needed to tell, and probably wanted to tell from the early stages of the first films development, and I think pushing more sequels out would be overkill. The characters are left in the best place they could be, and I think it's time Rocky was moved on from, to be remembered as one of cinema's true great characters, without muddying the waters any further.

In summary then, there's something here for everyone, long time Rocky fans will get a rush out of seeing what is said to be the characters last appearance, and new fans won over by Creed will be glad to see the characters move on from where they were left off. I'd call this a triumphant sequel, easily meeting its heavyweight (I just can't stop myself) credentials, and a more than worthy addition, and hopefully finale, to the long-running series.

Ralph Breaks the Internet (Originally published December 15th, 2018)
Directed by: Rich Moore and Phil Johnston
Starring: John C. Reilly, Sarah Silverman, Gal Godot and Jane Lynch

Disney has an alarmingly high batting average when it comes to films. This year alone has seen the release of Coco and The Incredibles 2 (with Pixar) and now comes this, a sequel to the beloved 2012 release Wreck-It Ralph.

Disney have only really recently embraced theatrically releasing sequels. Showing a lot of restraint for a Hollywood studio, but in their shoes, I'd do the same. Many of their films make up the foundations of childhood nostalgia, and the older their customers get, the more unforgiving they get. Luckily, Disney is one of the few entities that also handle their sequels with care (theatrically released ones anyway, the less said about their straight-to-video sequels of the late 90's, early 00's, the better.)

All this being said, Wreck-It Ralph is a great display of Disney moving with the times, and altering their output slightly, but the question remains, do they ramp up this self-awareness to unprecedented levels? Or just hit that nostalgia sweet spot?

Story

Six years after the events of Wreck-It Ralph, the arcade that Ralph, Vanellope and their friends live in gets Wi-Fi installed, this plants the seed for the two best friends to take an odyssey across the world wide web, where Vanellope must decide where her dreams lay.

Verdict

Every new sequel undertaken by Disney seems like a new opportunity to finally trip up and reveal themselves as just as clueless as any-one else, thankfully, this is not that time.

Ralph Breaks the Internet hits every note you wanted coming back a second time round from the first adventure, and a few you didn't know you wanted until you had it. It's also the film that probably made me laugh the most all year, which is never a bad thing, if anything it's a great sign that a Disney animated film is smart and funny enough to tickle the funny bone of jaded twenty-somethings.

This is probably the most self-aware Disney has ever been (and probably ever will be again.) Not in the cringe-worthy way certain mainstream films mock popular culture, but by holding a mirror up to Disney's characters and practices, while openly mocking them, in a way which just shows the obvious love the writers and directors have for the source material. (Incidentally, the princess sequence teased by the trailer is ten-times as good on screen.)

So onto the cast; John C Reilly once again leads the way as Ralph. Reilly is a great example of an underrated actor, quietly going about his career, gaining admirers, without needing the media profile of his peers. While on the surface, his career is mostly preoccupied with his comedic roles, he's proven himself an extremely capable dramatic actor, none of which matter here, what does matter is the way he can deliver lines through an animated character that make us sympathise with his character, while portraying the large faults his character has, that was the main draw of the first movie for me. The fact that at heart, Ralph is that guy overlooked by everyone around him, but never does himself any favours when he goes about trying to prove them wrong, it was heart-warming before, and it still is now.

Then, there's Sarah Silverman, who I'm not a huge fan of, in fact, I found Vanellope to be more irritating than cute first time around, I think she's probably been told to tone it down a bit for the sequel and she does, which makes for a much more enjoyable character and performance. There's a moment of Vanellope's that is the closest the film comes to a film-stealing scene, which I won't spoil, but suffice to say it's worth seeing.

Not that I don't have problems, I do, not huge ones, but problems, nonetheless. It sometimes feels as though we're re-tracing the steps of the first film, the example I gave of Ralph's character a few paragraphs ago might be endearing to watch, but re-tracing the same character moments seem like a loss of momentum, also, while some of the internet representation in the film is funny now, it's the kind of thing that won't age well, but frankly, if that's a films biggest fault, then it's not exactly the end of the world.

In conclusion, this film is exactly what you'd expect from Disney, moments of genuinely emotional storytelling mixed with some hilarious jokes, characters and references, with Disney's as-always flawless animation style, and they've got another massive success on their hands.

Aquaman (Originally published December 22nd, 2018)
Directed by James Wan
Starring: Jason Momoa, Amber Heard, Willem Dafoe and Patrick Wilson

Commenting on the DCEU on the internet is like poking a hungry lion with a stick, as there's a good chance you might be eaten whole by a terrifying beast.

There are several enthusiastic people on either side of the fence, people who defend the DCEU, and Zack Snyder in particular, and declare his work as masterpieces and decry the Justice League film for its bastardisation at the hands of Warner Brothers and Joss Whedon, and there are people who consider the DCEU a dumpster fire beyond the control of any fire department.

Myself, I sit in neither camp. I have stated my views briefly before; I do not want the DCEU to fail. In my eyes, the more good comic book movies there are, the better. My favourite superhero is Batman, despite how much I love the MCU films, it makes no sense for me to want the DCEU to fail, and truth be told, there have been highlights, Wonder Woman was great, Man of Steel was a great start to something that should have been so much more.

However, I am not here for a DCEU retrospective, I'm here to review their latest offering, Aquaman, so here we go...

Story

Arthur Curry is the son of a human lighthouse keeper, and the Queen of Atlantis, from his mother's side he is blessed with the gift to breath underwater, talk to fish and possesses incredible strength, with these powers he becomes the Superhero Aquaman, and when his half-brother, the current King of Atlantis threatens to declare war on the surface, Arthur must journey to Atlantis and challenge for the throne.

Verdict

The first thing I'll say for Aquaman is, it may well be the best-looking superhero film of all time. Its visual style is striking, and beautiful. Specifically speaking the underwater worlds are incredibly well realised by James Wan, which isn't to say the scenes on the surface were bad, they weren't, in fact there's a run of scenes in Italy which are amazing visually and practically, being home to some of the films best action.

Speaking of action, it is the films jewel in its crown, from the first five minutes, in a claustrophobic, closely-shot fight in the lighthouse to the grand-scale epic of the final battle between kingdoms, it shines brightest whilst focused on smaller skirmishes, with the aforementioned scenes in Italy shining brightest, two separate fights, effortlessly cut together to lead into each other, in a way which doesn't drop the pace, some of the year's best action scenes take place in this film.

In case you were still in the dark after that last sentence, I liked Aquaman, quite a lot actually. I'd even say it beats out Wonder Woman for best DCEU film, and if you'd have told me five years ago that the best film in a series that includes Batman, was an Aquaman film, I'd have been questioning your sanity.

When it comes to cast, the film doesn't boast a number of highly regarded performers, perhaps besides Willem Dafoe, but I can confidently say that all of the cast rise to the occasion brilliantly. Jason Momoa is charismatic and magnetic in his first lead outing for the DCEU, showing a surprising amount of depth too, in the more heartfelt scenes, I had in the past thought Momoa as someone who gets by on looks as opposed to ability, but here I see that he has that ability, and I am left to eat humble pie. Amber Heard is also impressive as Mera, I must confess to not knowing much of her work, but I liked what I saw here.

To me, Aquaman represents a new dawn for the DCEU, following the disappointment, critically and financially of Justice League, it needed a kick up the arse with a fresh, exciting film and it got it. Aquaman resets the path for the DCEU, in much the same way Wonder Woman did over a year ago. Not only has it brought financial success but a thematic departure from the DCEU's darker, grungier offerings, Aquaman offers a vibrant, bright world, going so far as to explore new worlds below the surface, it's a step in the right direction for the franchise, and a momentum boost that I hope they can carry on.

It is by no means a perfect film, of course. Clocking in at just under two-and-a-half hours, it is occasionally overstuffed, especially when juggling its antagonists, but at no point does it derail the pacing, it isn't a long film that feels long, like Justice League, it does feel like it deserves its run-time to flesh out the world. There are also an adherence to a fair few cliché's, none of which are deal breakers, the biggest recurring complaint from past films of forced humour isn't as apparent here, as the humour lands well, and is, more importantly, thematically appropriate.

In conclusion then, I believe this to be the high point of this franchise so far, those going in with a dislike of past films should be pleasantly surprised, and long-time DCEU fans have another film to hold up as a badge of honour, just know that we still don't agree on Batman v Superman though, sorry guys.

Chapter Nine: Other Writing 2018

Hollywood Has a Superhero Problem (Originally published January 11th, 2018)

Back in the 2000's, when I first started going to the cinema the big releases of Superhero movies were a rare commodity. The first one I remember seeing (bearing in mind my memory is terrible, so it is possible I saw one beforehand) was 2005's Batman Begins. I went with school and I really enjoyed it, as I do to this day, to tell the truth Batman is my favourite comic book character (there's probably a column in that someday.)

The year Batman Begins was released, 2005, only four movies based off mainstream comic were released. Conversely, last year NINE comic book movies were released that's one comic book movie every 5.7 weeks (hooray for calculators).

Therein lies the problem, we're being inundated with superhero/comic book movies faster than we can digest them, it's overkill and what's more, with Infinity War on the horizon and DC's universe staggering on, it doesn't look likely that they're going to slow down.

I took the liberty of looking up what comic book movies are currently slated for release this year and in total there is scheduled to be another nine movies to add to the increasing total, and that isn't taking into account straight-to-DVD animated releases, otherwise I could count to infinity (pun not intended).

The point I'm torturously trying to make is, the tidal wave of movies is potentially damaging not only to comic book movies themselves, but the movie industry as a whole. Hollywood now has a set precedent for how much they think these movies should make, it would only take a few high-profile flops for the kingdom to topple completely, leading to less being invested in genuinely interesting movies in favour of another production line Superhero film, mostly perfectly functional, but at this point, and with Marvel in particular, each movie just seems to serve as an advert for the next release, it's all one deadly cycle, which is destined one day to backfire horribly.

Please don't think I'm taking away from comic book movies, after all, my Top 10 of 2017 had no less than three comic book movies, so I understand if this rings somewhat hollow, but how can we enjoy these movies long term if we know there's always a new one just around the corner?

The effect of the comic book movie is spreading too, you can't seem to move now for 'Movie Universes' and it's a worrying trend, as I say it only takes a few failures for the whole thing to fall apart. Take for example last year's remake of 'The Mummy' before release day it was touted to be the start of a so called 'Dark Universe' of films, yet upon release and it's savaging at the hands of critics and audiences alike, this universe seems like it won't be coming back anytime soon.

I'm not asking for a complete veto on comic book movies, I just think the producers should take a step back and determine if the movie they're producing is actually a thing that's worth making for artistic merit, rather than as an extremely expensive advert for the next movie.

After all, what would you rather have? A few comic book movies a year that make an impact, or a production line of movies that leave no lasting impact? Audiences are sure to vote with their feet, and once they do, it's bad news for all involved.

Mr Opinionated's Oscar Predictions (Originally published February 28th, 2018)

The biggest awards ceremony in Hollywood, the Academy Awards, take place this Sunday. With the date fast approaching, I thought I'd look at each category and give my predictions for each, I won't be covering every category as I don't feel qualified to predict Best Costume Design, for instance, so only the creative awards will be predicted. Without any further ado, let's get down to it.

Best Original Score

Nominations:

- Dunkirk - Hans Zimmer
- Phantom Thread - Jonny Greenwood
- The Shape of Water - Alexandre Desplat
- Star Wars: The Last Jedi - John Williams
- Three Billboards Outside Ebbing, Missouri

Winner:

Star Wars: The Last Jedi - John Williams

One of the things I noticed during the first viewing of the latest Star Wars movie, was the epic and sweeping score by legendary composer John Williams. He never fails to hit a home run for the Star Wars movies, and this ranks way up there with the best.

Best Original Song

Nominations

- Mighty River (Mudbound) - Mary J Blige, Raphael Saadiq and Taura Stinson
- Mystery of Love (Call Me by Your Name) - Sufjan Stevens
- Remember Me (Coco) - Kristen Anderson-Lopez and Robert Lopez
- Stand Up for Something (Marshall) - Diane Warren and Common

- This Is Me (The Greatest Showman) - Benj Pasek and Justin Paul

Winner:

This Is Me (The Greatest Showman) - Benj Pasek and Justin Paul

This is one of the many categories where I don't envy the Academy. Really, it's a two-horse race between two great songs; Remember Me and This Is Me, both have equal chances of winning, and have great pedigree behind them, but I think This Is Me will edge it on Sunday night.

Best Animated Feature Film

Nominations:

- The Boss Baby - Tom McGrath and Ramsey Ann Naito
- The Breadwinner - Nora Twomey and Anthony Leo
- Coco - Lee Unkrich and Darla K. Anderson
- Ferdinand - Carlos Saldanha
- Loving Vincent - Dorota Kobiela, Hugh Welchman and Ivan Mactaggart.

Winner:

Coco - Lee Unkrich and Darla K. Anderson

Year after year the Academy show their contempt for animated movies, the fact that The Goddamned Boss Baby is nominated is all the proof you need of that, of the category there are only really two stand outs, Loving Vincent a strikingly beautiful and original animated piece of art and Coco, the latest Disney-Pixar masterpiece. I believe the Academy will go with old reliable and give the gong to Coco, God-forbid they push the boat out and give it to something original.

Best Adapted Screenplay

Nominations:

- Call Me by Your Name - James Ivory, based on a novel by Andre Aciman
- The Disaster Artist - Scott Neustadter and Michael H. Weber based on a book by Greg Sestero and Tom Bissell
- Logan - Scott Frank, James Mangold and Michael Green based on Marvel comic books.
- Molly's Game - Aaron Sorkin based on the memoir by Molly Bloom
- Mudbound - Virgil Williams and Dee Rees based on a novel by Hillary Jordan

Winner:

Logan - Scott Frank, James Mangold and Michael Green.

No surprises here, the best comic book movie since The Dark Knight, should walk away with the honours, however there's a chance Molly's Game could take the honours, or even The Disaster Artist, really in a just world, Logan should win, let's hope it does.

Best Original Screenplay

Nominations:

- The Big Sick - Emily V. Gordon and Kumail Nanjiani
- Get Out - Jordan Peele
- Lady Bird - Greta Gerwig
- The Shape of Water - Guillermo Del Toro and Vanessa Taylor
- Three Billboards Outside Ebbing, Missouri - Martin McDonagh

Winner:

Three Billboards Outside Ebbing, Missouri - Martin McDonagh

This could easily go to The Shape of Water, whose screenplay is also exceptional, but I don't think there's been a better script this year than Three Billboards. Sharp and darkly humorous as well as tragic and heart-breaking, it's a rollercoaster ride.

Note of apology:

I haven't seen enough of the nominated performances in the Best Supporting Actress category; therefore I don't feel like I can predict it, my apologies.

Best Supporting Actor

Nominations:

- Willem Dafoe as Bobby Hicks - The Florida Project
- Woody Harrelson as Chief Bill Willoughby - Three Billboards Outside Ebbing, Missouri
- Richard Jenkins as Giles - The Shape of Water
- Christopher Plummer as J. Paul Getty - All the Money in the World
- Sam Rockwell as Officer Jason Dixon - Three Billboards Outside Ebbing, Missouri

Winner:

Sam Rockwell - Three Billboards Outside Ebbing, Missouri

Another unenviable task for the Academy, two incredible performances in one movie from Sam Rockwell and Woody Harrelson, as well as a stellar performance from Richard Jenkins in The Shape of Water. But Sam Rockwell should claim the prize, for portraying a character with an incredible arc, and almost managing to steal the movie. Almost.

Best Leading Actress

Nominations:

- Sally Hawkins as Elisa Esposito - The Shape of Water
- Frances McDormand as Mildred Hayes - Three Billboards Outside Ebbing, Missouri
- Margot Robbie as Tonya Harding - I, Tonya
- Saoirse Ronan as Christine "Lady Bird" McPherson - Lady Bird
- Meryl Streep as Katharine Graham - The Post

Winner:

Frances McDormand - Three Billboards Outside Ebbing, Missouri

There can only really be one winner here. Frances McDormand gave a powerhouse performance that leaves everyone else in the shade. Only the Academy's obsession with Meryl Streep stands in the way of her winning a second Oscar.

Best Leading Actor

Nominations:

- Timothee Chalamet as Elio Perlman - Call Me by Your Name
- Daniel Day-Lewis as Reynolds Woodcock - Phantom Thread
- Daniel Kaluuya as Chris Washington - Get Out
- Gary Oldman as Winston Churchill - Darkest Hour
- Denzel Washington as Roman J. Israel - Roman J. Israel, Esq.

Winner:

Gary Oldman - Darkest Hour

I'm not a betting man, but if I was, this would be the easiest bet I'd ever take, the only thing that stands in his way is another Academy favourite Daniel Day-Lewis is also nominated, paired with the fact that it's allegedly Day-Lewis's final performance, that could be a factor, but I can't see it, there's only one winner here.

Best Director

Nominations:

- Christopher Nolan - Dunkirk
- Jordan Peele - Get Out
- Greta Gerwig - Lady Bird
- Paul Thomas Anderson - Phantom Thread
- Guillermo Del Toro - The Shape of Water

Winner:

Guillermo Del Toro - The Shape of Water

Had this been a post of who I would want to win as opposed to a predictions of who I think will win, then Christopher Nolan would take this award, although I wouldn't have any problem with Del Toro winning, he deserves it too, it's been a particularly tough year I think to pick any one movie over another.

Best Picture

Nominations:

- Call Me by Your Name - Peter Spears, Luca Guadagnino, Emilie Georges and Morabito
- Darkest Hour -Tim Bevan, Eric Fellner, Lisa Bruce, Anthony McCarten and Douglas Urbanski
- Dunkirk - Emma Thomas and Christopher Nolan
- Get Out - Sean McKittrick, Jason Blum, Edward H. Hamm Jr. and Jordan Peele
- Lady Bird - Scott Rudin, Eli Bush and Evelyn O'Neill

- Phantom Thread - JoAnne Sellar, Paul Thomas Anderson, Megan Ellison and Daniel Lupi
- The Post - Amy Pascal, Steven Spielberg and Kristie Macosko Krieger
- The Shape of Water - Guillermo del Toro and J. Miles Dale
- Three Billboards Outside Ebbing, Missouri - Graham Broadbent, Pete Czernin and Martin McDonagh

Winner:

Three Billboards Outside Ebbing, Missouri - Graham Broadbent, Pete Czernin and Martin McDonagh

What a list to have to pick from, as much as it's impossible to tell sometimes what the Academy will vote for, it's even harder here with such a stellar line-up, any of them could win it, but I've opted for Three Billboards, using the BAFTAs as a template for the Oscars isn't always wise, but I feel that Three Billboards is the kind of movie the Academy vote for Best Picture, therefore I'm plumping for that.

<u>Marvel Cinematic Universe Retrospective - Phase One</u> (Originally published April 14th, 2018)

This year marks the tenth anniversary of the Marvel Cinematic Universe, and to celebrate this, and the run-up to Infinity War, I'll be taking a look at every film released in the MCU at this point, starting from the very beginning.

Note: Due to the sheer number of films covered, these reviews won't be as in-depth as my usual posts, simply taking a brief look at the film and my opinions of it.

Iron Man (2008) - Directed by John Favreau

It's unbelievable that the MCU began ten bloody years ago with this strong start, Iron Man. This introduced everything the MCU is now beloved for, first and foremost, Robert Downey Jr as Tony Stark, who has proven to be the perfect casting.

Who knows whether when they were making this whether they knew the amorphous monster this franchise will become? It doesn't carry the burden of later movies; such as feeling like an episode in an unusually long TV series, it feels focused as a result on establishing Tony and Iron Man as the man and character, there were little glimpses of what's to come, namely the now prerequisite post-credits scene, featuring the first mention of the word 'Avengers' and appearance of Nick Fury.

The film was directed by MCU favourite Jon Favreau, who would return for the sequel and portray Tony's bodyguard, Happy Hogan, who's appearance would become more and more vital as the films progress.

This is one of the stronger franchise starters, it referred to a bigger future while focusing on the characters it is introducing, it's also one of the few early MCU movies that I personally enjoy going back to, it's enjoyable, funny and the action is honed to a fine shine.

The Incredible Hulk (2008) - Directed by Louis Leterrier

It only took until the second movie for Marvel to misstep. Now, The Incredible Hulk isn't a terrible film, there are worse movies even in the MCU itself, but it is crushingly dull, which is a big enough crutch for a film.

It is unfortunate that this will probably be the only solo Hulk movie in the MCU. Seeing as Universal still hold half of the movie rights for the Hulk, hence this is the only Universal distributed film in the MCU, apart from that Paramount distributed all the Phase One films before Disney came along with their sacks of cash and bought the burgeoning franchise.

The director of this venture, Louis Leterrier, never returned to the MCU, he went on to make the average at best Now You See Me and the terrible Clash of the Titans, so it's probably for the best.

When a franchise line-up includes films renowned for their entertainment value, it hardly makes a film like Incredible Hulk worth revisiting, except for revisionists sake, as I say it's not bad, the final battle is suitably city-destroying, apart from that there's not much else to it.

Iron Man 2 (2010) - Directed by Jon Favreau

Here is where the misstep off the path turns into a fall into a ditch. Can you tell I don't like this film?

So, two years have passed since the touchstone Iron Man was released, The Incredible Hulk didn't set the world on fire quite like Iron Man, it was time to return to the charisma of Tony Stark, it's just a shame that his charisma was wasted in such an inconsequential film.

There seems to be an unwelcome trend in the Iron Man sequels where the big villain ends up being just a businessman. Granted this was also the case in the first, but the thing with that is, Obadiah Stane was interesting, and his motivation was believable, conversely Justin Hammer (portrayed by Sam Rockwell, who deserves better) is just irritating and the secondary villain isn't much better. Mickey Rourke is so hammy in this you could stick him between two slices of bread and call him a sandwich.

There was also a focus on Tony's relationship with Pepper, which isn't what we're all here for, I don't know about anyone else, but I struggle to see why Pepper is portrayed as someone the audience is invested in when she's about as interesting as a cereal box with a frowny face drawn on it. I was relieved when she wasn't in Age of Ultron, only to come back in Spider-Man like your most unwanted neighbour, but we get ahead of ourselves.

I don't know what happened to the Jon Favreau who helmed the interesting original film, but it just shows how little this film was thought of, since he was removed from the director's chair for the sequel.

I wouldn't recommend watching Iron Man 2 now, since there are so many more MCU films worth your time, only touch it if you really, really want to watch all the MCU films before Infinity War.

Thor (2011) - Directed by Kenneth Branagh

So we've been left in a ditch after Iron Man 2 and Thor tries to claw us out of the ditch, but then fails and instead decides to recite Shakespeare to itself.

Apart from that incredibly contrived analogy, Thor is in the same category of Incredible Hulk, dull, yet functional and mostly just there to introduce the character before The Avengers must assemble.

Actually, that's not quite fair, we're also introduced to one of the franchise's most beloved villains (a paradox in itself really) Loki, Thor's adopted brother whose attempts to take over Asgard and later the Earth anchors the main post of the first phase, in that way it is significant to the rest of the series as whole.

You might be surprised, as I was when I remembered this, that this was directed by Kenneth Branagh, he of classical Shakespearean fame. You may remember that Branagh both starred in and directed one of my favourite films last year, but this is far from his finest hour. It's just not a great fit, besides the mildly Shakespearean tone that the Asgardians talk in, he's well acquainted with that at least, if not suited to superheroes.

This is the kind of film that is hard to critique. Functional, but not interesting enough to make me invested, I would rather watch this over Iron Man 2, but that's not really saying much.

Captain America: The First Avenger (2011) - Directed by Joe Johnston

And thus does the final jigsaw piece fall into place. A rather vital jigsaw piece too as the title tells us, Cap is 'The First Avenger' the guy who the rest orbit around, which makes it a bit of a shame that he's not all that interesting, at least in this film.

So, in somewhat of an emerging pattern in Phase One, this could have been so much more. It is, however, better than Thor, the World War II setting might be old hat, but here it is needed, Cap's character needs to emerge unblinking from the glory of the War, to set him up as the patriotic war-hero character to extract from the 40's into modern times for The Avengers.

It's a basic plot and will seem familiar if you've watched any WWII film, Hydra are a Cling film-thin facade for the Nazi's and Red Skull is basically Hitler with a red skull... obviously. It also plants seeds for later, Bucky for instance, we get the start of his story here.

The director responsible for bringing the iconic Captain America to the silver screen is Joe Johnston, who brought us childhood favourite Jumanji and the not-so-favourite Jurassic Park III, his career also boasts a credit as 'Art Director' for Empire Strikes Back. Another one and done director, his career has recently stalled unfortunately, as his direction here is admirable, even when the script is often dull.

If I had to re-watch Phase One, I would probably look forward to this after Iron Man 2 and Thor, which isn't exactly a point in its favour, but it at least isn't awful and does have redeeming features, I might be tempted to go back to it for another watch for revisions sake but wouldn't rank it as a favourite.

The Avengers Assemble (2012) - Directed by Joss Whedon

This is what four years of introducing plot points lead up to. At the time the biggest superhero movie ever released, Avengers was received with a rapturous response by critics and fans alike, and well deserved that praise is, it makes the dull moments in Phase One all worth it which is all you can ask.

This is the point where a thousand executives realised the potential in a Shared Universe and thus, ruined several films and properties, but you can hardly blame it for that, if you saw its profit, you'd probably want a share of it too.

It brought together all the elements introduced in the last four years and tied it up with a nice big bow, while leaving itself wide open for future instalments, as we all now know all too well, as we navigate the tidal waves of new superhero movies.

Joss Whedon was the guy trusted with the keys to the kingdom here and a lot of responsibility sat on his shoulders, either the film would be a runaway success and launch a monolithic, and highly lucrative, future or it was underwhelming, and faith would be lost in the project and it potentially trails off. Fortunately for us the first narrative came true and this movie is championed as one of the greatest superhero movies of all time.

Would I call it that? Maybe not, I think there's been better films in the MCU, but at the time it was mind-blowing, several popular characters come together for the first time in cinematic history, you'd think that is the kind of hype you couldn't replicate, but as we now know, with Infinity War on the horizon, this could not be more wrong.

If I were to watch Phase One out of choice, I'd probably only watch Iron Man and Avengers, which tells you more about the other films than it does about this, but this is still incredible amounts of fun to re-watch, even with the more modern films to watch.

Marvel Cinematic Universe Retrospective - Phase Two (Originally published

So having covered Phase One a few weeks ago, I figured it was time to revisit the world of personality disorders and spandex to recap the second phase of the MCU

Iron Man 3 (2013) - Directed by Shane Black

So we start with a cough. Not a bang, not a whimper, just a cough.

That was my diplomatic way of saying that it wasn't bad, yet not good either. Steps forward were taken from Iron Man 2, and a few steps back also, the Iron Man films still can't get out of the 'baddie is a businessman' angle that they trotted out again here. This was also the film that promised the on-screen debut of The Mandarin, one of Iron Man's most enduring comic book adversaries. Instead we got an old, drunk actor character. Not a bad swap, right?

There doesn't feel like there's a massive jump thematically. Except for the introduction of a new wrinkle to the character of Tony Stark in the form of PTSD, it gives an interesting new angle to not only Iron Man, but Stark himself too.

Overall not the best introduction to a new phase, given the extravagance of Avengers, and how this had to follow it, an impossible task perhaps, a better effort would have been required to come close.

Thor: The Dark World (2013) - Directed by Alan Taylor

Urgh. Well, here we are, the absolute nadir of the MCU, Thor: The Dark World.

The Dark World is the worst kind of bad, the kind that is as exciting as watching the Wall-Drying World Championships. The kind of film that's perfectly well put together technically, but is crushingly, crushingly dull.

Marvel seemed to take forever in getting Thor right, I would argue the only time he's been interesting was in Ragnarok, and arguably the Avengers films, they seemed to have him down as some kind of Shakespearean tragedy character, instead of the lightening-flinging Norse God that he actually is.

After the first Thor, I didn't think the character could get duller, but obviously I just wasn't being ambitious enough, as this is like a scientific experiment in how much boredom a human can naturally take.

The real shame is the amount of talent on display here. Firstly there's Alan Taylor, who made his name directing several episodes of the utterly sublime Game of Thrones, then there's your usual cast of badly used actors, this film particularly putting a bee in my bonnet for so utterly wasting Loki, and then there's poor Christopher Ecclestone. As if it wasn't enough to be underappreciated in his role as Doctor Who, the absolute tripe he has to work with here really wins my sympathy, his character pretty much being the antithesis of the 'Marvel can't write villains' argument.

So two films in, we have one resounding meh, and one complete wash-out, but don't worry, it can only get better from here...

Captain America: The Winter Soldier (2014) - Directed by Anthony and Joe Russo

Now, I'll be the first to admit that in my list of favourite superheroes, Captain America is nowhere near the top, which is why I was so struck dumb that this movie was the best instalment of the MCU up to this point and has rarely been topped since.

I think the reason I'm not a fan of Cap is, he's so often just a cut-and-dry character and I like characters to have complexities and flaws, whereas Cap often comes across as a goody-two-shoes boy scout, and while I understand that this is his character and I've criticised the DC film's for trying to make Superman broody, it doesn't make for a terribly engaging character. Here, however, they make him interesting by putting him against possibly his biggest failure, Bucky.

It doesn't surprise me that the Russo's were giving the Marvel baton to run with after this film as its direction and pacing are crisp and seamless, each film flows very well into the next and the plot is tightly executed using characters that we grow to sympathise with.

One particular stand-out scene for me is the fight scene in the crowded elevator, which could have seemed cramped and restrictive in some director's hands, but in the Russo's, it is a cinematic marvel (no pun intended).

Not only did this movie succeed in being an excellent stand-alone movie, it also lays the groundwork for many years to come, establishing Bucky's time as The Winter Soldier, something that becomes pivotal further down the line.

All-in-all this is an excellent recovery from two fairly mediocre films, but the pressure was on to follow this up with something equally surprising and successful.

Guardians of the Galaxy (2014) - Directed by James Gun

In a few years, we will look back on 2014 as the year where Marvel truly hit its stride. Not only did they release The Winter Soldier for our pleasure, but also the single most surprising superhero movie of all time, Guardians of the Galaxy.

I think it's safe to say that not many people were familiar with the Guardians prior to the film's release, maybe hardcore comic fans, but even then, they weren't long-time mainstays of the comic world. So leave it to James Gunn to take a relatively obscure superhero property and make a genuinely surprising, hilarious and generally fun movie out of them.

From what I can remember, hype wasn't at an all-time high surrounding this movie at release, people only truly got excited post-release when everyone was gushing about how fun it was, and fun it certainly is, it's by no means a perfect film, and I think the low bar of expectation really helped it at the time, but it really is just pure entertainment, not tremendously deep, but self-aware enough to not need too.

The success of the movie instantly launched the characters into the stratosphere, characters like Groot and Star-Lord are now among the most beloved in the MCU, but it also did wonders for the careers of its main actors, Chris Pratt was merely a sitcom actor before Guardians, he can now count himself among Hollywood's elite, former wrestler Dave Bautista defied any and all expectations to really grow into the part of Drax, in such a way that you could swear it was written for him, he has since built a respectable career as a reliable character actor.

With all the hype around the film post-release, the sequel was green lit, signalling the next phase of Marvel's plan to expand into space with the true arrival of Thanos. It also spanned thousands of people attempting Vin Diesel's "I Am Groot". It almost felt like the start of a revolution.

Avengers: Age of Ultron (2015) - Directed by Joss Whedon

The year is 2015. Marvel have just released two massively successful blockbusters that have steadied their franchise immeasurably and now they have the enormous task of not only following those, but also following the original Avengers movie.

After vanquishing Loki in Manhattan and leaving a mess in their wake, the Avengers have gone their own separate ways somewhat, but are brought back together when an over-zealous Tony creates an artificial intelligence that then gains sentience and decides the sensible thing to do is to wipe out humanity.

What feels different this time around is that it feels like Ultron is a problem the Avengers themselves caused, of course only one of them, arguably two, is directly involved, but still they're fighting their own creation, in a throwback to Frankenstein almost.

Age of Ultron had a mountain to climb from the word go, which is probably why it hits us straight out of the gate with a big action set-piece, it doesn't want to waste a minute less we think they're getting complacent, granted it slows down a bit later, but the frantic pace remains for most of the movie, book-ended by two excellent action set-piece fight scenes.

At the time of release, I rated Age of Ultron higher than the first Avengers, having watched them both again since, my position has changed somewhat, as I find them difficult to compare. All the characters are in completely different places to where they were when Loki and his alien chums invaded. They feel weighed down with extra baggage, which on one hand makes them relate-able, while sneakily planting seeds for future events, but on the other it struggles to match the sheer scale of the first one and the scale of the first Avengers is what made it special.

I don't want to be too harsh on Age of Ultron because I still think it's a great superhero film, but I do think it was the right time for Joss Whedon to move on, not that I have anything against him, but I couldn't see his style of writing working in say, Infinity War.

In summary, it was a film brimming with ideas, with some great moments scattered about, but it felt like a lesser film for lacking in the scale of its predecessor.

Ant-Man (2015) - Directed by Peyton Reed

And so we reach the final film of the MCU's second phase. A film I consider to be a bedfellow of Guardians of the Galaxy, Ant-Man.

To add to a list of confessions in the column, I'll freely admit to laughing at the concept of an Ant-Man film before release. Knowing little about the character, I found the concept absurd (really, Nathan? A comic book movie being absurd? What next? Sci-fi being a bit unrealistic?) but I have a friend who was, and still is, into Ant-Man comic books who assured me we were in for a treat. Lo and behold he was right.

While not being as re-watchable as Guardians, in my opinion, Ant-Man is still an incredibly surprising thrill-ride, anchored by an extremely love-able protagonist, but let-down somewhat by a less-than-stellar villain, a common theme in some Marvel films.

The cast is very impressive here, led by Paul Rudd, someone competing with Chris Pratt and Robert Downey Jr for the prize of 'most charismatic man in the MCU' who gives a funny, yet sometimes touching portrayal of Scott Lang, a convicted thief trying to stick to the straight-and-narrow so he can see his daughter. He is supported by Evangeline Lilly, who portrays Hope van Dyke, the daughter of the original Ant-Man, Hank Pym, who himself is portrayed by Michael Douglas, who it was great to see in a prominent role again, and rounding out the cast is Michael Pena, who plays Luis, Scott's hilarious, Hispanic friend/accomplice. They all gel incredibly well together, chemistry between the cast is swiftly becoming Marvel's bread and butter at this point.

The reason I say Ant-Man is kind of a bedfellow for Guardians is that feelings were very similar towards it before it's launch. Being a riskier release than say, an Iron Man film, the creators really have to work hard to make their film worth watching, and Ant-Man is very much worth watching, and I look forward to how they build on it in the sequel.

Ranking the Star Wars Movies (Originally published June 6th, 2018)

Now, for the fervent cinemagoer like myself, the current times are one hell of a mixed bag. On a positive side, all the blockbusters have been released a few weeks apart, but on the other side of the coin, when you're like me, you see all the films in the first week and then spent the following few weeks digging deep for something to watch. This was my long-winded way of saying I've already reviewed all the big movies so I'm going to witter on about an opinion that no-one asked for. Enjoy.

In case you didn't figure out this fact over the last year or so of me writing these pieces (which I still have no idea of what to call, I hate the word blog and column sounds too formal, but I digress) I love Star Wars. Love it so much that over the last few years I've stayed up until the early hours of the morning to watch these films at midnight, like a complete loser, so I could see them early and bask in their splendour.

Ranking these films is a double-edged sword, on one hand, the bottom half is simple, as you'll see later, but the top half may see me lynched by certain segments of nerd culture, so bear in mind that this is MY opinion, and mine alone. With that said, there will be more spoilers here than usual, so in case you missed the bold writing at the start of this list, here's another warning; HERE BE SPOILERS!

One rule before we start: only theatrical releases are eligible, so no Holiday Special or Caravan of Courage, more's the pity.

Eleven - Star Wars: The Clone Wars (Directed by Dave Filoni)

I'll forgive you if you told me that you forgot that there was a cinema-released Clone Wars movie, I certainly wish I could.

If you'd sat through the Prequel Trilogy and thought you'd like to see more of whiny Anakin and the faceless, character-less Clones, then here's the movie for you, you weirdo.

It was certainly an odd choice to launch a TV series with a movie, specifically one released in cinemas, fans of the extended TV universe will be quick to point out that Rebels also launched with a movie, the difference being that that one was made for TV and was essentially a pilot episode, which is exactly what this feels like, a pilot episode and not a very good one at that. Probably best to leave this one forgotten to history.

Ten - Star Wars: Episode II - Attack of the Clones (Directed by George Lucas)

From one movie with the word 'Clone' in the title to another with 2002's *Attack of the Clones*.

I've seen this movie defended by some as the best movie in the Prequel saga, but honestly, I just can't see it. I do truly believe that each of the saga has **at least** one redeeming factor, and this has very, very few of those. The stadium battle scene probably being an albeit brief highlight. It doesn't have the fleeting spark that made Episodes I and III slightly more watchable.

It's main flaw for me is it's casting of Anakin. After the backlash (as harsh as it was) towards Jake Lloyd in Episode I, the pressure must have been on to choose the perfect Anakin, and George Lucas could not have missed the mark more had he been in a different star-system.

Admittedly, not all blame lays on Hayden Christensen, some of it has to lay on Lucas' reportedly slapdash directorial style, but Anakin really comes off as a whiny, entitled little brat here, and while this may have been the intention at the scripting stage, it's hardly in-line with the Darth Vader character that we all know he's going to become.

Not helped by this is the romance subplot between Anakin and Padme. This mostly falls flat because of the two actors involved having as much chemistry as two dead fish, every line of dialogue sounds awkward and almost as if the writer hasn't heard genuine conversation (when was the last time you flirted by mentioning sand?) they don't feel like two people pre-destined to fall in love as two awkward wallflowers on prom night.

In this movie's favour it does introduce a somewhat interesting side villain in Count Dooku, played by the legendary Christopher Lee, but even he can't save this damp squib, and all we're left with is another two hours of wasted opportunities, which will become a running theme in the prequels...

Nine - Star Wars: Episode I - The Phantom Menace (Directed by George Lucas)

Imagine people's disappointment in 1999, when after all that anticipation, they're treated to this dull, often incoherent and frustrating mess. After this film, all the goodwill people had for George Lucas drained away, along with several glaringly missed opportunities.

The reason this film is so frustrating is it could and should have been so much better. All the pieces were there for a worthy continuation of the Star Wars mythos, building up to the genesis of Darth Vader, it's just a shame that the film assembled these pieces as poorly as French carmakers.

On the face of it, Episode I was a success. It made over $1 billion at the box office after all, of course we know that making a lot of money doesn't mean the movie is good, the Transformers films are testament to that, but not only that but it formed the basis for the rest of the prequels, which as we were to find out, is like building a house on quicksand.

Just like its sequel, in fact probably even more so, this is a film built on missed opportunities. A new, interesting Sith lord is introduced and promptly killed in the same movie (a mess that future animated series would clean up), massively talented actors are wasted with a weak script and practical effects that helped characterise the series up to that point were thrown out in favour of gaudy CGI monstrosities. Not only that but we got Jar Jar Binks, and it isn't often I swear in these write-ups, but fuck Jar Jar Binks.

So after all that, why isn't Episode I below Episode II? Well, that's because despite it having an incredible number of flaws, there are simply more redeeming factors in Episode I. The Pod-Racing, derided by some, but seen by me as a bright spark in a dark period of Star Wars, yes it isn't perfect and young Anakin is incredibly irritating, but it's exciting and actually feels like a thrilling scene in a Star Wars movie, set aside from the dreary trade disputes that make up the rest of the movie.

Most of all, however, this movie is almost completely redeemed by Darth Maul and the subsequent fight scene with Qui-Gon and Obi Wan. Take away its ant-climactic end, and you have one of the greatest lightsabre duels in the franchise, brilliantly choreographed and even competently shot, a surprise given who directed, this is the real gem which nudges Phantom Menace above Attack of the Clones. It still doesn't excuse the decision to kill off your trilogy's most interesting villain though George, you mad bastard.

Eight - Solo: A Star Wars Story (Directed by Ron Howard)

First, let me preface this entry with the sentiment that there are very few Star Wars films I consider 'bad'. They pretty much consist of the previous three movies, every one of from here on in has merits that out-weigh positives, but the more I think about Solo, the more complaints begin to emerge.

As a whole, I enjoyed the movie (the full review is available on this blog itself) but found it occasionally lacking, specifically in its pacing, which had a habit of screeching to a halt.

I feel like as a spin-off, it is a welcome slice of Star Wars canon, but it doesn't feel as pivotal as Rogue One felt a few years previous, which portrayed an event which enabled the rest of the saga to continue as we knew it, this merely serves as the backstory for one of the series beloved characters, and had significant pressure to deliver the moments we wanted to see, which for the most part it did, but it also showed us some things that could have been better left to the imagination.

Its performances were where this movie shone, with Alden Ehrenreich leading the charge as Han Solo, although he is arguably outshone by Donald Glover's portrayal of Lando Calrissian, never before has both a character and actor oozed charisma quite like this.

Its failings become clear towards the middle of the film where it runs out of an interesting narrative to tell before the climactic final act and the ending twists can be jarring, but the cameo near the end of the film is one begging to be paid off, but whether it is remains to be seen.

All in all, Solo is an enjoyable Star Wars romp, but runs out of steam and ends up as nothing more than a middling outing.

Seven - Star Wars: Episode III - Revenge of the Sith (Directed by George Lucas)

As I said earlier in this piece, I don't feel like the prequels are completely without merit, and usually I point to this film as proof of this, the prequel where everything seemed to come together finally and there were more hits than misses.

This is the film that I feel most resembles the classic trilogy, its ambitious beyond anything that the previous two attempted and it executed the turn of Anakin to Darth Vader with sufficient weight and brevity.

Hayden Christensen is still nothing more than mediocre in the film, he does start to feel like he's hitting his stride after he becomes Darth Vader, and Ewen McGregor proves the star turn of not only this film but the entire trilogy, as he meshes successfully with the Obi-Wan character that he spent the last few films building.

Whereas I struggled to find more than a few positives with Episodes I & II, there are more than a few more examples of redemption from this film, with my stand-outs being: the opening space sequence, Anakin's defeat of Count Dooku, Order 66 being executed on Kashyyyk and the subsequent fight and last and most importantly, the duel between the newly-minted Darth Vader and Obi-Wan. This sabre duel is actually the longest in Star Wars history and is presented over many different stages, each of which raise the already considerable stakes higher until a well-timed climax leaves Anakin without legs by the lava flow, it's quintessential Star Wars at its very best.

That's not to say that it's perfect, not, this is still a prequel after all so not everything worked, the romance between Anakin and Padme is still forced and stilted, even more so now that they're having a baby and Anakin's angst is through the roof, and let's not forget General Grievous, the slice of prequel nonsense before which this film was almost sacrificed. Yes, the fight with him was exciting but the fact he put up more of a fight than most of the Jedi's would later is extremely disappointing.

Despite this being the undisputed (for me at least) peak of the prequels, it still falls short against even the worse moments of the original trilogy, which is why it can only make it as high as seventh.

Six - Star Wars: Episode VI - Return of the Jedi (Directed by Richard Marquand)

It may seem like blasphemy to place any of the original trilogy outside of the top five, but hang on, there's reasons.

Return of the Jedi is by no means a bad film, as I said earlier, I consider very few Star Wars films to be 'bad' such is the quality of the first two that even this perfectly acceptable film feels somewhat inferior. Mind you, following Empire Strikes Back must have been like following Queen at Live Aid.

It has its moments, the climactic battle between Luke, Vader and the Emperor gives a good feeling of closure to the trilogies arc and even the rebels mission to blow up the Death Star is suitably impressive, if not giving us a sense of Deja vu.

What does send it over into more negative territories is the Special Edition changes, firstly, that bloody CGI singing monstrosity is absolutely terrifying, not only that but it adds nothing, in fact it takes a hell of a lot away, then there's the addition of Hayden Christensen as a force ghost at the end, which feels like painting the Mona Lisa with a dried turd.

Apart from that, Return of the Jedi has its moments of excellence, but fails to shine like its two predecessors, but you can't really blame it for that, you can't always release solid gold, unless your name is Quentin Tarantino, of course.

Five - Rogue One: A Star Wars Story (Directed by Gareth Edwards)

My big argument about big franchises, and in broader strokes, spin-offs (as I've said in the past) have to have a reason to exist for me to care. Solo, had a threadbare reason in seeing more of that beloved smuggler Han Solo, this feels like it does have a reason to exist, the events of this film enable the plot of A New Hope to take place, so its importance is paramount.

This of course could be mishandled, like most things in Hollywood, happily this story was handled incredibly well, it ticks all the boxes of what fans were expecting (most fans that is, there is of course a section of Star Wars fans who live with a psychotic constant hatred of any female characters, who can all do us a favour and jump off a large cliff) not only did it tick boxes but it stands up as good film, not just as a Star Wars story, but in general.

Character was the main draw here, Jyn Erso is not just a typical bad ass action girl, she has depth and reasons to help the rebellion that go beyond her sense of justice, her problems with the Empire mount up until it becomes a personal mission as well as a Rebellion mission. Also, there's another fun robot character to carry on Disney's streak of fun (and also marketable) robots that the audience can all enjoy, and hopefully buy pricey plushies that look roughly like the characters.

I think my favourite part of the film is the fact that it had the balls to end without pulling a happy ending out of their arse, the characters knew this was practically a suicide mission and that's exactly what it ended up being, but despite this, we get closure for the characters. Of course we knew that they would succeed as we've already seen the results, but the way the characters were written off is a suitable enough emotional punch to write off the characters as selfless heroes sacrifice themselves for the greater good.

Also, before I close this section, there is a big elephant in the room and that's the CGI reincarnation of Peter Cushing's Grand Moff Tarkin. Now, I'm the first person to call out unnecessary CGI in movies, and this recreation does have an 'uncanny valley' look about it, but I do think that it looks suitably like Peter Cushing and doesn't look TOO much like obvious CGI Mo-Cap. Would it have been better to just let the actor who played him on set and voiced him, Guy Henry, play him fully? Would it have been disrespectful to Cushing? I am not the person to answer this, I will however say that the rendering of Princess Leia looks considerably worse.

In brief, Rogue One is a welcome addition to the canon with strong performances and a tight focus, exactly what we want from a Star Wars spin-off.

Four - Star Wars: Episode VIII - The Last Jedi (Directed by Rian Johnson)

Well, here's a choice that will split the fan-base. Here is my viewpoint of The Last Jedi: It will be remembered as the Star Wars film of this generation, and I don't say that lightly, especially as I haven't got to The Force Awakens yet. But I truly believe that in twenty years, we will look back on this as on par with Empire Strikes Back. Fighting words, right?

Firstly, this film is bloody beautiful. Beautifully directed, beautifully paced and beautifully acted. The high point for me is the shot after Vice Admiral Holdo launches through Snoke's ship. It's the kind of shot that would bring the most jaded cinematographer to a shuddering climax. Then there's three scenes on Crait, where the landscapes look like they've been lifted from picture postcards, the red salt only adds to its overall thematic style.

Mainly, I like it because it takes risks, not for risks sake, but to make interesting character and narrative moments. It would have been easy to make Luke take up the mantle and stand up to The First Order without invitation, but with all the character has been through, building up to it not only works on several narrative levels but it shows a level of balls that many wouldn't have. Luke isn't the same wide-eyed Jedi hero we left in Episode VI. He's a broken man, emotionally and psychically, all of his dreams have crumbled before him and the person who burned down his ambition is also his nephew, I'm not surprised someone like that isn't in a rush to take up arms again, he has lost his faith in the force.

We also saw development between Kylo and Rey, we saw flashes of humanity in Kylo Ren that adds another dimension to the already complex characters, sure, there could have been more development and him killing Snoke doesn't really lead anywhere except back into his villainous ways, and Rey goes through the character development in finding more of herself, she broke away from Kylo's influence and is well on her way to becoming the last hope of the Jedi by the end, but in the middle we have the intrigue of how much influence Kylo will have on her. As I say, the plot point doesn't go far enough for me, but I do like both of their characters arcs as is, and their inevitable climatic battle has a lot to live up to.

The Last Jedi is by no means perfect, and it's those imperfections that don't put it any higher. I still find "Super Leia" absurd like I did on first viewing, it doesn't take me out of the film like it almost did the first-time round, but still annoys me. Also, the whole Canto Bight sequence is self-indulgence personified, it's over-blown and unnecessarily complex, we didn't really need to spend that much time in that environment, it was a style clash nightmare against the rest of the film.

It is the above complaints that stop it going any higher than fourth, but it gets this high because of its style, character and narrative development and breathtakingly beautiful direction and cinematography, give it another try, you'll thank me later.

Three - Star Wars: Episode VII - The Force Awakens (Directed by JJ Abrams)

After 10 years in the Star Wars wilderness (not counting the animated TV series) we were all breathless with enthusiasm for our return to the Star Wars universe, and this is where the universe split into two parallel universes, one where the reboot was so awful that we gladly crawl back to George Lucas and his midichlorinans, or, one where a new filmmaker breathes life into a long-dormant franchise, thank Darwin for JJ Abrams.

Rather than wallow in the old characters and making what would have essentially been a fan film, JJ Abrams and Laurence Kasdan instead concentrate their efforts to create new heroes for a new generation and use the old characters to advance the new stories.

Our main two new heroes are Finn: A First-Order Stormtrooper fighting his training and on the run from the very organisation which enslaved him as a child to make him into the perfect soldier, and Rey, a scavenger from Jakku with a mysterious background and untapped power of which she is unaware.

There are other additions, of course, most impressively is Kylo Ren, who surprisingly enough isn't just a Darth Vader clone, he's a heavily troubled man, turned to the Dark Side by a sinister authority... okay maybe his backstory is a bit like Vader's but Kylo has dimensions and layers that Vader didn't have. Firstly, he's the son of Han Solo and Princess Leia, estranged from them after he slaughtered Luke's entire Jedi temple and burned it to the ground (which is totally different to how Vader killed all the younglings, shut up) and suffice to say, his slaughtering isn't over, unfortunately for his dad in particular.

All of these characters are brought to life effortlessly by a trio of talented young actors, John Boyega, Daisy Ridley and Adam Driver, respectively, all of which go through an arc in this movie alone, they all feel like they've moved on from where they were at the start of the film, not only moved but in a position that will launch them into the rest of the series.

As for the old guard, as I mentioned they mostly function to advance the new characters, Han's death in particular marking a particular turning point for Rey and Finn, then there's Leia who has moved on from Princess to General, she's no longer the damsel in distress but a perfectly capable battle-trained tactician and often the wisest character on screen, in other words they also have gone through a journey, although theirs has been off-screen, which we'll no doubt see in some future inevitable spin-off.

There are quibbles, the most glaring one being that it's almost a direct remake of a New Hope, but for each similarity there's something that sets it apart, the mission to blow it up does it no favours, but there's a nice lightsabre fight thrown into the mix in a forest between two people completely untrained in lightsabre combat somehow defeating a highly trained master of the Dark Side, but we should probably ignore that.

For all the similarities to A New Hope, there's new life breathed into every corner of the film, the characters, the setting and the direction, even Abram's love of adding lots of bloom is reined in somewhat, it's simultaneously a love letter to the series it follows, yet adds just enough to stand up on its own, this is how you perfectly add jump leads to a previously dead horse.

Two - Star Wars: Episode IV - A New Hope (Directed by George Lucas)

For all the manure fanboys throw at George Lucas, you can't deny that he knows how to make a strong start. This is the film that of course launched the multi-billion behemoth we know today, and it all started with this comparatively conservative effort. Adjusted for inflation to today's money, A New Hope had a budget of $46.6 million, which nowadays would barely get you the Cantina scene.

A New Hope works because it takes stock character traits and transplants them into a new setting, in this case, a sci-fi setting. To judge this film we have to realise how well this movie holds up in sci-fi settings in modern times. Let's not forget that this is only 9 years after 2001: A Space Odyssey, who's influence is felt heavily in this film, specifically in its very first shot, way to get off on the right foot George.

This is the point where our beloved characters began their journey, Luke was a simple farm-boy, unaware of his genes, Han Solo was busy making the kessel run in 12 parsecs and Princess Leia is busy being a princess and getting kidnapped, like she's in a Mario game.

For a movie that's over 40 years old, this film is still jaw-droppingly beautiful. The two suns shot in particular is practically a work of art on its own. For being the starting point for all our beloved characters, it's impossible to not love A New Hope, not only does it hold up but it exceeds all expectations even to this day, it's a film that's infinitely re-watchable even today, and still absorbs you into its lore, and that's all you can really ask.

As much as it pains me to point out flaws in this movie, it does have them, one of which is one we realised in a more concentrated way 20 years later, and that is that George Lucas writes dialogue about as well as a salmon climbs trees, it's not as noticeable here as it is in, Attack of the Clones, say, but it is occasionally noticeable, mainly when Luke is being a whiny little bitch on Tatooine. Also, there's the inevitable problems that the special editions create, but we have de-specialised editions now (even if they are of questionable legality) so that really shouldn't prove a problem.

In brief there's a reason this film launched the franchise it did, it's because it was such a strong launching point that it practically needed to continue, the story wasn't over and there was a long journey ahead...

One - Star Wars: Episode V - The Empire Strikes Back (Directed by Irwin Kershner)

So here we are, eleven films of varying quality and we finally reach the peak, the first sequel released nearly 40 years ago. The perfect storm of everything that makes this series great, epic sci-fi drama, relatable characters and some climactic battle in a floating city, what more could you ask for?

Everything that annoyed in A New Hope is fixed here, George gained a new writing partner in Laurence Kasdan, who presumably kept George well away from dialogue, who would also be attached to the franchise to this very day. Even the lightsabre fights were improved, as much as I like Ben and Vader's duel in A New Hope, it was somewhat threadbare, Luke and Vader's first meeting, conversely, is epic and extremely well directed and thought out.

There's also character development from the place where we left the characters in A New Hope, the rebellion are gaining traction put are somewhat brutally misplaced after the Battle of Hoth. Han is no longer as mercenary as he was in A New Hope, now a fully-fledged member of the Rebellion, and Leia has moved on from being a damsel in distress to being a key member of the hierarchy of the Rebellion, while Luke seeks further training on the new, fresh environment of Dagobah and the introduction of another long-running character, Yoda, who is introduced here as a somewhat bumbling, senile old man, before transitioning naturally into the wise Jedi master, when the facade he puts up is no longer necessary in the face of the prophesied chosen one.

There are very few films that I find difficult to criticise, that's because I'm picky and I like to find nit-picks no matter how small, I'm sure, if I tried, I could find one here, but you know what? I don't want to. It's a shining jewel of a sci-fi epic in the churning sewer that is most of Hollywood's output and it's one of the few films that I love, something that built my love of films, and for that reason alone, it has to stand atop the galaxy of Star Wars films.

Conclusion:

Star Wars is a franchise I spend a lot of time defending recently, and the top three films remind me why it's worth defending that what you love, it's not all perfect (far from it) and I feel like I've baited a hell of a lot of fanboys a few times here, and I'm at peace with that, I've been as honest and thorough as possible and I hope you've all enjoyed it.

My Top 10 Best Superhero Films (Originally published August 14th, 2018)

So, I don't know whether you've noticed, but superhero films are quite popular at the moment. Shocking, I know, but they're all over the place right now. With Marvel and DC both reliably churning out movies of varying quality and given my longer editorial pieces like this tend to get more views, I thought it was time to compile my own list of what I consider to be the best superhero films.

Some house rules before we start:

- This is a list of MY personal favourite Superhero films, based on my own enjoyment of the film and NOT its Rotten Tomatoes score.
- Some of the film rankings are inconsequential, as I like the films equally, so I've taken into consideration its impact on the broader world of superhero films and films in general.
- And, finally, I've tried my best to not linger too much on one particular franchise of films, and have done my best to make it balanced, that being said, if one franchise is named more than others, it's because I enjoy those films more, not because of any bias to any particular brand, I want as many great superhero franchises as possible.

With that being said, let's get started... with some honourable mentions! (Give me a break it's difficult to just pick 10)

Honourable Mentions:

The Incredibles (2004) - Directed by Brad Bird

Now, I love Pixar and Disney, and I love superhero films, so a superhero film made by Disney/Pixar? Count me in. But besides this, it has a genuinely interesting story and complex characters, especially the films villain, Syndrome. However, however much I like it, there are others I like more, and I couldn't justify putting it in my Top 10.

Avengers Assemble (2012) - Directed by Joss Whedon

We have a lot to thank the first Avengers film for, it's the first of its kind, the massive blow-out epic team-up movie that managed to be both enjoyable and re-watchable. I do feel like there has been better MCU movies since, so this just makes my honourable mentions. Also, I'd like to mention two other really strong MCU movies that didn't make the list, Iron Man, which kicked the whole party off and Captain America: The Winter Soldier, a film that finally made me care about Captain America, which given how dull I found the character in the preceding films, is an achievement all of its own.

X-Men: Days of Future Past (2014) - Directed by Bryan Singer

The X-Men prequels really breathed new life into the series; after the disappointment that was X-Men: The Last Stand and the cinematic dog turd that was Origins: Wolverine, it really did seem like there wasn't much life left in the series. Enter Bryan Singer, who successfully got it back on track with the also excellent First Class and then topped even that by producing this, a time-travel plot that has high stakes for both the present and future, Singer really showed us how to properly refresh a series. It isn't my favourite X-Men film however, and only just missed out on the final 10.

Batman Begins (2005) - Directed by Christopher Nolan

My love of Christopher Nolan is well documented, given how much of my saliva ended up on Dunkirk last year, and his Batman films are some of my favourites, it was the series that showed us that superhero films can be dark and gritty (for better and worse). I did also really enjoy The Dark Knight Rises, although I do think it's the weakest of the trilogy, and who knows, we may end up revisiting this trilogy by the end of this list.

The List Itself

10. Wonder Woman (2017) - Directed by Patty Jenkins

With the DCEU being the hypothetical consolation prize that it is, expectations weren't exactly high for Wonder Woman. However, her arrival was one of the few things usually liked in Batman v Superman (which, by the way, I don't really think is that bad) so maybe we should have known better.

For me, Wonder Woman is the very best of the DCEU (which is a bit like being the best-looking patient on the burns ward) its action is tight and exciting, its direction is a bit brighter than other DC films and its story actually manages to be comprehensible for the entire film.

While I will freely admit to exaggerating the low quality of the DCEU for comic effect, but I will always have hope in the series because of this film.

9. Guardians of the Galaxy (2015) - Directed by James Gunn

Guardians was one of the biggest surprises of the last decade. It's safe to say that anyone who says they knew about the Guardians prior to film release was incredibly dedicated comic fans or liars.

Unlike other films, Guardians isn't here for its stellar storytelling, because truth be told it's nothing new, especially in the villain stakes, but it is the film I go back to whenever I want to watch a superhero film I can really, really enjoy, with characters I've come to like over the length of the film, it also does an excellent job of world building, and genuinely seems like a product of passion, which is a rarity in this nightmare-ish 1984 existence we have.

Guardians was a true watershed moment in superhero films, as it reminds us that no matter how minor the character, Marvel can be trusted to give us entertaining movies, and also, the turning point for comedy in superhero films, it's a compact, easy story with likeable characters with great world-building and genuinely funny and exciting set-pieces that made us wish we'd known the Guardians sooner.

8. Captain America: Civil War (2016) - Directed by Joe and Anthony Russo

I'll be the first to admit that I'm not all that into Captain America character, he has the same character traits I don't like about Superman. He's (mostly) a bland, all-American white-bread hero and that is incredibly dull in a character.

Having watched The Winter Soldier and seeing that he can be interesting at times, I was still firmly in Team Iron Man come Civil War time, co=incidentally, it's a point in the films favour when hype is at such a peak that people are picking sides between two fictional characters, it shows how the MCU has pulled the audience in in the past 10 years.

It is a prime slice of Marvel-branded fun that we're all used to now with the added tension between Cap and Iron Man, and it manages to pull us into the fight, making both sides of the argument make sense in their own way, as well as introducing two new key characters in Black Panther and Spider-Man, both introductions are well handled and well executed, the first time we meet Black Panther is in a high speed intense chase with Cap and Bucky, a great introduction to lay out what we can expect from the character.

I also hold up the airport fight scene as a high-point in superhero action set-pieces, it's perfectly choreographed, directed and performed, and my respect for the Russo's knows no bounds.

7. Black Panther (2018) - Directed by Ryan Coogler

Okay, so I'm leaning heavily on Marvel at the moment, which I promise won't make up the rest of this list there are other films to talk about. However, I make no apologies for including this film, which blew me away the first time I saw it, and just gains depth with each watch.

What really drew me in to the film was the way it built the world of Wakanda, it made it feel completely new in the Marvel universe, not only did it take us to Wakanda, it took the time to introduce us to its traditions and rivalries, all wrapped up in a neat, two-hour package.

Let's also talk about the 'villain' of the piece, Erik 'Killmonger' was a deep, complex character with relatable problems, Marvel had been criticised for shallow, uninteresting villains, and in one year they gave us Killmonger and Thanos, granted Thanos had been built for years, but Killmonger had a smaller, personal story that made you care for him, despite his villainous behaviour, it was pure magic from Marvel.

Special mention should also go to its direction, from Ryan Coogler, a great leading performance from Chadwick Boseman, as well as the rest of the incredibly strong cast, and finally, its visual effects, which at times, were absolutely breath-taking, an all-round stellar effort from all involved.

6. X2 (AKA X-Men 2) (2003) - Directed by Bryan Singer

The first X-Men film changed the game for comic-book adaptations. It successfully made a comic-book movie that was interesting to both an older, mature audience and a younger, impressionable ones. Of course, people had tried making darker comic-book movies, but none had found the right balance, and more importantly, made an actually decent film.

X2 is everything a sequel should be, it takes what was built in the first film and expanded on it, starting with an incredibly exciting action sequence in the White House with Nightcrawler, who is introduced in this film.

Its story also builds on the original and raises the stakes, putting all of mutant-kind in danger from a power-hungry, paranoid military General, it also gives purpose for Magneto and Professor X to work together, and their relationship is the one I find the most interesting. They're two people with similar goals, but go about it in two diametrically opposed ways, Xavier wants to integrate mutants and humans, Magneto wants to make mutants the superior race, by killing any humans that stand in his way. However, their background gives them extra dimensions and their on-off friendship makes for entertaining tension.

X2 is an early high-point in the early development of comic-book movies and we have a lot to thank it for, let's just forget the third instalment, yeah?

5. Deadpool (2016) - Directed by Tim Miller

For a while, it was a universal truth held by Hollywood executives that R-Rated superhero movies didn't sell, of course this isn't true, as Blade did alright for itself in the early 2000's but that didn't stop the crotchety old men, I imagine make up the Hollywood powers that be believing it. Then Deadpool walked in, farted in their face and defiantly had sex with all of their mothers.

Deadpool is a jolt of light in a landscape that increasingly gets darker and darker, while other films tests boundaries in storytelling, Deadpool joyfully skips along and laughs, and that's what's great about it, it shows that you don't always need dark, gritty stories to make a good movie. Sometimes all you need is a wise-cracking smart-ass in a skin-tight suit.

While it wasn't tremendously deep, it was still engaging, to the point where you actually cared for Deadpool and wanted him to rip Francis' spine out, whether the smug prat felt pain or not. It also pushed the boundaries of love interests in superhero films, neither Vanessa or Wade are particularly good people, but they're both still incredibly lovable and their chemistry pops off the screen.

Besides the humour which lends Deadpool its unique charm, it was also proficient at stringing together a great action scene. Whether that be the opening fight on the bridge (which I love for the uniqueness of his lack of bullets factoring into the fight) to the balls-out final fight with Francis, it didn't have the biggest budget, but it made-do with what it had until it was fit-to-bursting with charm, humour and most importantly, violence. It's a rainbow-patterned unicorn in a world of dull, grey horses, and I love it.

4. Spider-Man 2 (2004) - Directed by Sam Raimi

Spider-Man is one of Marvel's most popular characters, arguably THE most popular, so his transition to screen was always going to be closely scrutinised. Thankfully, his big-screen debut in 2002's Spider-Man was well-received by fans and critics alike, and despite being a bit flabby at times, could well have ended up on this list too, eventually though, I realised that I much preferred its sequel, so here it is.

Spider-Man 2 was a perfect storm, and in many ways, the perfect formula for a sequel, as I said in an earlier entry, a good sequel builds on the original's formula, however, it's also important that the original's focus isn't too large as to over-shadow any potential follow-up. In the first, the larger series plot-line - Harry Osbourne's hatred of Spider-Man - is established in given context, here, not only is it expanded and given more depth, but a more powerful threat emerges for Spider-Man, one that is his intellectual and physical equal.

Dr Octopus' origin is tragic to the point of us sympathising with him, only for that sympathy to drain away as his villainous actions ramp up, only to bring us full circle into sympathising again by the end, all while not feeling rushed, as some films with a one movie arc might do. It's extremely well-paced and has enough emotional heft for us to sympathise, and demonise him, all within a two-hour run-time. Now that's a masterclass in pacing.

Tobey McGuire is nostalgically labelled by fans as the 'best' Spider-Man, while I don't completely agree, I will say he was the perfect

Spider-Man for that time, someone who carries the weight of the world on his shoulders all while lacking the crucial experience afforded by age, and Tobey finds his peak in his performance here, his relationship with Mary-Jane is explored in depth, his devotion to being Spider-Man and maintaining a healthy home life is tested, as well as his strength and intelligence in the face of an equal threat. It is a Spider-Man that struck the perfect balance of showing both Peter Parker and Spider-Man, and still holds up as his best solo outing to date.

3. Avengers: Infinity War (2018) - Directed by Anthony and Joe Russo

Okay, okay, I'm indulging one more film from the MCU, but in my defence, it isn't any old MCU movie, it's THE MCU movie.

Ten years, and nineteen movies of varying quality, lead us here and it could have quite easily have played it safe, but instead it gave us the most epic superhero film in history in scale and in quality.

I could go on singing the films praises, but I've already said all I wanted to say in my review of the film earlier in the year, which can be found here: https://mropinionatedweb.wordpress.com/2018/05/17/avengers-infinity-war/

All I have to add is that ten years of ups and downs lead us to the most ambitious superhero property of all time and showed that in the hands of a competent studio, a superhero team-up can be the most epic movie in recent memory.

2. Logan (2017) - Directed by James Mangold

Oh, how I agonised over my top 2. You see, when I started this list, I knew my Top 2 would-be set-in stone, and the rest would fall into place, but how to separate two films that I love so dearly, well in the end, I left my choice up to fate, and flipped a coin. That was the only way I could decide which order to put the top two in.

Where to begin with Logan? It served as a perfect swansong for Hugh Jackman's almost two-decade stint and the regenerating mutant, and he delivered the performance of a lifetime.

It wasn't just Jackman that made this the masterpiece that it is, it was all the factors the film juggled, which came together so perfectly on film. The post-apocalyptic setting with no mutants, the culmination of the father-son dynamic between Logan and Charles Xavier, the tight brutal action and most of all, the gorgeous direction. Despite a dystopian future being somewhat overdone at this point, this film still manages to make it look like a work of art.

Logan may not have the scale of Infinity War, but what it has in spades is character and emotion, every person in the film seems broken, and this film isn't showing how they become fixed, but how they cope with being broken in a dying world. It shows that a family is more than just blood, it's who you love and who you trust. It's a smaller, more personal story, a story fronted by a character we've come to love over nearly 20 years of films, this wasn't just the perfect end for Logan, but the perfect way for Jackman to hang up his claws and ride off into the sunset. It was a well-deserved final piece of cinematic gold that was the final piece of the larger jigsaw that is Logan, the character, by the end he was a redeemed man, and even in death, fulfilled.

1. The Dark Knight (2008) - Directed by Christopher Nolan

As I say, this and Logan were nailed on for Top 2 the second this idea crossed my mind, and this eventually won my game of eenie-meanie-miney-mo. However, it is not an undeserved victory, as The Dark Knight is the absolute pinnacle of superhero films, and arguably, films in general.

It's a rare merit to find a superhero film that appeals to hardcore comic-book fans, film fans and general movie goers in general, and that's because of its incredibly compelling nature.

It is a flaw of deep films that multi-layered story can turn off casual movie-goers, but The Dark Knight is such a good time that it's enjoyable no matter what your grasp of the story is, after all, the film is almost worth it for just one performance.

It feels like we were robbed out of the follow-up that this film was supposed to have (not that its actual follow-up was bad) because another chance to spend two hours with Heath Ledger's Joker would have sold a ticket to me alone. It's one of those performances that you can't tear your eyes from, every aspect gives a new depth to his character. The little quirks added by Ledger himself only add to his magnetism.

It's not just Ledger that gets this film top spot, but the all-round package The Dark Knight provides, it's beautifully shot (as can be expected from Christopher Nolan), keeps a good pace so there's no chance of getting bored, the performances are staggering and just as an extra cherry on the cake, it has a wonderfully atmospheric score, that makes Gotham City feel that bit more dangerous.

Another thing I really love about the film is the Harvey Dent/Two-Face origin that happens both alongside and together with the main plot, the wires cross over from time to tie and tie the story together, but it never feels like Harvey is overshadowing the Joker, and vice versa, they exist within the same vacuum, yet are still equally compelling, this is how you pull off a narrative with more than one villain, you don't have to clutter your movie, and this shows how screen time can be properly shared between two equally relevant villains, even if Aaron Eckhart gets somewhat forgotten, unfairly I'd say.

Overall, The Dark Knight is as close to a perfect superhero package as you're going to get, each aspect weaves itself together to create something truly special, a once in a lifetime movie made by the perfect cast, and the perfect filmmaker. It just doesn't get better.

Conclusion

So that's my list, feel free to comment on this with your own ranking, and please remember this is just a bit of fun, and just because a film didn't make the list, doesn't mean I don't like it.

Hope you enjoyed reading!

My Top 10 Worst Superhero Movies (Originally published August 30th, 2018)

Sir Isaac Newton once said that: "Every action has an equal and opposite reaction." But what did he know? He probably had concussion from sitting under apple trees, the silly sod.

Basically what I'm trying to say is, last week I did the Top 10 Best Superhero Movies, so naturally I'm following it up with the yin to that lists yang. To remind everyone of the rules:

- This is a list of my own personal opinion. If you like the movies I don't, that's cool.
- A Films appearance here reflects how I didn't enjoy the film, not any preconceived bias towards any studio.

Before I go into some dishonourable mentions, there's a particular movie I'd like to address on its own, as it feels like an albatross hanging over these lists, so here I present my opinions on...

Special Mention: Batman v Superman: Dawn of Justice

Right, I touched on this film very briefly in the last list, and truth be told, it was on the shortlist, for BOTH the best, and worst lists. Why is this? Well, I think there are genuine bright spots that stand out as positives, but each one is balanced by the film's flaws.

Ben Affleck is great, but there isn't enough narrative reason for Batman and Superman to hate each other. Superman feels like he's been listening to a lot of Linkin Park, and Jesse Eisenberg seems to think he's in a Social Network sequel.

All this being said, I still think BvS is enjoyable enough, the extended cut even more so, and yes I enjoy poking fun at it for its numerous flaws, but I really don't think it's that bad to belong on this list, neither do I love it enough to place it on my best list.

So with that being addressed, it's time for some (dis)honourable mentions!

Dishonourable Mentions:

Superman III (1983) - Directed by Richard Lester

So, no Superman movie made it into my Top 10, and that might shock a few, but there are reasons. The first two, while undoubtedly classics, are products of their time and haven't particularly aged well, Superman Returns is so mediocre its memory becomes white noise the minute it finishes and Man of Steel is good, but not good enough to break into 'favourite' territory.

Then there are the 1980's sequels, boy oh boy. Their reputation, or should I say infamy, is fearsome, and of the two, Superman is the least horrible, which is a bit like being the smartest Kardashian.

Richard Pryor is enjoyable, but not in a particularly good way, and Superman is already feeling played out and tired, if you're feeling nostalgic, best to stick to the first two.

Batman Forever (1995) - Directed by Joel Schumacher

Fun fact: this film was released the day I was born, and this we learn that my birth was cursed from the start.

On a serious not, going from the Tim Burton Batman films to the Schumacher ones is like going from driving a Ferrari to a Robin Reliant. Gone is the series gothic charm, in its place are Bat-nipples and acting so hammy it could be sold at a butcher's shop.

In my younger days, I had a soft spot for this. Jim Carrey was my favourite actor, and this was at his peak, of fame and silliness, now however I can only watch through my hands as he parades around in a deeply unflattering costume in the cinematic equivalent of a late-night kebab, in that it has no value and you'll probably regret it the next day.

Amazing Spider-Man 2 (2014) - Directed by Marc Webb

One of the main lessons that should have been learnt from the fiasco of Spider-Man 3 is that too many villains spoil the broth, to paraphrase a popular proverb.

After the reboot of the series was basically okay, they duly ignored history, and were thus doomed to repeat it. Too many villains and not enough plot do not a good movie make, and the series was rebooted again two years later.

If past history is anything to go by, Tom Holland shouldn't get too comfortable in those tights.

That's the honourable Mentions over-with, now let's dive headfirst into the slurry and hope we come up with the will to live by the end.

10. Spider-Man 3 (2007) - Directed by Sam Raimi

Oh hello again, Spider-Man. I didn't recognise you with that emo fringe.

Spider-Man 3 is an odd duck really. The first two films in Sam Raimi's trilogy are now considered classic, and those who read my previous list know that Spider-Man 2 in particular made it very high in my list, so what went wrong? Everything, everything went wrong.

First of all, and perhaps worst of all, was its balancing issues. With a two-hour run-time to play with and THREE villains to establish, as well as cramming in an amnesia storyline for Harry Osbourne, the film was spreading its butter on an extremely large slice of bread so to speak.

Out of all the villains though, it was Venom who came out looking the worst. Played by Topher Grace as an absolute goofball, and the entire arc is rushed, with Spider-Man going through an infamous emo phase in the movie that included a cringe-worthy dance sequence and the worst fringe since cousin It.

What really makes this bad is the missed opportunity the film represents, there was real promise there that was squandered by including too many villains in a short space of time, maybe a more focused movie that included just one of the villains could have been enjoyable, as it stands, it's a complete mess, made worse by the fact that no-one at Sony learned a bloody thing.

9. Suicide Squad (2016) - Directed by David Ayer

How do you go about re-introducing an iconic character such as the Joker, not long after Heath Ledger's iconic interpretation? I don't know, but I'll tell you what you shouldn't do plaster the Joker in 'edgy' tattoos, and give the actor playing him a script that could have been put to better use as toilet roll.

Another day, another film with incredible balance issue, but somehow made even worse by the inclusion of the Joker, who spends most of the film locked in a cupboard somewhere. It felt like the writer's maybe had enough ability to write one good character, but had to share it among seven different people, and arguably just gave it all to Harley Quinn.

This film offends me, not just because of how they used The Joker, but because it doesn't know what it wants to be, is it dark and gritty? Or is it light and goofy? Be either one or the other, Suicide Squad, or even better, don't be anything at all.

All in all, this asinine film did its franchise no favours by being released so close to Batman v Superman; given all the uproar that caused, it meant an even bigger microscope was placed on this, you could practically feel the panic from DC as they churned out a new trailer each week, each with its own different tone and feel, it's almost as if they didn't have any faith in the property, and I can hardly blame them.

8. X-Men Origins: Wolverine (2009) - Directed by Gavin Hood

After the stumble that was X Men: The Last Stand, it can be understood why Fox chose their most marketable character to front his own film to revitalise the franchise. However, if The Last Stand was a stumble, then this was a fall off a bridge in comparison.

The usual thing at the top of the list of the worryingly large list of problems with this film is the portrayal of Deadpool, a particular mouthful of sand in the sandwiches of comic-book fans, whereas we now know that Deadpool works as a loudmouth, who turns most goons into a pile if chunky beef. However, in this film, he starts as a loudmouth, then gets his mouth sewn shut, which is a bit like telling Clint Eastwood he can't squint.

It's also fails at bringing Wolverine's relationship with his half-brother Sabretooth to the screen, as that aspect is thrown away to make way for more God-awful Deadpool scenes, also, and this is a bit nit-picky for me, Wolverine's claws looked bloody awful, I don't see how CGI claws can look worse in sequels than they do in the originals, shouldn't technology be moving forward, not backwards.

All that being said, X Men Origins: Wolverine can claim the award for 'Worst X-Men Film'. Which I'm sure will sit alongside the Golden Globe on Hugh Jackman's award shelf.

7. Thor: The Dark World (2013) - Directed by Alan Taylor

For me, the worst thing a movie can be is boring. A good film is great because it affects you in a positive way. A bad film may have things to laugh at and enjoy in a way which probably wasn't intended. Whenever I have a bout of insomnia, I watch Thor: The Dark World. It's that boring.

Granted, the first one wasn't a Criterion Collection classic to begin with, but it was a two-hour thrill ride compared to this. It's amazing that it took Marvel so long to finally get Thor right, Ragnarok was a blast, and that potential has always been there, it's just been buried under the rubble of pseudo-fantasy blubber that was unnecessary, but the filmmakers seem to think we wanted from Thor.

Not only is this comfortably the worst Marvel Cinematic Universe film, it also has comfortably the worst villain in franchise history. It really hurts to slate Christopher Ecclestone in this way, being the massive Doctor Who fan that I am, but it barely feels like he's there, he'd checked out long before the film wrapped and given the dross he had to work with, there's no wonder he lost faith in big movies.

6. Fantastic Four (2015) - Directed by Josh Trank

The early-2000's Fantastic Four films weren't great to begin with, so think about how bad this film has to be to get the backlash it did. The tragic thing is, there was promise here, it had a promising new director, looked to distance itself from the cartoonish earlier films, so how did it end up being this much of a mess?

It's easy to blame studio interference, but the cracks were there. From reports of Trank's on-set behaviour, to the terrible re-imagining of Doctor Doom, it must have been in a state before it was released in the mess it was.

The failure of this film led to Josh Trank to be fired from his directors' position in a Star Wars spin-off movie, and he hasn't been heard from since. This film was so bad that it ruined a career, or maybe he ruined his own career if you believe the stories, whatever you choose to believe.

Its biggest crime is taking a talented cast and making them all look terrible. This film had Miles Teller, fresh off his career-high performance in Whiplash, it had Michael B. Jordan who would win hearts in Creed later in the same year as this film's release. It had all the tools to be special, and it takes a perfect storm of idiocy to mess that set-up off.

5. Justice League (2017) - Directed by Zack Snyder

Speaking of having all the potential in the world, here's Justice League, a fantastic idea on paper, screwed up by too many cooks and that old favourite: 'studio interference'.

I believe that this was a completely different movie when Snyder left the project (for very understandable reasons I must add). It's not for me to say whether this hypothetical version would be better than the theatrical cut, but I will say that re-shooting an entire movie with a completely different director, who has a completely different style couldn't have helped the final product.

The film suffers from feeling like two different drivers are in charge, Snyder feels like he's favouring the darker side of filmmaking (like Batman v Superman) and Joss Whedon is... well, Joss Whedon. Inserting humour where it isn't needed and lightening the tone when it feels disingenuous. You can tell when Whedon has taken over, because it feels like a B-grade Marvel film, it doesn't feel like its own product, it's a knock-off, trying to win a race that ended five year ago. It was afraid of its own identity, so it stole what was popular. All of this makes for a complete mess of a film, one that isn't even enjoyable for being 'so bad its good' it's just sad, really, really sad.

4. Green Lantern (2011) - Directed by Martin Campbell

If you want a perfect example of CGI becoming a problem, here it is: Green Lantern.

Hated by everyone who's seen it, including the actors involved, especially Ryan Reynolds, judging by his jibes in the Deadpool movies. Every aspect of this film has something to hate; the story, the effects, the characters, the acting and so on and so on.

This film has devolved so much in recent years that it's no longer a film, it's a joke, to be looked back on and laughed at, maybe mentioned in the next Deadpool movie in the same breath as a dog shit, because that's how fondly it's remembered.

To get back to that CGI again, I refuse to believe that suit was looked on by human eyes and passed as anything close to passable. The point of CGI is to create something that isn't currently possible, it can be used to create alien worlds and whatever the mind can dream up, a superhero suit is something that can be tangibly created in real-life, so why wasn't a real suit commissioned? CGI is really out of its depth when creating something that already be realistically made, as it will always look worse than the real thing. Surely someone must have seen that. Or is no-one allowed to talk up at Warner Brothers or else be fed to the company crocodile?

3. Elektra (2005) - Directed by Rob Bowman

Remember when Ben Affleck played Daredevil? Remember how utterly putrid it was? Well they made a sequel/spin-off. Thanks Hollywood, that's everything I ever wanted.

As you can expect from someone who was as wooden as a picket fence in the first film, a Jennifer Garner led Elektra movie is as welcome as a fart in a lift, in particular, a lift you're stuck on for 10 more floors, and you're dying of Ebola. That's the level we're working at here.

As if expecting us to sit through Daredevil was bad enough, having the gall to release this, in the same year Batman Begins hit cinema no less, shows a massive pair of brass balls that are beyond the remit of any regular polish.

This film is as enjoyable as sticking forks in your eyes, less so in fact, at least the spoons give you something to talk about afterwards.

2. Superman IV: The Quest for Peace (1987) - Directed by Sidney J. Furie

The 80s were a weird time. A time the rest of humanity has looked back on with great regret, mainly about the music and fashion, but just as the decade was nearing its conclusion, it deals this final kick in the testicles.

Superman had started out as a ground-breaking entity on the big screen, the first had people believing they could fly, the second had them believing they could be superheroes, the third introduced audiences to feelings of despair and finally, the fourth makes us think that Christmas at the in-laws isn't so bad.

Pretty much everyone had checked out at this point, you can see Christopher Reeve's spirit get crushed in every scene, the effects are deliberately re-used from earlier films (and some shots re-used entirely). For as bad as Superman III was, at least it had a somewhat interesting performance from Richard Pryor, the only enjoyment to have here is by sadists, that's the only way I think you can actually enjoy this film, if you enjoy punishment, probably best to call a dominatrix services, after all, this movie is two hours long, and sex only takes about 12 seconds. 15 if you're feeling frisky.

Superman IV euthanised it's series so thoroughly it took nearly 20 years for Superman to appear on the big screen again, it took a further 6 to get a half-way decent Superman movie again (Superman Returns is the Tesco's own brand of superhero films, bland and digestible but hardly the highlight of your week, Man of Steel was a good Superman movie soaked overnight in a grimy pond) this was the film that drove the stake through Superman's heart, poor Chris Reeve's career was in tatters and not long after, his life was destroyed, a true tragedy, and it's all Superman IV's fault.

I refuse to believe that anyone thought this was up to par, and my standards are pretty low, I sat through The Boss Baby for Christ's sake (albeit only for the sake of my relationship, my partner is odd) but this... thing is a cinematic equivalent of a barbed-wire baseball bat colonoscopy.

1. Batman and Robin (1997) - Directed by Joel Schumacher

Batman and Robin. Batman and bloody Robin. Superman I can take or leave, but Batman? You've just made this personal, Schumacher.

I make no secret of the fact that Batman is the greatest superhero of all time, so think of how bad, how utterly appalling and creatively bankrupt a Batman movie must be, for me to declare it the worst superhero movie of all time.

Superman IV may have felt like a barbed-wire baseball bat up the backside, but this is like being beaten to death with a plank of wood, with all your life's failures written on it, while Mother Theresa looks on cheering. This is not a film, this is desecration. It took Christopher Nolan (arguably one of the greatest filmmakers of our era) to resurrect the Batman character after he flounced around with protruding nipples and a bat codpiece. Not only did he resurrect it, he made every effort to be everything this film WASN'T.

This is the blueprint, not just for bad superhero movies, but bad movies in general. It should be shown in film schools as a "how not to do it" guide, its awfulness decreed from the tallest rooftop and its director kicked off said building.

Batman & Robin is the closest I've ever been to hating movies, no sentient being involved in its creation could possibly be making it out of passion, a genuine love for the character and for film, no, they made it to be a 90 minutes toy commercial, and they were so god-damned blatant about it. The fact that Joel Schumacher can be allowed near a film camera after producing this shambles makes me despair for humanity, you see what you did to me Schumacher? You are responsible for me losing hope in humankind, I hope you and your bat-nipples are happy.

Conclusion

All in all, Superhero films are in a good place right now, apart from the odd misstep we're spoilt for choice for quality, so be grateful for the next marvel film, and think, it could be worse, we could be watching Batman and pissing Robin.

My Top 10 Films of 2018 (Originally published December 31st, 2018)

So, here we are again...

Another year has passed, which means it's time for critics the world over to compile their Top 10 Films of the year list in an effort to feel more important and, more importantly, to boost site traffic. As the old saying goes, if you can't beat them, join them.

It's been quite a year in cinema with lofty highs and crushing lows, I've set myself some proper rules this time out, after receiving complaints last year, complaints that were entirely justified in hindsight, over the inclusion of too many comic book movies, only one of these movies feature in my main list, I'm also not counting cinematic re-releases or live-streams to cinema, as good as I though 2001: A Space Odyssey was in cinema, it is 50 years old, and therefore it could be incongruous to include it here.

Also, this list is due to go out on New Year's Day, when you're all in the midst of. A monster hangover, staring down another year on the march to the grave, so this list is here to brighten your entry to 2019, by looking back at the best bits of the past year.

With that said, straight on... with the honourable mentions!

Honourable Mentions

Black Panther - Directed by Ryan Coogler

While I set myself the goal of only one Superhero film in my Top 10, I allowed myself a bit of freedom with the honourable mentions, seeing as they aren't part of the top 10, but exist on a plain of existence just outside of the Top 10.

It was honestly a tough choice between this and Aquaman, the last film I saw before my self-imposed deadline of the 21st December. As I honestly enjoyed them both equally, but I've chosen to go with Black Panther for what it represents, a step forward in terms of Hollywood representation, along with a simple, yet enjoyable, story focused around a likeable protagonist and an interesting antagonist, had a certain film not been released this year and utterly blown my socks off, this would comfortably Top 10, but as it stands it remains an honourable mention.

Isle of Dogs - Directed by Wes Anderson

I am a big fan of animation, as I see it as an interesting way of telling a story, not to mention my admiration for the hard work and passion that goes into most productions, I especially like when an animated film thinks outside the box in terms of traditional animation and utilises a much more rare form of the art in the form of stop-motion.

Wes Anderson is renowned for his quirky storytelling, and truth be told this isn't his first foray into stop-motion animation, Fantastic Mr Fox was his first, and you'll struggle to find a film as charming as Isle of Dogs. Its visual style is captivating, and it does a tremendous job of building a world around the dogs and the human characters. All in all however, it was just nice to spend time watching a movie made out of obvious passion and love. The story is simple, but it has heart, and that's all it really needed, it's as enjoyable a time watching a movie as you could have, but just doesn't manage to break my Top 10.

Ralph Breaks the Internet - Directed by Rich Moore and Phil Johnston

From one style of animation to the other, it's the highly anticipated Disney sequel, Ralph Breaks the Internet. I mentioned the word 'charm' when describing Isle of Dogs, and that's the word that also springs to mind when describing this film, and the original film even more so, it's a concept that you'd have thought would have been done years ago, and other films may have tried it, but done nowhere near as good of a job (looking at you Emoji Movie, now get back to the cellar where you belong).

Disney have this knack of reading a situation and audience so well, that they very rarely fail, and the perfectly judged humour from the first film makes the jump to internet humour very well, and there's enough inside jokes and Easter eggs to merit re-watching, it maybe isn't as focused as the first but it's still another undeniable hit from the house of mouse.

The Top 10.

10. Coco - Directed by Lee Unkrich

Now, my American readers may well be scratching their heads in confusion; they may think: "Didn't Coco come out in 2017?" To which I say, yes, it did for you, but we didn't get it until March, so there, it counts.

Coco is yet another example of how Disney can be when they get things right, together with their team at Pixar, they create animated masterpieces seemingly for fun, and together they created another one here.

I often feel that Disney/Pixar are at their best when exploring new worlds, be it the world in which toys are sentient or the world in which your emotions live inside your head, and here they create a world surrounding Mexico's 'Day of the Dead' ceremony, something ripe for the picking, imagination wise at least.

The animation is beautiful, the world is vibrant and full of life, and the songs are catchy and thematically correct, Pixar really went all out to make this world come to life, be it in the world or the tremendous voice cast, Coco is one of the few films this years to get to me emotionally, given that it deals with a sense of loss, it is a universal struggle and one that is impeccably realised here.

9. A Quiet Place - Directed by John Krasinski

For someone who doesn't really like horror films, I sure do like to include them in my Top 10's. It was It last year (what an odd sentence) and now, it's A Quiet Place.

In my defence, it is hard to not see the appeal in A Quiet Place, it doesn't fall into the usual horror tropes, choosing to build suspense rather than go for the low-hanging fruit of jump scares. It also has a unique and interesting concept, something as rare in the horror genre as an Amish YouTube star, and it uses this concept to its fullest effect, utilising the effect of silence on its characters and the world around them.

As for the world, it's a bleak and depressing place, highlighted excellently in the first few minutes when a child is picked off by the roving monsters of the film, that is its very early statement of intention and it never really lets up, setting your stall up with something like killing a child ups the stakes indescribably, as we now the lengths the film, and the creatures are willing to go to threaten us.

Its direction is effective, its tension is nerve-shredding and its characters are sympathetic, you'll have to walk a long mile to find a more effective, and strangely enjoyable, horror film.

8. Bohemian Rhapsody - Directed by Bryan Singer

This is a film that may not have won over all critics, but every Queen fan I have spoken to has gushed about the film and I myself practically wrote a love letter in the form of a review to it just last month.

It is probably the film that is mostly here because of personal taste, but what do you want? It's my list after all. I think it's a marvellous film, highlighting all the features that made Freddie an icon, and some of which showed him in a more negative light, and more the better, we want to know the real Freddie, but know that that doesn't detract from the God we've all watched perform, be it on recordings, or live in person if you're extremely lucky.

Not only is the film a love letter to all things Queen and Freddie, it's also brilliantly shot, and acted. Rami Malek rightfully has Oscar buzz about him for the role, but Gwilym Lee was also an astonishing Brian May, and the cast in general were great.

It may not be a perfect film, but it is a treat for Queen fans, young and old and contains one of the year's best all-round performances, so for that reason, it makes the list.

7. BlacKkKlansman - Directed by Spike Lee

Now, I'd never watched a Spike Lee film (or 'joint' as he refers to it, a term I feel too white to use with any seriousness), but I knew him by reputation. From taking a look at his past works, it seems like his career has been up and down, but obviously I can't judge.

What I can judge, however, is BlacKkKlansman. It's completely grammatically incorrect title aside, BlacKkKlansman is one of those stories that makes sense in both its own time period and in modern times, and Spike Lee recognises this, which is why the film works, its mainly in the timing, we needed this film to remind us of the huge steps backwards we are currently taken.

It's not just in the films social attitude where it shines, but in its performances and smaller story points. It has natural story progression, with some incredible intensity completely out of left field. Including a lie detector scene that I will hold up as one of the year's best scenes, and the performances of John David Washington and Adam Driver, I can't see either getting a nod in awards ceremony, but they are incredible here, I'd say I preferred Driver slightly, but both can lay claim to two of the best characters of the year, and Spike Lee can lay claim to being one of the more relevant directors of our time.

Finally, I couldn't move on from this film without mentioning its ending. Which is one of the greatest things I've ever had the pleasure of being surprised with in a cinema. It is worth the price of admission alone and cemented its place here in the top 10.

6. The Shape of Water - Directed by Guillermo Del Toro

The Shape of Water doesn't really need my acclaim, as it already had the saliva of every other critic all over it, but I'd say it deserves it. After all, it won Best Picture and who am I to argue with the Academy?

Despite my obvious sarcasm, it is an absolutely beautiful movie, which is to be expected from Del Toro, he's practically a Picasso with a film camera, visuals are his bread and butter, but here he goes beyond visual beauty and into beautiful storytelling.

He crafts likeable characters with such ease, and makes his antagonist instantly hate-able, and the scenes with him are creepily uncomfortable, he's one of those villains that you know is probably evil from his first appearance on camera, maybe it's because he's played by Michael Shannon, that would help, and we feel attached to the main character because she's vulnerable, with her being a mute and all, so we are made to sympathise with her quite easily, even more so when she's victimised by others.

In summary then, beautiful world with a unique love story and engaging characters, helmed by an extremely talented auteur director, the world could do with more films like The Shape of Water.

5. Mission: Impossible - Fallout - Directed by Christopher McQuarrie

On the surface, placing the latest Mission Impossible in front of The Shape of Water exposes how little I actually know, to which I say, drop the elitist attitude and you'll realise how great a time at the cinema Fallout is.

As I stated at the time, I only recently caught up with the world of Ethan Hunt and his film series, and I'm astonished at how a series can still be getting better in its sixth instalment. I think this may have something to do with the series finding its true rhythm under the direction of Christopher McQuarrie and allowing Cruise to produce these films may be another masterstroke, as he finds new ways to push himself in ways men in their 50's really shouldn't.

Of course, to compare Tom Cruise to a regular 50-something would be a grave error in judgement, as he's better than he's ever been in Fallout, it isn't just that the stunts get better, it's that they have focus to go with them, it's girdle-tight action sequences that have a reason to be action sequences, because the stakes get bigger in each film.

The film also toes the line between that action, and character development, the previous films antagonist makes his return to trouble Ethan Hunt and his team once again, and we dig further into Ethan's past and into his relationships with his crew.

Mission Impossible - Fallout, is what happens when summer blockbusters actually make effort, when they decide not to be vapid, fill in the spaces money vacuums, they really can be great, and this is one of the best examples, smart action paired with characters we've grown attached to will always be a winning formula, if only more studios would realise this, it'd be a much happier world.

4. Avengers: Infinity War - Directed by Anthony and Joe Russo

The award for most obvious inclusion goes to...

Seriously though, following on from what I said about Mission Impossible, this is another example of another blockbuster that tries. Mind you, having to follow 18 other films and satisfy a rabid fan-base should be all the motivation you need.

To say this film had to top off an epic 10-year arc put an enormous amount of pressure on any production and is usually an impossible task in Hollywood, yet the Russo's rose to the occasion and hit it out of the park like.

Earlier in the year, I ranked this film as my third favourite Superhero film of all time, which should give you an indication of how much I loved this film (and the fact that it only made fourth on my year list is a testament to the quality of some of this year's releases) but I also don't want to risk repeating myself too much, so here's a few brief reasons why it worked.

Firstly, and foremost, is its balancing of its characters, working with an unprecedented number of heroes must have been a thankless task, but they manage to highlight all of the characters strengths in the short time they had on screen, it made every character important, every development important, it was a huge production with a tight focus. Secondly, it made itself feel 'epic' without straining too much to make itself look like it's trying too hard to be epic (good luck making sense of that sentence) and last but not least, it offered closure for the journey, whether you're a long-time fan, or watching for the first time, it made you understand the story and offered closure for its characters.

There have been technically better films this year, but none that offer the roller-coaster Infinity War offers.

3. First Man - Directed by Damien Chazelle

Very few films manage to make my jaw drop with visuals, but First Man managed it in the very first scene.

So, there's that, I'm willing to go on record as saying that First Man is this year's most beautiful film, and when we get this far up the list is where the job of arranging these into order gets a **LOT** harder, honestly, I left all three of the top 3 films in stunned silence, and still haven't found adequate superlatives for any of them, I don't even think my full reviews scratch the surface of praise I could give it, much less in a few paragraphs in a list, but here goes.

On the back of the equally eye-catching La La Land, one of Hollywood's most promising filmmakers, Damien Chazelle, announced that he would adapt to film one of history's greatest moments, the Apollo 11 moon landing, and straight from the go, I knew that, if nothing else, it would look spectacular, and even with my lofty expectations, the film surpasses them, by quite a distance.

It isn't just how this film looks that lands it so high up though, it's its focus on the personal story of Neil Armstrong, the part we didn't know about, to say this film is about the moon landing would do it a great disservice. In reality, it's about the life of an ordinary man, who had experienced heartbreak, getting his life back on track, and how his life escalates into becoming the hero of a nation.

But, for the most part, we don't see that, we see him at his lows, his struggles with grief, and with his place in his family, his relationships, his successes and his failures, all conveyed in one of the year's best performances from Ryan Gosling.

It is all of these things, and more besides, but in the centre, this film has a heart, it has the feel of a film made with love, and the best intentions, and my only regret is that I didn't see it in cinemas more than once, it was the kind of cinema experience that makes you remember how important the cinema is for watching films.

2. A Star is Born - Directed by Bradley Cooper

I'll let you into a secret, dear reader. I'm a soft touch, this characterisation as a grizzled critic? It's all a front, films make me cry. Not often, but they do. Sometimes this is a good thing, I cried at Coco (don't judge) and this film, because they awakened an emotional response, they hit me right in the soft spot for emotions, and sometimes I cry at films like The Boss Baby because I actually wasted money and time on it, but that's another thing.

Upon first hearing about this film, my eyes started rolling like a Ferris wheel pushed down a hill. Not only a remake, but the FOURTH version of a film, and directed by an actor who we hadn't seen step behind the camera, it smelled like an ego trip if there ever was one. How wrong I was.

Even as the reviews started rolling in, praising the film and specifically the performances, I kept a cynical eye, safe to say I wasn't expecting one of the most emotional cinematic journeys I've ever been on.

So, straight on with the obvious, yes Lady Gaga is phenomenal, if there's a more deserving Oscar winner, I haven't seen it yet, but it wasn't just her acting talents that she brought to the table, but her musical ability, and that is another place in which the film shines, its soundtrack. I've always admired Gaga from a distance, her music isn't up my street, but at least she's an artist, with her own style, and that is why she fits so well here.

The music is great, the acting is great, but the surprise package is Cooper's ability as a director. The film has a distinctive feel, an important thing for a director to realise, and it has focus, some of the shots are works of art in their own right, and for that Cooper deserves praise, I look forward to what else he can bring to the table, we may have a new Clint Eastwood on our hands.

In conclusion then, this is what a remake should be, a timeless story updated for a new age, which is probably why this film has been made so many times, its story will always resonate, it has an legitimate a place within cinema history as any, and it was made by someone with a clear passion and love for the source material, potentially the greatest remake there's ever been.

1. Three Billboards Outside Ebbing, Missouri - Directed by Martin McDonagh

Anyone who knows me will not be surprised by my number one pick, it's practically been sewn up since February.

Another film on this list that was a late release over here in Blighty, Three Billboards was released in 2017 Stateside, but I'll be damned if I miss another opportunity to trumpet this film from the rooftops again.

Three Billboards isn't only my favourite film of this year, it may just be my favourite film of all time, and if it isn't definitively my top pick, it's up there. I adore it so much, and I knew from the second the credits rolled way back in February when I saw it, that it would take nothing less than a titanic effort to unseat it as the year's best, A Star is Born ran it close, but in the end, there was no competition.

It goes to show how much I loved this film that, even now, almost a year on, I am still talking to anyone with even a passing interest in cinema about it, I want more people to see it, so I have more people to talk about it with.

It's hard to say why I enjoyed it so much, I think it's because it's a perfect storm of a film, it has great characters used to their full potential, and it's even better to know that their effort paid off come awards season, usually I'm not always a big fan of occasions like the Oscars, I think they're a bit too self-aggrandising for their own good, but this year I was actively hoping it would clean up, in the end they only left with two wins, nothing to be sniffed at of course, and I was overjoyed that McDormand walked away with a well-deserved Best Actress (its other award also being an acting award; Best Supporting Actor for Sam Rockwell) but left with less than perhaps I think it deserved.

This is partly the reason it occupies top spot, not just because of my own opinion, but because it's the film I think most deserves the praise, the one that deserves to be remembered, I could have put Avengers, or Shape of Water at number one, but everyone remembers how good they were. I feel that Three Billboards has been forgotten, and anything that inspires that amount of passion from me, should tell you why it's so deserving of the golden crown of 2018.

So, that's me done for another year, I hope you enjoyed this run down of the year's best films, in a few days, I will provide a counter-point in the form of the worst films, but until then, thank you for reading, and I hope 2019 brings you all health and happiness.

The Worst Films of the Year (Originally published December 31st, 2018)

It's all very well and good being positive and all that, but we all know that the world is not a positive place, it's a dull, unforgiving place, and Hollywood is no different, in fact it's probably worse, if Hollywood were a person, it would have the worst mood swings in human history. On one hand it gives us films like Shapes of Water and Three Billboards, and with the other it slaps us with Transformers films, and Titanic.

I've chosen not to go about this in a Top 10 format, as I don't like doing too many Top 10's seeing how bloody popular, they are on every site in the world, I am instead going to address the worst films I've seen this year in an extended rant/autopsy. Bear in mind before you read that this is **MY** opinion, if you liked these films then that's cool, and you should also probably seek help.

Molly's Game - Directed by Aaron Sorkin

Probably the most disappointing cinema experience I had last year, Molly's Game had a fair amount of positive critical reaction early last year, but to me was nothing more than a damp squib.

I only remembered how disappointed I was in this film when going back through the films I've seen, truth be told, the film hadn't crossed my mind in the whole year since I saw it, which is never a good sign.

It had all the ingredients to be great but was hampered by a glacial pace and uninteresting characters, not a great start to the year all in all.

Hereditary - Directed by Ari Aster

After It and A Quiet Place, I had a much more open mind towards horror, and this is the film that closed my mind again.

The two films I used as examples both had creativity and life, Hereditary was happy to trot out the same dated horror clichés that we've seen for 30 years, all while having an air of smugness of a film that thinks it is so much cleverer than it thinks it is.

It also irks me that the film was advertised as 'this generations Exorcist'. Now, I put it to you, dear reader, that any film that uses another films name front and centre in its advertising campaign, doesn't have faith in its own film to succeed on its own. If this film was any good, it wouldn't need that prefix.

I was excited to see another exciting horror film that further changes my mind to the genre, all it did was show me all the things I don't like about horror and put me off the genre further.

The Festival - Directed by Iain Morris

I'm an Inbetweeners fan, you know. I'll willingly concede that it's hardly high-brow comedy, but it was lightening in a bottle, a mirror to a whole generation of youths. That's why the show worked, because people my age, who were watching, knew a Jay, or a Simon. We grew connected to the characters over three series and two movies, and clamour for any potential reunion.

However, The Festival really tested my patience with Inbetweeners nostalgia. It is the kind of film that refuses to move on from a past film, hell they even cast one of the main actors from the series that we're all nostalgic for, that's not moving on from your comfort zone, that's building a den over your comfort zone.

It was also irritating because of its use of humour, sure it's the same kind of low-brow humour as The Inbetweeners, but when Inbetweeners used gross-out humour, it had build-up, paced brilliantly until the climax (pun very much intended) here it has all the subtlety and pacing of a sledgehammer to the face. If you want my opinion, watch The Inbetweeners again, and forget this film ever existed.

The Happytime Murders - Directed by Brian Henson

When I posted this review to Facebook, I made the very hilarious joke of calling this: 'The Crappytime Murders' and I stand by that solid gold burn.

I could go on and on about how awful this film is, its tone-deaf humour, unlikable characters and stupid, stupid plot. But all of this can be summed up by the fact that the screening I was in had a fair few people in, and nobody laughed, once, and that is pretty damning for a comedy movie. But, in all honesty, The Crappytime Murders (I said it again for maximum humour) is about as funny as bowel surgery.

Slaughterhouse Rulez - Directed by Crispian Mills

A few paragraphs ago, I scolded The Festival for playing off the nostalgia of The Inbetweeners, and right here is another great example of the same sort of thing.

At the front and centre of the advertising for this film was Simon Pegg and Nick Frost, also the way it's trailers were edited suggested that we were in for a comedic romp similar to their brilliant 'Cornetto Trilogy' but what we got was a tepid, clunky film about fracking, of all things, one in which Pegg and Frost do not even appear in a scene together, and includes a God-awful performance from Michael Sheen, it's the kind of film that will make you like the 'Cornetto' films a little bit less, even though this film is unrelated to those films.

It's cynical marketing is a trend that runs through most of these films, be it Hereditary or Slaughterhouse Rulez, I find it to be a good rule of thumb that if a film is pointing you to anything outside of those films, then those films don't have enough about them to stand up on its own, and most if not all of these films are guilty of this tactic, basically, be wary of advertising.

This brings us to the end of the run-down of these years' flops and disappointments. You'll notice there are considerably less than the

Best list, this is because I saw more good films than bad, I like to think that I can spot bad films, but the fact that I spent two hours of my life watching Hereditary would suggest otherwise.

Chapter Ten: January 2019

Bumblebee (Originally published January 2nd, 2019)
Directed by Travis Knight
Starring: Hailee Steinfeld, John Cena, Jorge Lendeborg Jr. and John Ortiz

Well, it's the rise of a new dawn, a New Year and a fresh start, so what have you got for me film industry? A Transformers spin-off movie? You are too kind.

Sarcasm aside, I thought I'd be going to see a slowly paced French film at the cinema before a Transformers film, but I thought, what the hell? It's a New Year (well, almost, I saw it on the 29th December, but that's practically the New Year, right?) so why not broaden my horizons, for better or worse. Besides, other critics seem to think that it isn't God-awful, so how bad could it be?

Story

It's 1987, the Autobot B-127 escapes the war on Cybertron to the planet Earth, where he disguises himself as a yellow VW Beetle, whereupon he is found by social outcast Charlie Watson, and an unlikely friendship blooms. Meanwhile, the Autobots arch-rivals the Decepticons have tracked B-127 (AKA Bumblebee) and will burn the planet to ashes to retrieve him.

Verdict

I understand that the above plot synopsis might fly over many heads, it would have flown over mine before I watched the film, while it just looks like technobabble to the untrained eye, but the film, to its credit does a good job of making it all understandable.

It surprises me more than it could ever surprise anyone else to say that I enjoyed this film. I know, I enjoyed a Transformers film, is the sky about to fall?

No, you hypothetical sarcastic sods, and the reason I liked it so much is because of how much it DOESN'T feel like a Michael Bay Transformers film, first and foremost, it treats its female lead as an actual human being and not a sex-doll in a miniskirt, and for this reason, the character is actually likeable and sympathetic, in fact, there's a significant improvement in characters overall, they've taken a big step away from cookie-cutter archetypes (for the most part, more on that later) and they're all much better for it.

I also liked that it took time to explore the Transformers conflict, between the Autobots (good guys) and the Decepticons (bad guys) in the bad Transformers films, that was put to the background for copious explosions, lazy stereotypes and puerile leeriness. We get to see a part of a battle on the Transformers home planet, Cybertron. Even though its CGI base creates a certain amount of disconnect, it's still somewhat exhilarating to see the base of the war that we see so little of in the main series.

As for the characters I mentioned earlier, I really liked the lead character, Charlie (played by Hailee Steinfeld) she has very relatable character traits, there are parts that seemed shoehorned in, the catty girls at school and the dead dad spring to mind, but that doesn't bring her character or the film down, Steinfeld should be commended for carrying the weight of the films narrative, emotionally at least, and for making us buy into a relationship between a teenage girl and a robot.

Elsewhere in the cast, there's strong, if unspectacular performances. John Cena was far better than I thought he would be, his strong charisma carries across from his wrestling persona, he sparkles when given comedic lines, but when things get a bit more serious, it is more difficult to buy into, then there's the predictable nature of his soldier character, but the strong base is there to build on. There's also Memo, Charlie's neighbour and love interest (played by Jorge Lendeborg Jr) who was good in a somewhat limited, not to mention cliched, role of nerdy love interest, his performance brought the character to life in his hands, he'll be one to watch in the future I'm sure.

I do have complaints, though. As I mentioned earlier, some characters are predictable and tread the same ground, there's the bitchy high school girls, the stepdad who tries too hard to be liked and the corrupt government officials. There have been steps forward taken, but these cheap and lazy characters drag down the overall quality I find. Also, I was quite annoyed by a certain narrative device in the climactic battle, it's a well-worn cinematic cliché that hasn't aged well, at all. It again quickly drags down the moment by artificially heightening tensions.

Overall though, this film is worlds apart from the terrible, awful main series films, part of that is down to a fresh director, a fresh perspective and likeable characters, that's how you bring people back to a franchise, now I just hope they build on this success, and don't regress into their old form, it's all very well to praise steps taken forward, but we now need to hold them up to that standard going forward, which will be its real challenge, that being said however, this film did endear me to the Transformers much more than Bay's output, which is unprecedented, and says all I need to say really.

The Favourite (Originally published January 3rd, 2019)
Directed by Yorgos Lanthimos
Starring: Olivia Colman, Emma Stone, Rachel Weisz and Nicholas Hoult

I've never really been into period dramas. I find Downton Abbey about as interesting as a maths lecture at a paint-drying convention, and they're always paced like a snail going across the Sahara.

But the Favourite caught my eye as it looked as though it was trying something different, and I'll say it achieves that at least. I was also drawn in my it's leading cast, Olivia Coleman is one of my favourite actresses, as is Emma Stone, so it had my attention, but could it keep it?

Story

It's 1708, and Britain is at war with France, the Queen, Anne, is in increasingly poor health and is reliant on her 'favourite', Sarah, the Duchess of Marlborough. Suddenly, Sarah's cousin, a Fallen Lady by the name of Abigail Hill arrives and begins to work her way into the Queen's inner circle.

Verdict

That little synopsis is as about as much as I understood the plot, as it is a bit abstract in parts. A period drama fever dream is perhaps the best way I can describe it, if you can try and imagine Terry Gilliam remade Pride and Prejudice but turned Mr Darcy into a sarcastic ballsy woman. If you can imagine such a thing, then that's as close as I can describe The Favourite.

You know the kind of film that you know is good, accomplished and artistic and what not, but it fails to grab you? That's where I was for most of The Favourite. The dialogue and acting drew me in the most, but the underlying surrealism makes some of the film difficult to grasp, I enjoyed the film when it was focusing on character moments, specifically with Queen Anne, played brilliantly by Olivia Coleman, she really stands out as a sympathetic, yet still powerful feeling.

Other characters loyalties are wavering, however, and as such can be hard to get behind. Abigail for instance, starts the film as a sympathetic figure, cast down the class system by the actions of her father, yet over the run-time, she evolves, into what would usually amount to an antagonist (really trying not to spoil) whereas, Sarah starts as a bossy controlling character and swaps places with Abigail to being a devoted, and loving aide. Done right, I'd usually say it was a clever subversion of character roles, but here it just feels a bit incongruous, it doesn't feel like Abigail *needs* to do the things the does, there's no reason why they couldn't work together for a mutually beneficial end, but then again, maybe that was the thing in the 1700's and being a bastard was just the way of life.

There were, however, things I really liked about the experience, the acting, as I previously mentioned, was top-notch. I do believe Olivia Coleman received a Golden Globe nomination for her performance, and if so, I thoroughly approve, as she was the film's most watchable element. Stone and Rachel Weisz (who played Sarah) were also characteristically excellent, I didn't like their characters as much, but they gave everything they had to what they had.

I also really liked the direction in the film. There are certain scenes which look as though they are filmed with a 360 degree camera, which works very nicely in this setting of lordly halls and distinguished gentleman, and as I previously mentioned, I really liked the dialogue, there were certain lines that gave me a good chuckle, far more than I was expecting of a period piece anyway.

All in all, The Favourite is like not being into fine art, but going to an art gallery, you appreciate the artistry, and might even find one or two things you liked there, but it ultimately isn't for you. Perfectly acceptable as a piece of art, but it failed to thrill me, despite its acting and intelligent filming.

Spider-Man: Into the Spider-Verse (Originally published January 11th, 2019)
Directed by Bob Persichetti, Peter Ramsey and Rodney Rothman
Starring: Shameik Moore, Jake Johnson, Hailee Steinfeld and Mahershala Ali

Okay, so I'm a bit late to this particular party. My viewing of films is dictated by my local cinemas showing times, and they often don't match my usual schedule, in this situation I miss certain big releases, or am late in reviewing them, and the review seems pointless as everybody already knows whether the film is good/bad.

Either way, I've watched it now, and not reviewing it would be foolish in my position, whether everyone else has made their mind up or not.

Story

Miles Morales is an ordinary high school kid, his father is an over-bearing police officer, and he's just been transferred to a private school for geniuses. Then he's bitten by a radioactive spider, and you all know the rest...

Verdict

When I first heard of this, my expectations were set on the basement of Satan's wine-cellar. ANOTHER bloody Spider-Man? Before long I'm going to need a flow-chart to keep track of all these universes. Then, the trailer came out and I was even less impressed, I didn't like the animation style at first glance, it felt like staring into the uncanny valley, caught mid-way between comic and realistic style and as a result looked odd.

But, as is usually the case, I was wrong. Into the Spider-Verse is a wonderful film, and one of its strongest aspects is its animation, which surprises me, given my original aversion to it.

I think the thing I liked most about it, was its change away from the Peter Parker story we've seen too many times (and we didn't need to see Uncle Ben die, which is always a plus) it explores different aspects of Spider-Man, even beyond Spider-Man as there's also a Spider-Woman a Spider-Mech and a Spider-erm-Pig (not the same one from The Simpsons Movie)

I also found Miles to be an extremely likeable protagonist. He's a nice change of pace from Peter Parker, who does appear in this film, but instead of a sprightly young teenager, the Peter Parker of this universe is an older-slightly overweight man in his thirties, therefore making him more relatable to his main fan base.

The expanse of Spider-People (is there a collective noun for a group of Spider-related heroes? Let's go with Spider-People for now) was another thing that put me off from the trailer, that and the Sony Animations logo, because that certainly did the trick too, but the mix of styles from Miles to the Anime styles of Peni and the Looney Tunes-like Spider-Ham (yes that really is his name) maybe it's because I've been so engaged in live-action Superhero films, but it was a red flag to me.

In reality, however, the film is very well-balanced, there is the goofy comedy aspects, but there's also some fairly touching moments, unexpectedly, and it all balances quite nicely alongside each other.

I think what makes me like this film is the characters though, not only do we get the ever-lovable Miles, but there's older Peter Parker, Spider-Gwen and even Spider-Ham turn in some nice moments, not only that but the growing character dynamics between certain Spider-People (and ordinary people) I like the relationship between Miles and Peter, and the relationship between Miles and his Dad, which just brushes the border of cliché-town without ever building a camp there.

There aren't really any massive criticisms I can levy at the film, it isn't a film that sticks in my mind like, say, Infinity War, but then again it's working with one-tenth of the scale and budget, maybe it's a little forgettable and I'm not sure I'd rush to watch it again, but that's about the worst I can say. Oh, and some of the twists are very predictable, but at a film that is essentially aimed at kids, I wasn't expecting Inception.

In conclusion then, Spider-Man: Into the Spider-Verse is a lovely-looking, well-written film that will entertain you with likeable characters and interesting story points. But it probably won't stick in your mind for the long-run, and that's not a bad thing, I'd certainly watch a sequel should one be made. It may even surprise you from time to time as well, a well-made film for the whole family.

Colette (Originally published January 17th, 2019)
Directed by Wash Westmoreland
Starring: Keira Knightley, Dominic West, Elenor Tomlinson and Denise Gough

So, you'd think with my cards laid on the table a few reviews ago when I said that period pieces weren't really for me, so much so that a period film that is hoovering up awards wherever it goes didn't hold my attention very well. But I am not one to dismiss a genre on one film, it usually takes at least two to turn me off a film.

Still, there was promise in Colette, Keira Knightley is front and centre, giving her chance to show off her often misused talent, Dominic West is also in it, who is a Yorkshireman and therefore superior by default and its director made the Oscar-winning Still Alice, so all looks rosy on the surface, maybe this could be the film that turns me onto the side of period dramas, or maybe it'll reaffirm my feeling that they're dry, very dull affairs for sexually-frustrated housewives, let's find out.

Story

In Paris at the turn of the 20th Century and a failing author, Willy, played by Dominic West falls in love with a country girl, Gabrielle Colette, played by Keira Knightley. When Willy's stuttering career threatens to put the both of them on the street, he turns to his wife to ghost-write his next novel, which becomes a surprise success, as Colette starts to realise being an un-credited writer isn't all it's cracked up to be.

Verdict

Remember those two possible outcomes I listed before the story summary, of course you do, it's probably still on screen, well let's just say I'm swaying more towards the latter conclusion.

The thing about these films is they're so hard to criticise from any respectable level. I can say how much this film bored me to tears, to the point I was checking my watch at regular intervals, but fans of period dramas will just tell me that it 'isn't for me' and that's fair enough. I was lucky enough to be born white and male in a first world country, so most things are already made for me, I accept that not every film genre will be to my liking, but the thing about it is, there always seems to be something that I might enjoy hidden away underneath the faff and nonsense that comes with historical period settings.

Hidden away within Colette is a perfect allegory to be related to modern times, gender oppression and sexuality. No matter how boring the experience of the film was, I still found myself rooting for Colette, which I suppose is a point in its favour, but it helps that Willy is a self-satisfied, smug little tosser, thereby making Colette much more sympathetic, it doesn't even really need to try.

As I said, it feels like somewhere buried deep in Colette's narrative is a period drama that can relate to modern issues, and I like that. BlacKkKlansman made my Top 10 last year for doing something similar, but that also had the added advent of being interesting and fun to watch even if you're watching in a vacuum. Its on-the-nose allegories for modern times were made all the sweeter by the feeling that it had earned it, whereas Colette never gets that far, instead giving us a bland story populated by bland characters, even if Colette was sympathetic, this wasn't because of her character, it was because of the actions of another character, there are insinuations that Colette has more in the brain department than she is given credit for, but it's never properly explored.

I could go on all day about how films such as Colette and The Favourite are well-directed, well-acted and generally nice looking, but that doesn't change the fact that my eyes glaze over about half an hour into each film, which can never be a good thing.

I understand that they aren't made for me, and that's fine. I gave them a good chance and that's all that can be asked, but I never feel engaged with any films of their ilk, so I suppose they shall go on my list of things that 'Just Aren't For Me' whose current occupants include: anything Michael Bay has done, and being stuck in a conversation with a family member you haven't seen for a while and don't particularly like.

In conclusion, if you get a kick out of Colette, that's fine, and I'm happy they have an audience, as they're clearly made with love and passion, however, this film, like The Favourite before it, failed to draw me into the genre, in fact, it probably even drew me in less than The Favourite, which at least had some quirky stand-out moments, whereas Colette is like having porridge for breakfast, it's competent and gets everything right where it should, but it's as interesting as a game of golf during the paint-drying appreciation weekend.

Stan & Ollie (Originally published January 19th, 2019)
Directed by Jon S. Baird
Starring: Steve Coogan, John C. Reilly, Nina Arianda and Shirley Henderson

I'm willing to bet that most, if not all, of us have come across Laurel & Hardy in our lifetime. For me it was my granddad, who would watch the films in fits of hysterics as the duo got into "another fine mess".

This past week, I got to take the very same granddad who remembers seeing the two of them the first time around to see the biopic of the duo, Stan & Ollie, starring Steve Coogan and John C. Reilly, respectively, as the titular duo.

I am usually cautious in approaching biopics, as sometimes they seem as though they're just a little bit too in love with their subject matter to convey a worthwhile narrative, but that being said, one of my top films of last year was a biopic, and exploring stories from little-known periods of a famous career can give plenty of drama for the casual cinema fan, and the long-running fans of the person it is immortalising. With that being said, let's look at the Stan & Ollie.

Story

It's 1953, and Laurel and Hardy are in the twilight of their careers, with their greatest successes a distant memory. To try and get a new film off the ground they embark on a music hall tour of the UK, which brings to light old grudges and new health problems for the ageing duo, as they try and regain the spotlight.

Verdict

If there's one prevailing word I can relate to Stan & Ollie, it's: nostalgia. It hangs thick over the films many twists and turns, and in many different forms. Nostalgia for old Hollywood, nostalgia for music-hall comedy and nostalgia of a post-war Britain, still recovering from its heavy losses less than a decade earlier.

There's also a twinge of sadness in the film, in the most unexpected ways, it's a sadness of a duo who know their days in the spotlight are numbered, but they push on for the adoration of their fans, all the while knowing that this tour might be what kills them off completely.

As a film, it's held up wonderfully by its two leads, Steve Coogan gets to show off his more dramatic side, which is often under-used, and John C Reilly continues to be one of Hollywood's most underrated actors. They have the same quality in their performances that Rami Malek brought to Bohemian Rhapsody, you don't think of them as actors playing real people, rather as the real people themselves, telling their story, and that's a rare kind of thing to bottle in a film.

The film comes to us from director Jon S. Baird who could not have made a bigger departure from one film to the next, as his previous film was *Filth* the James McAvoy vehicle, based off the Irvine Welsh book, a tale of alcohol and drug abuse, a million miles away from the inherent sweetness of this film, not that this is a bad thing of course, if anything it shows the directors ability to adapt to the subject matter, and showing a broad wealth of range between the two films can only be the catalyst of a bright future ahead.

It is by no means a flawless film, no matter how charming it may be, a lot of side-characters are heavily stereotyped, especially the wives and concert promoter, the latter of which seems to lack any sort of credible nuance, being the very essence of a typical film concert producer, i.e.: will do anything to get the show on, and more importantly his money in the bank.

The wives conform to other stereotypes though, Stan's wife is practically a cartoon of a Soviet female in some scenes, whereas Hardy's wife comes across as the nagging wife we've seen so many caricatures of over the years. The difference between the two wives and the promoter, however, is they gain nuance and subtlety towards the films climax, in a way that doesn't feel anticlimactic, it's another feel-good moment in a film full of them.

If I had to pick a favourite thing about the film, I'd look beyond its nostalgia-heavy presentation, its charm and likeable leads, and point towards the film's final scene, a lovely pay off of a full films build to show the duos genuine affection towards each other, perfectly encapsulated in one of the pairs most iconic routines.

In conclusion then, Stan & Ollie is a wonderful, feel-good experience, dripping with charm and anchored by two committed lead performances and a capable guiding hand of its director. If you're seeking a bittersweet film, over-flowing with love and passion, you could do far worse than Stan & Ollie.

The Upside (Originally published January 23rd, 2019)
Directed by Neil Burger
Starring: Kevin Hart, Bryan Cranston, Nicole Kidman and Golshifteh Farahani

I am torn on whether or not I actually like Kevin Hart. That may seem like an odd way to start a review but go with me on this. Putting aside the recent furore over past tweets, and judging plainly on his film performances, you can't really say he's anything special, he certainly has charm, but has never shown any signs of real growth in his performances, so upon seeing the trailer for this film, it made me think that this might be the film where he flourishes in a more dramatic setting.

While this is a point for debate, I did think the film looked like an interesting choice for Hart, and Bryan Cranston, his co-star, whose acting talent is never in question, to take on this remake of a popular French film, which has flown comparatively under the radar recently, bar a few news stories on the ethics of Cranston playing a quadriplegic, which isn't a topic for discussion here, I'm just here to review the film, so here we go.

Story

Phillip Lacasse (Cranston) is a quadriplegic billionaire who is understandably tired of life, he strikes up an unlikely friendship with ex-con Dell Scott (Hart) who is hired as his unlikely carer, through unorthodox means, Dell helps Phillip find the joy in life once more, as both of their lives improve.

Verdict

While I surmised in my earlier paragraphs that this might have been Hart's dramatic breakthrough, I wasn't entirely accurate. While it has dramatic moments, it is heavily entrenched in its comedic settings, rarely embracing its flair for the dramatic.

There is a fair amount of chemistry between Hart and Cranston, enough to make the film an enjoyable watch, but it doesn't feel like we're getting the full effect of either of them. Hart's usual antics are toned down, but still evident, I can see a glimmer of potential for the dramatic in him, however, should he be willing to embrace it. He's certainly not lacking in charisma and magnetism, especially in this film, Dell comes across as likeable, but highly flawed, a conclusion we're naturally brought to given his status at the start of the film.

Whilst it is an enjoyable enough watch, and the two leads bring what they can to the table, it is still quite an insubstantial film, frequently missing opportunities for dramatic tension in favour of more outwardly comedic moments, if that's what they were going for that's fine, but it seems given the subject matter, there were ample opportunities to take the film down a more serious path that are missed.

One particular incident springs to mind when thinking about this, and its somewhere in the middle of the film, when Phillip and Dell go for a hot dog, and Dell speaks up to the cashier who ignores Phillip, and instead asks Dell what Phillip wants. Right there is an ideal message to drive the film, one that is sorely lacking in Hollywood, but it's never really brought up again, and we're back to comedy antics right afterwards, I think that's the biggest disappointment, knowing the potential was there for something more, but the opportunity was missed and they just made a bland, but fairly enjoyable, comedy.

For all of its flaws, there are parts I enjoyed about the film, Dell has a nicely paced arc, even if there are elements of his character that contradicts itself. I actually felt that Hart was better during the few dramatic moments than in the comedy moments, even if that is somewhat out of his wheelhouse.

In the end though, while it isn't particularly memorable, and I probably won't watch it again, there are enough elements of The

Upside that are enjoyable to make it worthwhile, even though it is disappointing that an opportunity for something more complex was passed up, which I think will be my prevailing memory of it when I look back, perhaps unfairly, but when a chance for a film to convey a more important message is missed, I feel that that is the important factor to take away, no matter how enjoyable the end product.

Glass (Originally published January 24th, 2019)
Directed by M. Night Shyamalan
Starring: James McAvoy, Bruce Willis, Anya Taylor Joy and Samuel L. Jackson

M. Night Shyamalan has a very mixed history, which is the kindest thing I can say about his filmography really. On one hand there's modern classics such as The Sixth Sense, Unbreakable and some of Signs and on the other hand there's After Earth, The Happening and, God help us, The Last Airbender.

In fact, Shyamalan was on somewhat of a low streak, in fact, he hadn't made a good film in well over a decade, when 2016's Split came around. So, the fact that Split ended up being one of that year's stronger offerings was a bit of a shock, and what's more, there was another shock awaiting at the end of the film, when Unbreakable's David Dunn appeared, confirming the films were linked.

So, after a career revival and revisiting one of his most popular characters, anticipation was high for what many were hoping would be a new Shyamalan masterpiece, so let's see what the resulting film brought us.

Story

Following the events of Split, Kevin Wendell Crumb/'The Horde' has left groups of murdered teenage girls in his wake and has another group ready to feed to The Beast. He is traced down by David Dunn (now given the name 'The Overseer') and following an altercation between Dunn and The Beast, the two are detained in a mental institution, where Mr Glass awaits...

Verdict

There was a fair amount of critical storm towards this film upon its release, with many citing its slow pace as its biggest negative, these people have apparently never seen a Shyamalan film before, which are characterised by their slow builds with explosive finales, and it's the same thing here.

While I can see why there would be disappointment, as Split was more briskly paced, but this was the exception as opposed to the rule. Unbreakable was a slow-burn, building tension and intrigue until the final reveal blew our minds, and Glass tries to follow this formula, as a result, it builds nice tension and character moments, a challenge for a film that is based almost entirely in an asylum, but each new development gives us a tease of what's to come, a glimmer of a clue for us to guess the inevitable Shyamalan twist.

So, about that twist then, after leading us through a slow burn plot building tension and drawing us back into the characters, the twist ends up falling somewhat short.

Obviously being hampered by my 'no spoilers' rule isn't exactly helping here but following two films with arguably Shyamalan's strongest twists with this really seems like he was desperately scrabbling for a twist just for the sake of one. While I wouldn't say it's a bad twist, it actually ties in with a previously innocuous scene in Unbreakable, it simultaneously manages to be too lazy, and too convoluted, which is an achievement in itself.

One thing I will give M. Night credit for though is giving us a definite ending to the story, once again trying hard to not spoil here. It's rare in this age of franchises and shared universes that a creator draws a definitive line under their property with next to no chance of a sequel, so I applaud the fact that he isn't going to draw this out longer than necessary.

Apart from the effective tension building, the films main strength is in its acting department. James McAvoy is once again outstanding, seamlessly transitioning between 24 distinctive characters is a titanic achievement for an actor, as most would make their performance overstretched or corny, but McAvoy avoids this by actually making each character distinguishable from the last, all helped along by some strong character writing from Shyamalan.

Alongside McAvoy in the lead roles are Bruce Willis and Samuel L. Jackson, who both bring their 'A' game back to two of their most familiar characters. Willis eschews his habit of sleepwalking through roles to produce a thoroughly engaging performance as David Dunn, a seemingly ordinary man with extraordinary powers, he comes across as tired and unsure of himself and above all, he's still the same likeable every-man he was in 2000. Sam Jackson brings his undeniable presence and I'm not too ashamed to admit that seeing him back as Mr Glass gave me goose bumps.

While this film may be a disappointment to some, I came away very happy with Glass, I felt it gave me everything I wanted from the concept, while not fulfilling them as I imagined and suffering from being a tad over-written, I found real joy in the film, especially in its effective building of tension, acting and characterisations.

M. Night Shyamalan is an extremely flawed filmmaker, just as this is an extremely flawed film, but I can't hold it against him because among the drudgery of some of his works shine bright, pure diamonds of ideas and concepts, he is never afraid to try something that might not work, to take a risk, which we see very little of in film. Sometimes his ideas don't come off, and he ends up being the butt of jokes, but sometimes he creates things with great ideas and depth, and to me this shows one thing sorely lacking in the film industry: humanity. Yes, he may not be perfect, but who is? Just as that applies to him, it applies to Glass, on the surface, very flawed, but underneath it's human and driven by passion.

In conclusion then, if you look past its flaws, you'll find an enjoyable tension ride that compares unfavourably when compared to the original film, however, has enough to make it stand-out to make it a nice way to cap off the series. You may come away disappointed by it, and that's fair enough, but for all its flaws, Glass is an effective thriller, with some great performances and if nothing else, gave us the opportunity to see Mr Glass ride again, which can only be a positive thing.

The Mule (Originally published January 31st)
Directed by Clint Eastwood
Starring: Clint Eastwood, Bradley Cooper, Laurence Fishburne and Michael Pena

It was once said: "no one directs Clint Eastwood, like Clint Eastwood." Which is a sentiment I agree with completely. Furthermore, I think the list of actors who are as good, if not better as directors is a very short one, even when Eastwood is absent in front of the camera, he remains one of the most underrated directors of all time. From directing himself to stellar performances in films such as Gran Torino and Unforgiven, to stepping away from the acting spotlight in films like Letters from Iwo Jima and Mystic River, Eastwood is a man of many talents.

So, when I heard he was stepping back in front of camera to direct himself once again, I was understandably excited, not to mention the story seems like prime late-era Eastwood material, an older character doing something uncharacteristic of the elderly, with the unmistakable feel of his films, the dry, gritty feel that characterized Gran Torino seemed like it was also present here. So, does this latest offering compare with his impressive rap sheet?

Story

Earl Stone is a 90-year-old horticulturist who is facing losing his business, as well as his family. Through a series of chance encounters he ends up wrapped up in the Mexican cartel's drug operation as a 'mule' a driver delivering packages across the border, and pretty soon, the authorities are on his tail.

Verdict

Right now, Clint Eastwood is 88 years old, he has been in films since 1955, he is one of Hollywood's most experienced heads, so the material here seemed like prime material for Eastwood to show he still has what it takes to compete in an ever-increasingly competitive market, which is why it breaks my heart to report that this film falls short of Eastwood's mighty reputation.

As a director, he still remains nearly flawless at capturing an image of stunning beauty, and some of this films long shots rank among some of his best, capturing the dusty, dry American desert in Eastwood's typical style and flair. It feels very similar to Eastwood's 2009 offering Gran Torino, which long-term readers will know I am very fond of, which makes sense as it's from the same scriptwriter, but it feels several steps removed from that films heart, depth and character.

Perhaps it is understandable that Eastwood is considerably slower as an actor, it's true that he's still incredibly watchable, his trademark squint doesn't lose its endearing nature despite his advancing age, he just generally seems slower and more pained in front of camera, which really stands out among his co-stars, which include recent Oscar-nominee Bradley Cooper and Laurence Fishburne, it's very sad to see, as he does generally look like he's doing his best with what he has, but age finally seems to be catching up and his performance suffers because of it.

To be honest, even his co-stars don't dazzle as they usually do. The aforementioned duo of Cooper and Fishburne often seem to be phoning in their performances, as if this film was a contractual obligation rather than something they looked forward to, mind you, having said that, they didn't strike lucky in the character department, playing a couple of cookie-cutter DEA agents, it all feels like it's so far below both the cast and director that it comes across as false.

It is, as I mentioned, the direction where this film shines, and for what it's worth Eastwood still seems incredibly capable of that at least, but the rest of the story hits the same predicable beats as you would think from its premise, and what was once a promising idea shrivels into becoming another run of the mill film about Mexican drug cartels, something we've seen a million times and done a million times better, I'm not sure if this is a late attempt to catch the trend of current cartel-related media, and if it is, it's a cynical attempt.

Overall, this is a film that is simply not worthy of Eastwood's name and reputation. A predictable, and often cliched, script, occasionally brought to life by some great direction and cinematography and the advent of seeing Clint on screen even loses its appeal after seeing him shuffle through the mediocre script, served up from a scriptwriter who you would hope could do better.

In conclusion, I wouldn't recommend this movie for those wanting another slice of prime Clint Eastwood, as it comes nowhere near his lofty standards, the praise I give the way it looks is overshadowed by my indifference to its characters, and my contempt for its script. Lovely direction and vision, ruined by a sub-par script, and phoned-in performances.

Green Book (Originally published January 31st)
Directed by Peter Farrelly
Starring: Viggo Mortensen, Mahershala Ali and Linda Cardellini

So, we're well into Oscars season now, the cinemas are full of films with more banners than a Jubilee street party, all three months late into UK cinemas for *some* reason (seriously, sort it out Hollywood) so now I'm just catching up on the big nominations, the first of which is Green Book.

Now, we're all familiar with the setting of the Jim Crow South, in all its disgraceful backwardness, but there's always room for more interesting stories whatever this setting, anyway, this film has the talent, is it worth the hype?

Story

Tony 'Lip' is out of work due to the closure of the Copacabana night club, he is offered the job of driving a Black concert pianist around on a tour of the Deep South and keeping him out of trouble along the way.

Verdict

The most interesting thing I found about the film pre-release and during the film, is its director Peter Farrelly, who some might recognise as one half of The Farrelly Brothers, makers of wacky, gross-out comedies such as: There's Something About Mary and Dumb and Dumber, and the fact that someone with 25 years of experience makes the decision to take a turn for the dramatic, moreover without his brother.

Actually, the truth is, there are laughs to be had in here too, mostly from Tony themselves, but what really drew me into the story was the heart behind it, the difference between the two main characters made them all the more magnetic.

There's a scene in the trailer, where the two main characters are eating fried chicken and get rid of the bones by throwing them out of the window, in what is representative of a character breakthrough for Doc Shirley (Mahershala Ali) which the trailer makes you think is a big build-up to that moment, but in the film it feels like it peaks too soon, as it happens maybe earlier than it should. Which is odd, as for the rest of the run time it's very well-paced.

While I'm griping, I was also put off by the caricature of Italian-American people, in a film that makes a stand against the treatment of African-Americans later in the film, and their even-handed treatment of Black culture, the Italians were representative of any Italian-Americans you've ever seen in a film, which seems mis-placed in a film trying to make a point, for them to rely on stereotypes on that side of character.

All that being said however, there's a lot to recommend about Green Book, Peter Farrelly makes the jump to dramatic film-making very well, and there's some lovely shots to enjoy here, I especially like the cinematography inside the car and how many perspective that can give, and also framing Doc Shirley on stage incredibly well, balancing portraying the prejudice of the era, and the sympathy of the Doc Shirley character.

Speaking of Doc Shirley, Mahershala Ali was far and away the best thing about the film, he worked extremely well with Viggo Mortensen, their chemistry pops off the screen, but Ali just grasps the nuances of the character and makes them thrive, at the same time you're admiring Doc Shirley's talent, you're feeling sympathy for his innate loneliness, and Ali was the perfect person to bring this across, as he is very quickly becoming one of Hollywood's best actors

To be honest, the film took until the final third to fully draw me in, it seemed like Farrelly was hesitant to let go of the comedy roots entirely, and it was only when they focused on the dramatic story that it come alive, with material like this comedy can seem incongruous, and I can understand why this director was perhaps trying to leave his fingerprint of comedy on it, but when it came together, it was incredibly gripping, especially when focusing on the characters and their relationship.

In conclusion then, an incredibly interesting character study is in this film, it is sometimes lost behind mixed intentions and sometimes heightened by clean and focused direction, and entirely worth a watch for Mahershala Ali's performance if nothing else.

Chapter Eleven: February 2018

Beautiful Boy (Originally published February 2nd, 2019)
Directed by Felix Van Groeningen
Starring: Steve Carell, Timothee Chalamet, Maura Tierney and Amy Ryan

This is a film that had flown under many people's radars but was one of my most anticipated films of this year. Most of the reason for that is the leading actors, Steve Carell, who is an incredibly underrated dramatic actor, rightly starting to get recognition now, and Timothee Chalamet, the most promising acting talent in Hollywood, best known for his Oscar-nominated performance in Call Me by Your Name, itself a beautiful account of love in unorthodox circumstances.

Then there was the source material, seemingly perfect for the talent involved, the story of a father and son whose relationship is ravaged by the son's drug addiction, a seemingly transformative role for Chalamet, and an emotionally-driven character for Carell to flex his dramatic muscles, so the opportunity is there for one of the year's best films, does it live up to expectations?

Story

David Sheff (Steve Carell) finds himself stuck in a vicious circle of supporting his Son, Nick (Timothee Chalamet) through his addiction troubles, only for him to keep relapsing, as David starts to reach the end of his tether.

Verdict

Beautiful Boy is not a happy film about overcoming addiction. It is a stark, and at times harrowing, account of how the disease ravages addicts and their families. In some scenes, it builds up the hope for a happy ending, only for it to come crashing down time and time again, in a startling allegory for addiction itself in some ways.

I will apologise right now for this review being short on laughs, but I find it very hard to joke about a film depicting such serious issues in such unflinching, uncompromising ways. In many way, I think that's what the film deserves the most plaudits for, many films have skirted around the issue of drug addiction, but few have managed to take us so deeply into the heart of the issue so effectively.

It manages really well to balance showing the right amount of respect to the issue without shying away from showing some of its worst sides, in ways that can sometimes make it incredibly hard to watch, it creates a great sense of disappointment when Nick once again reaches for the needle, as we've grown throughout the course of the film to see he's just a scared kid, unsure of the way out of the situation he's found himself in, which brings me nicely around to the characters and the actors portraying them.

Earlier on in this review, I said that this film presented an opportunity for a transformative role for Chalamet, and he grasped that opportunity with both hands. His presence on screen is that of a shadow of a once bright young man, ravaged by the effects of drugs, his face conveying a million different thoughts and emotions in each scene, as his character withers away in front of us into a shell of a person.

What the performance and the writing make us do is empathise with Nick, and with David, when he disappoints David, he disappoints us, we feel sorrow when he reaches for the needle or the pipe again, and that is such a rare thing for a film to achieve.

Steve Carell is also playing a character going through a whirlwind of emotions, he is perhaps on more of a roller-coaster than Nick, as he tries his best to play the supporting father, but is taken advantage of one to many times, which climaxes towards the end in a heart-wrenching scene, involving a phone call between father and son, one that feels like it pushes the narrative from above average to phenomenally important.

There are complaints I could mention, the film sometimes seems unfocused and slow at times, not giving each event sufficient time to breath, but any complaint I could levy against it is overshadowed by the films immense importance in highlighting the dark recesses of this deadly disease.

Another area in which the film thrives is its direction, it's conservative, never reaching a grand scale that could overshadow the narrative, which just lifts the heart-breaking moments even higher, there are some truly incredibly-shot moments between Nick and David that aid in telling the story via the framing of the scene, it is not a film that aims to be the best-looking, as I said, it's an account of an unsavoury corner of life, one which does not need beauty, but honesty, and that's what this film is, it's honest, it could have ended with an uplifting climax of a young man beating addiction, but it knows that the reality is often not like that, and its honesty is what will define it, it's an astounding achievement in narrative film-making and it has been criminally over-looked by the powers that be in Hollywood, as a film that deserves more nominations but also as a tool of warning, and as a visceral reminder that drug addiction is not beautiful, it's a struggle for every day.

I'm not one for doing this but seeing as this subject matter is one that affects too many, I'm listing several phone numbers where help is available for anyone struggling with addiction. It is a disease and there are people out there who can help.

UK:

Talk to Frank: 0300 123 6600

The Mix: 0808 808 4994

Community for Recovery: 01785 810762

Help can also be found via the NHS on this site: https://www.nhs.uk/Service-Search/Information-and-support-for-drug-misuse/LocationSearch/339

US:

Finding Recovery: 1-877-958-9735

Boys Town National Hotline: 1 (800) 448-3000

National Council on Alcoholism and Drug Dependency: 1 (800) NCA-CALL (622-2255)

Local services can also be found via Google search, don't suffer in silence and seek help.

Vice (Originally published February 5th, 2019)
Directed by Adam McKay
Starring: Christian Bale, Amy Adams, Steve Carrell and Sam Rockwell

In my last review, I briefly mentioned 'transformative' acting roles in relation to the film I was reviewing, and the actors involved, and if there is a modern master of this art, Christian Bale is certainly a front-runner.

From losing an incredible amount of weight for The Machinist to bulking up once more for his three appearances as Batman in the 'Dark Knight' trilogy, Christian Bale is transforming himself once again in his latest role, as former US Vice-President Dick Cheney.

As a Brit, my foreknowledge of American politics is rather ropy. I know of Cheney by name, mainly from his name being mentioned by various comedians as some curmudgeon who values human life slightly less than he values his third doughnut of the day, that is to say, not much. So this film will serve as a crash course in Cheney, but is it a worthwhile one?

Story

Charting the rise of Dick Cheney from college drop-out to the most powerful Vice-President in history, we see the rich tapestry of American politics through the eyes of Cheney himself, and the many people he comes across.

Verdict

If, like me, you aren't all that knowledgeable of American politics, this film serves as a crash course in the past 50 years, charting the swings in power and all major points of contention along the way. From Nixon all the way through to Obama, Cheney was there, and this film shows that.

This film is currently riding a wave of success on the back of the release of the Oscars nominations, where it has amassed eight nominations across many categories, including the much sought-after Best Picture award, in the grand scheme of Best Picture nominees, it stands out as a bit more experimental than most, utilising jump-cuts through various issues and flirting with non-linearity, the director's background on comedy is on show in some stages, much like Green Book before it, although it is quite even-handed in its genre definition.

What isn't as even-handed is the director's position on who he is portraying, it is quite clear from the outset that Adam McKay is not a fan of Dick Cheney, even though later in the film he makes more of an effort to portray him as a more sympathetic figure, the directors own views are made very clear in how he chooses to portray the subject material.

Putting political views aside, Cheney isn't the most interesting figure to document on the surface, it is only when you start digging that you realise that Cheney was at the heart of almost every decision the Bush administration ever made, while the film is hardly a documentary, the points it makes are well-researched enough, and even referenced in some cases, it helps to build a full working view of the political climate.

Whatever McKay's view on Cheney as a person, he clearly had the best intentions in mind when choosing who to portray him, Christian Bale's ability to become his character is almost chameleon-like and it's no different here, seeing the lengths he goes to embody Cheney, gaining weight, shaving his head and learning his mannerisms are only the tip of the iceberg in an intriguingly layered performance, it's hardly surprising it has got a nomination for Bale at most film awards, him having already won a Golden Globe for his performance, with the BAFTAs and the Oscars still to come, he may be one to watch for these awards.

The cast a whole is one of the films main strengths, using an ensemble cast to bring to life various political figures from the late 20th, and early 21st, century. There's Amy Adams as Cheney's wife Lynne, Steve Carell as Donald Rumsfeld, and Sam Rockwell as George W. Bush himself, a performance which earned Rockwell his second Best Supporting Actor nomination in a row.

While boasting a cast that would make any film-maker jealous, there does feel like there's a lack of spark in the early stages of the film, I think the problem lies with how unsympathetic Dick Cheney is, and quite frankly that extends to most characters in the film, we do get glimpses of a softer side, particularly surrounding his daughter Mary, where the film's emotional heart ultimately lies, but beyond that we have no real reason to warm to Cheney, I'm well-aware that that may be the intention, but to make a main character deliberately unlikable is usually either pretentious or misguided, but I don't quite get that impression here, it feels like the director is trying to make a statement, which is all very well, but in doing so you sacrifice a fair bit of investment.

As far as filmmaking goes, the method flits between the surreal and intense and the naturalistic and simple. There are a few scenes which completely take you by surprise, as the film's general tone is one of a natural, realistic approach, simply portraying the vents as they are planned bureaucratically, which make the cut-away to the actual events all the more effective as a tool to shock the viewer, and are well-spaced as to not become routine.

There is a fair amount of style here then, enough to cover the unsympathetic main character. On that point I'm on the fence, however there is enough in here to see why it has gained its plaudits, but it is also a bit hard to engage with at its worst, yet it can also be a gripping political thriller, so it has variety to itself, and once the film is rolling towards the finish it becomes more gripping.

In conclusion, there are enough merits to recommend Vice, namely its cast and varying direction style, but it also struggles to make its protagonist likeable, however, making Dick Cheney likeable seems to be like making a king cobra cuddlier, so I can overlook that. It's a good look at exactly how much power the American President has, and that is almost enough to make it a horror film, but it's an entertaining ride while it's there.

Can You Ever Forgive Me? (Originally published February 9th, 2019)
Directed by Marielle Heller
Starring: Melissa McCarthy, Richard E. Grant, Dolly Wells and Jane Curtin

You may recall that I said a lot of nasty things about Melissa McCarthy last year, after her turn in The Happytime Murders, but here she is months later with an Oscar nomination to her name, something I wasn't expecting when I was watching her share a screen with an ejaculating puppet last August.

Now, I'm all for a good-old career turn around, the best example of which in my opinion is Jim Carrey, going from his wacky mid-90s comedies to winning two Golden Globes in a row for The Truman Show and Man on the Moon, the latter of which is one of my favourite films of all time. These turnarounds are somewhat rare however, not nearly enough do we discover an actor's true talent for their fear of taking a risk.

Not only does McCarthy now proudly have an Oscar nom, which is apparently her second, but undervalued British actor Richard E Grant has earned his very first Oscar nomination, which leads me to wonder why it's taken so long, and why McCarthy had a nomination before him, not that I hold it against her, by the end of this review I may have given her a lot of praise, which is giving too much away, so let's get on with the review.

Story

In the early 90's biographer Lee Israel (Melissa McCarthy) has hit a slump in her career, her books aren't selling, her agent is ignoring her, and she is increasingly turning to drink. By chance, she discovers the value of letters written by prominent writers, so she begins a career of embellishing letters which eventually spirals out of control.

Verdict

Wherever this Melissa McCarthy was hiding, I'd like to know why she stayed hidden for so long. This could not be more opposing to the last film I saw her in, not only does she make the character both likeable and flawed in an impressively dramatic way, but also brings her comedy chops to the table in a much more subtle and, more to the point, smart way.

While watching two hours of an author writing letters might not sound interesting, that's really only the first layer of this surprisingly deep film. On the surface it's about someone forging letters, but deep down it's about loneliness, and its effect on a person, who may outwardly choose to be on her own, but really, she needs a friend as much as anyone.

Before getting into the acting, I should address the film's technical attributes, as it's very well-made behind the camera too. I really like its colour palate, it's not your typical dark and gritty one, there's enough colour in there, but the backgrounds mirror the characters, faded and slightly falling apart, along with some excellent framings for its settings, mostly in dusty bookshops, as I say, it's like the film itself is a reflection of its characters and as a stage for conveying the performances it does a great job.

As you may have gleamed from past statements in this review, I really, really liked Melissa McCarthy in this film, it's the most subtle I think she's ever been, in the best way possible, while there are moments of comedy, they are well thought-through and balanced by an extremely grounded and engaging dramatic performance, making us emotionally invested in what really should be a really unlikeable character. It makes me wonder where this talent has been hiding, there's an extremely emotional scene later on in the film where her character really comes together and cements her place in the audience's heart, and this moment is carried excellently by McCarthy.

Along with McCarthy, Richard E Grant is another bright spot in this film. Once again, he plays a character who should really be unlikeable; he's arrogant, a compulsive liar, and a thief but you still feel sorry for him. Mainly because it feels like a lot happened in the characters past to bring him to this point, it's established early in the film that he's down on his luck, so what unfortunate circumstance brought him to this? He also carries a fair weight of emotion, he, like Lee Israel, is desperately lonely. On the outside he has this facade of popularity when he's really a troubled, and very lonely man, all of this is handled with expertise by the seasoned Grant, who should really have had more recognition by now.

There aren't really any big criticisms I could levy against it, I suppose there are moments where the pace noticeably slows, and there's a lot of peripheral characters who don't get enough development, but these are small troubles with a largely excellent film.

It is not a typically plot-driven narrative, while the plot is there and important to the story, I'd say the real effectiveness of the film lies in its lead characters, Lee Isreal is simultaneously sympathetic, yet obnoxious and Jack Hock (Grant's character) has all the necessary character traits to be an antagonist, but it's the strong writing that make these characters three-dimensional enough to not rely on those kind of labels. In many ways the main plot of Lee and the fraud she commits becomes the background of a blossoming friendship between two interesting, yet deeply flawed, people.

Can You Ever Forgive Me is probably my favourite film of the year thus far for acting and characters alone, but the idea behind the story is turned from its bland-sounding premise, into an intriguing account of someone striking lucky in the most unlikely circumstances, only to come crashing down once again.

In conclusion then, there's not much left for me to do but recommend Can You Ever Forgive Me, and say that it is a genuine pleasure to be proven wrong by such a genuinely enjoyable performance, even critics can be wrong, who knew?

The Lego Movie 2 (Originally published February 25th, 2019)
Directed by Mike Mitchell
Starring: Chris Pratt, Elizabeth Banks, Will Arnett and Tiffany Haddish

So, The Lego Move was a bit of a surprise when it landed back in 2015. There's a tendency for these films (film adaptations of popular things; see Angry Birds and The Emoji Movie) tend to be cloying, brain dead activities in endurance, that only those with half a brain cell (or under the age of 5) could extract any entertainment from.

The Lego Movie changed this however; it brought on board some filmmakers with some comedy pedigree, who wrote a script brimming with charm, character and copious amounts of in-jokes.

It was then followed a few years later by the Lego Batman Movie, a film I found so incredibly fun that I named it in my Top 10 of that year, so safe to say Lego Movie 2 had some big boots to fill.

Story

Immediately after the defeat of President Business at the end of the first film, a group of Duplo figures invade Bricksburg, turning the once-mighty utopia into an apocalyptic wasteland. During this time of hardship a new threat arrives and kidnaps the master builders and it's up to Emmett to rescue them all.

Verdict

One thing that stuck with me about the first film, and is still prevalent here, is the oceans of charm the film possesses. Every character is crafted lovingly with enough humour to entertain the very young to the very old, there's the simple jokes for the younger audiences, and the deeper reference humour in there for the eagle-eyed adult.

The dialogue is another thing that stood out from the first few films, they are scripted with the aspirations of a high-concept film, rather than a brightly coloured film essentially made for kids. The script is densely packed with meta humour and in-jokes, which in itself presents another challenge for there is a fine line for this sort of humour, and leaning on it can be somewhat of a crutch, however this film, and its predecessors skate around the edges gracefully, never leaning on it enough to be pretentious and providing enough fun for everyone involved.

Since the first film there has been a change in director but not much of a change in direction, if you get my drift. The scriptwriters remain the same; Lord and Miller return to provide their magic in the screenplay department, but it is Mike Mitchell who takes the directorial reins this time around. This gives us enough focus on the tone from the first, but perhaps some fresh visual flair brought to us by Mitchell.

For what it's worth, the animation of the Lego Movies is phenomenal, crisp and detailed, the closer you look the more detail you discover, like a magic eye picture, everything conceivable is rendered in Lego, and the levels it goes to too properly present the construction toy that inspired it is awe inspiring.

This gives it a feel of a film spreading its elbows to a wider scope, including other Lego lines such as Duplo and Lego Friends that the success of the first film afforded them, but in widening the scope you lose a certain amount of focus, and thus, the threat doesn't feel as tangible second time around.

The sense of adventure branching through many different lands and characters remains, but the tight plotting of the first is lost somewhat by the less-focused antagonists. However, this is made up for by a few incredibly smart twists in the final act, that are telegraphed well enough if you look closely, but still enough of a surprise to take you by surprise first time around.

The idea and execution don't feel as 'fresh' per se, but they hardly needed to. The first film broke the mould, this was there to expand what was already there, add in an eager voice cast and an incredibly catchy soundtrack and you've got yourself all the makings of an incredibly enjoyable film.

What this film does, as well as the previous ones, is capture a feeling of childlike nostalgia, even if not for Lego then for all the characters it packs into its smorgasbord of a character list, with subtle jabs at other franchises for good measure, the Lego film franchise has yet to take its eye off the ball, and there is creative ideas enough to carry on this franchise in new directions for years to come, and long may it continue.

Cold Pursuit (Originally published February 26th, 2019)
Directed by Hans Petter Moland
Starring: Liam Neeson, Tom Bateman, Tom Jackson and Emmy Rossum

Oh, to be Liam Neeson's PR team. The actor proved himself to be a bit of a PR nightmare in the past few weeks, with the media swarming the story and circling like the vultures they are.

While I certainly don't condone Neeson's words, all of that bears no effect on this film or my review of it, I don't think he's a bad man, he said the wrong thing, obviously, but I'm merely interested in films, there are only a few people whose films I refuse to watch because of their outside activity, and I don't think what Neeson said deserves the discrediting of his career.

So, with that out of the way, let's get on with the review.

Story

In the snowy landscape of Kehoe, Colorado, Nelson Coxman's world is turned upside down when his Son is murdered by a vicious drug gang, this sets him on a path to revenge, which, inadvertently, sparks off a turf war.

Verdict

I'm not sure whether this film will ultimately be remembered for the quality of the film, or Neeson's comments to the press, I am leaning towards the latter, as while the film flirts with fresh ideas, it suffers an identity crisis and ends up being painfully generic.

The aesthetic of the snowy ski resort is a nice touch, if a little too close to Fargo, in fact, while I'm on the subject of Fargo, the female police officer bears an uncanny resemblance to Frances McDormand's character in some scenes. Whether this is purely coincidental or a knowing homage, I couldn't say, but I theorize that it's more likely the latter.

Which brings me nicely round to the characters of the story, the cast is densely packed, yet unfocused, by juggling so many names it loses a certain edge to its characters, to the point where they all start blending into one. The respective drug gangs are good examples of this, as they was very rarely a distinguishing feature to each character, and even when there was in one particular case, there was no reason or pay-off to the proposed side-plot, it was just there for the sake of being there.

That last sentence could actually sum up a fair amount of the film, it's overly stuffed with needless faff and nonsense, when it could be driving home key plot points. The end product is a film that doesn't quite know what it wants to be, sometimes it flirts with knowing humour, only to drop that to quickly become a po-faced gangster drama a few minutes later, it's almost as if the screenplay was written by two people who didn't talk to each other, and an editor had to work out a way of blending two completely different scripts, and it just ends up being a mess.

That being said; however, it does have some nice ideas. There's a nice recurring motif of the people killed in the story getting named after they're killed with an on-screen graphic, which works nicely, and the police intrigue teased throughout could have been interesting, but it remains unexplored, to the point where it makes you wonder what the point of using these characters was.

The performances in the film are another unremarkable aspect. Liam Neeson appears to sleepwalk through a familiar feeling role for him, he gives the impression of being tired of this kind of thing. Laura Dern is barely used and has disappeared from the story by the time an hour has passed, and the various gangsters and henchmen all blend into one gelatinous mass of uninteresting stereotypes.

The characters are also widely inconsistent, and all of them incredibly unlikable, even Neeson, which is a feat in itself. There's a rather jarring plot point towards the end of the film where a child is kidnapped and it's so widely out of character that it makes you question everything about the film up to that point.

Overall then, besides being stylish and having a few nice ideas, the film is over-long and under-ambitious, using a nice aesthetic to draw you in, before telling a story we've seen done a million times, and much better executed. I can't really find much to recommend Cold Pursuit, unless seeing Liam Neeson is all you need in a film, I would say there's much better versions of this narrative out there, some of them even star Liam Neeson. I guess what I'm saying is, save your money, and watch Taken while imagining it's snowing, then you'd have had the overall experience.

Fighting with My Family (Originally published February 27th, 2019)
Directed by Stephen Merchant
Starring: Florence Pugh, Lena Headey, Nick Frost and Vince Vaughn

I'm a wrestling fan, you know. Have been since I was about 5, I used to watch Smackdown with my cousin, my favourite was "Stone Cold" Steve Austin (then again, he was everyone's favourite. Nowadays, I'm in my mid-20's and still love a good wrestling show, and you'll usually find me at independent shows, whenever I can be there.

Of course, I know it's fake, but then again, so is Game of Thrones, and most films you see that aren't documentaries. It's not exactly high-brow entertainment, but it's a method of storytelling as good as any other.

So, imagine my delight when it was announced that a film would be made, based around a documentary surrounding the Knight Family, a family of wrestlers from Norwich, England. I actually remember watching the documentary in question when it was first broadcasts, I remember certain events depicted here, from when they first happened, so all in all, it looked like an ideal film for me.

But, on the other hand, films tend to have a habit of portraying wrestling as a pass-time enjoyed only by slack-jawed rednecks, and treat the whole business, and its fan-base with vitriolic contempt. This isn't always the case however, the pinnacle of wrestling-based films is of course 2008's The Wrestler, a jarring, and very touching, story of a past-his-prime wrestler trying to cling to fame in a world that has passed him by. But there also exists films like Ready to Rumble, where the heroes of the piece are a pair of man-children, making fart jokes and generally showing about as much respect for wrestling as George Lucas shows his own franchises.

Given the fact that Dwayne "The Rock" Johnson was producing this film, however, it does give me hope that this film might be more on the side of The Wrestler as opposed to Ready to Rumble, but let's find out.

Story

A young wrestler, Saraya 'Paige' Knight, who comes from a family of wrestlers achieves the dream she shares with her brother and makes it to the WWE. However, along the way she will have to contend with family tensions and the struggles of living thousands of miles from home to achieve her ultimate ambition, becoming Diva's Champion.

Verdict

The story here, was on set-up perfectly by the documentary and real-life itself, Saraya (who I'll refer to as Paige from here on in for clarity) was from a different world to the one to the one most of us grew up in, her whole family were wrestlers, but beyond that there's a darker history to the Knight's. Her father spent time in prison, as did her brother. Her mother is a former addict, these are all aspects of an underdog story waiting to happen, and credit to Stephen Merchant (the writer-director) he captures most of that story pretty well.

The film has the feel of a modern fairy-tale. A dreamer with a seemingly impossible dream, who achieves her goals and then some against all odds, it's all very cheery stuff in itself, but consider the circumstances of her background, it's made all the sweeter.

I don't think the film does enough with the darker history of the Knight's to take full advantage however, I can see why, this is Paige's story rather than a family history lesson, but the more a character has to overcome the more we invest in their story, and while it doesn't shy away from portraying the harsh training a wrestler undergoes, it feels like it skates past details to get there.

It feels like this is done to achieve a PG-13 rating though, to reach as broad an audience as possible, which is fair enough, but I feel there is more to this story that was, if not untouched, then underutilised.

That's not to say I didn't enjoy it however, because I did. In fact I think it may only miss out on the label of 'best film about wrestling ever' because The Wrestler exists. Which isn't to take away from the film's achievements, it's a charming, heart-warming tale, that is well-acted and sharply directed.

The film is helmed by a strong performance from Florence Pugh, who I must admit I'd never heard of prior to this film, I'll be keeping an eye on whatever she does next. The supporting cast is strong, boasting such names as Lena Headey (of Game of Thrones fame) and Nick Frost, as well as cameos from wrestling world figures, most noticeably Dwayne 'The Rock' Johnson in an extended cameo. I was especially impressed by the performance of Jack Lowden, who plays Paige's brother Zac, who brings a few emotional dimensions to the story, as the one whose dreams were crushed, while their sisters come true.

Its sharp direction comes courtesy of Stephen Merchant, emerging from the shadow of friend and former colleague Ricky Gervais in the past few years has done him the world of good, as the world sees that he has more to offer than simply being Ricky's tall friend.

Where the direction, and camera work, comes alive for me is during the wrestling segments, where create camera angles and cuts create a solid impression of the emotions being conveyed by the wrestlers, it's very solid work.

Overall then, while not being anything ground-breaking cinematically, Fighting With My Family delivers a solid story, held up by charismatic performances and eager direction, you could do a lot worse in terms of wrestling films, and I mean a LOT worse, but Fighting With My Family sits firmly in the upper echelons of this particular sub-genre.

Chapter Twelve: March 2019

The Aftermath (Originally published March 7th, 2019)
Directed by James Kent
Starring: Keira Knightley, Alexander Skarsgard and Jason Clarke

It's safe to say that we've seen more of World War 2 in films than perhaps we need. The war's been over for 75 years and still we mine it for more narrative opportunity. But apparently, we haven't mined everything as here comes The Aftermath.

I must admit, what first attracted me to this film was its concept; I've often wondered what became of Germany in the immediate aftermath of the war, and this film offered to show that. What attracts me to the idea is the thought of the human story to tell, sure Germany were most definitely the bad guys of the narrative, but what of the millions of citizens who didn't really have much to do with the Nazis? I hoped this may offer some answers, and while it didn't answer all of the questions I had, it offered newer ones along the way.

Story

Germany. 1946. Britain are in the midst of rebuilding German cities and rooting out the remaining Nazi sympathisers. In the midst of this, British soldier Lewis Morgan (Jason Clarke) brings his grieving wife Rachael (Keira Knightley) to live in Germany while he finishes his duties. Living with them is the German family who owned the house prior to British occupation, flaring tempers between camps.

Verdict

I'm having a case of Deja-vu right now. You see, I only just reviewed a historical drama starring Keira Knightley, and now I'm reviewing another one. Although in fairness, this film isn't much like Colette, her other recent historical drama, it's set in a different time period, a different country, and it actually managed to keep my attention.

Where the Aftermath succeeds is in portraying a story of human nature in the most extreme of times. There are multiple factors and parallels at work at once. I think the angle the film is aiming for is that, beneath nationalities, we're all human, as that's the way it seems. It shows us that there were innocent causalities on each side, and how it handles grief is commendable, it doesn't use it to introduce unnecessary melodrama to an already dramatic film, it is used to remind us of the losses suffered by each side.

The acting is also a strong point of this film, I enjoyed Keira Knightley's performance immensely, her character is one in constant flux, on one hand putting up a front of social respectability, whilst harbouring incredible grief, and seemingly dealing with that grief on her own.

Opposite her is Jason Clarke, an actor I must admit I aren't very familiar with, and who was in danger of simply becoming set-dressing to Keira Knightley's performance, he does come into his own when his character has some meatier, emotional scenes later in the film, he managed to make me change my mind on his character within the space of one scene, in which his facade of social coldness melts into an outpouring of emotion, which made me warm to his character more than any other moment in the film.

Competing for Rachael's affection is Stefan Lubert (Alexander Skarsgard) whose character is complex enough on his own, dealing with his own grief, his anger at both his country, and Britain, but I found his daughter, Freda, to be a more intriguing character.

She is harbouring her own share of grief, and a larger share of anger than her father, which threatens to lead her down a dark path, which goes to show how easy it is for disenfranchised youth to fall in with extremism, in a startling allegory for modern times, her arc is probably the most complete in the whole film, while the rest of the film is by no means bad, I found Freda's story to be the glue that held it all together.

It's by no means a perfect film. There are several parts that feels like a re-tread of old territory, it's that feeling of war-time nostalgia that is most evident of this, against the backdrop of an interesting set-up, this is no longer war time, and they stand among the ruins of a country they bombed, there are many much more intriguing ideas within that that the film misses, disappointingly. It's not terribly visually imaginative either, I know there's no way of making ruined buildings look stylish, but it looks pretty much like every other film set around this time period, visually.

There were also a few attempts made at erotic scenes, which I felt fell flat amongst the emotional narrative backdrop, it's not too egregious, and most importantly, doesn't over-stay its welcome, but it seems out of place.

Overall then, The Aftermath is nothing mind-blowing, or fresh in its thinking, but it offers a nice little narrative, with incredibly good acting and a few good lessons within it. While not being everything I wanted it to be, it offered something I didn't know I wanted, and that in the end, is enough.

Captain Marvel (Originally published March 10th, 2019)
Directed by Anna Boden and Ryan Fleck
Starring: Brie Larson, Samuel L. Jackson, Ben Mendelsohn and Djimon Hounsou

So it's taken 21 films and nearly 11 years, but we finally have a stand-alone female hero in the MCU.

I won't be dwelling on the background politics in this review, that is not my job. I will be looking at it as a film, which given Marvel's near-faultless record in the last few years, I was bound to enjoy right?

Well, with us well on the road towards Endgame, Captain Marvel is the final piece of the puzzle, so to speak. Named as the MCU's most powerful hero by Kevin Fiege and other powerful film forces, this film will surely set the stage for round two with Thanos next month.

In the past I have commented on how certain MCU films seem to be an advertisement for the next one, and that was a risk for this film too, with so much riding on Captain Marvel's appearance in Endgame. So will this be the case?

Story

In 1995, Kree soldier Vers crashes to Earth amid a violent war with the shape shifting Skrulls. With no memories of who she is or where she came from, she slowly rebuilds her memories with the help of Nick Fury.

Verdict

The MCU have an undeniable formula when it comes to films, they're made to appeal to as broad an audience as possible, yet still offer enough to keep most people happy, occasionally they'll make a riskier film, like Black Panther or The Winter Soldier, and while Captain Marvel seems like a riskier film from the outside, once you get into it, you'll see how much it actually follows the formula.

Don't get me wrong, the film is fun, it's typical entertaining Marvel fare, but that's all it is. It's good, acceptable, run of the mill.

There are times when it tries to make a bigger issue out of the identity struggle out of its main character, but once that's resolved it's a pretty cookie-cutter film, to be honest.

It does have its moments though, especially surrounding Captain Marvel herself, when she finally realises her true power, and subsequently becomes the most over-powered hero since Superman started taking steroids. There's some nice space-y elements and the action is smooth and exciting, but never carves out an identity for itself.

It suffers from the aforementioned problem of feeling like an advertisement for Endgame, rather than a film in its own right. Almost like the powers-that-be realised they needed Captain Marvel in the film, so hastily knocked-up a film to show her off in as broad a way as possible, so that audiences were familiar with her when next month comes around, incidentally, I don't think the short gap between films will do Captain Marvel any good in the long run. Once Endgame is strutting up and down the box office catwalk, Captain Marvel will be consigned to history.

All of this is sounding very harsh, as I didn't dislike the film, I found it entertaining in the typical MCU mould, but there have been several better films released in the franchise in the last few years, I suppose it serves its purpose of introducing the character, and the third act twist is effective in making her a more likeable character, but it could have been more, we know it could have been more as we've seen much better from the MCU.

None of this falls on Brie Larson, who I felt really grew into the role over the course of the film, she's doing her best to produce something special, and set an example for generations of young women, which is commendable, and she's obviously extremely passionate about the character and that comes across, but when you have a character as all-powerful as Captain Marvel, you lose a touch of personality (what I like to call the Superman conundrum) and while attempts are made to give her personality, this is lost by the time she unlocks her true potential.

Don't go away from this review thinking I disliked Captain Marvel, it was a fun two hours at the cinema, with effective performances and accomplished, if a tad bland, direction, I just know it could have, and should have, been so much more.

In conclusion then, while it's an important chapter in setting up Avengers: Endgame, as a stand-alone adventure it's ultimately bland, a fun time at the cinema with the usual Marvel shine to it, but nothing truly special. One die-hard Marvel fans will enjoy simply for it being more of the thing they love; casual viewers might be better advised to wait for Endgame.

Alita: Battle Angel (Originally published March 14th, 2019)
Directed by Robert Rodriguez
Starring: Rosa Salazar, Christoph Waltz, Jennifer Connolly and Mahershala Ali

A while ago, on this very site, I published an opinion piece on James Cameron's promotion of this film, within that, I was highly critical of the way in which he promoted the film, choosing to promote its visual effects over its story, while that's a point I stand by, every film should hold up on story first and foremost, I was still determined to go into Alita with an open mind.

It's taken me a while due to times not lining up with my own schedule, but I finally got a chance to see it on the big screen, I was still unsure of what to expect, I hadn't exposed myself to any reviews prior to watching, as is my method, so from my perspective, it could have gone either way, with that being said let's get on with the review.

Story

It's the 26th century, in the aftermath of a catastrophic war known as 'The Fall' only on legendary 'sky city' remains, Zalem, with the people living below in a constant battle for life. A cyber-surgeon Dyson Ido (Christoph Waltz) discovers the still-living remains of a girl in the scrapyard below Zalem, she soon gains a new life in searching for her old identity.

Verdict

One thing I'll say for Alita straight out of the gate, is it builds an impressive, immersive world right from the beginning. In one (admittedly clunky) passage of dialogue, we establish the history of the world. It is the kind of sci-fi world dripping with atmosphere and background detail, the sort where new stories lurk behind every corner.

I might as well establish right now that I liked Alita, quite a lot in fact. More than I could have imagined. It took a while to draw me in, but there was a point around the middle where the intrigue broadens and the lore deepens that sucked me in, it was the point where our heroes were duly established, and all of their goals clearly set out.

It's not terribly original, I must say. Something that should be obvious given the lead characters amnesia, a plot device about as old as time itself, and her somewhat generic goals, but generic goals aren't always a bad thing, they can be used as building blocks for a deeper story, and Alita's story has enough satisfying twists and turns to keep its audience invested.

While the visual effects are staggering and do a great job of building the world, there was still an 'uncanny valley' effect in certain moments, mostly concerning Alita (Rosa Salazar) herself, I think it's the CGI work on her face, it looks human, but not human enough, and took a while to get used to, the same can be said of the world and its surroundings, but once you allow yourself to get immersed, you soon get used to it.

By the end of the film, I had grown to like its characters, too, even if Alita herself may look a bit jarring at times, she shows herself as having flaws and imperfections, even when she becomes a ruthless fighting machine, and her relationship with Hugo (Keenan Johnson) is probably my favourite thing about the film, you know it's coming , from the moment they meet, but it builds organically, to an effective conclusion.

Whereas other such films made in such an environment of prevalent CGI left me feeling cold and disconnected, Alita drew me in with the warmth of its characters, and the depth of its brutal, yet still beautiful world, even the CGI fight scenes delivered spectacularly, which, to be honest, was an aspect I wasn't much looking forward to. They're visually busy yes, but not to the extent of say, Transformers, where it becomes difficult to watch and follow, they go at a steady enough pace to follow, and deliver enough visually to be as exciting as possible.

Direction-wise Robert Rodriguez does a great job of portraying this world, calling back to years of cyberpunk films, there were even moments that put me in mind of Blade Runner, a comparison that can only really be viewed positively. the main word that I think describes this world is 'atmosphere' it never feels like a bare world; each corner is carefully constructed and full of life.

In conclusion then, I can see myself catching some stick for criticising the film's marketing only to highly praise it down the line, but I don't really care, I still stand by that it was poorly marketed, even more so now that I know it has more to offer than visual effects, it just goes to prove my point in a way, Alita had a very effective story, and I enjoyed it immensely, I'll even welcome a sequel to continue the story, which it left itself wide open for, another thing that would normally annoy me, but this time seems necessary. Alita is a real blast.

Us (Originally published March 24th, 2019)
Directed by Jordan Peele
Starring: Lupita Nyong'o, Winston Duke, Elisabeth Moss and Tim Heidecker

I must admit I missed Get Out when it was in cinemas, horror really isn't a genre I follow too closely so it completely passed me by. By the time I got around to watching it, I had already been surprised by a few horror films and was astonished by its depth and social commentary, it was the very opposite of the 'dumb horror' films I found myself rolling my eyes at whenever I watched one.

Given Get Out's massive media profile and acclaim, Jordan Peele's next project was always going to be one to watch, he had proven himself an original thinker in the horror stakes, but could he follow it up with a film that can match his first success?

Story

A young woman traumatised by a life event in her childhood goes on vacation with her family to the same beach resort where the traumatic event took place, the family then find themselves being hunted down by mysterious doppelgangers.

Verdict

The above synopsis doesn't do the plot a whole lot of justice I must admit, but it is the best I can describe Us without getting too spoiler-y and ruining the films more interesting facets. It really is a film you should know as little as possible about going into it.

There's a unique sense of dread that hangs over Us right from the first frame, layers of atmosphere become apparent right from the word go, as Peele sets out a world for his audience to become immersed in.

There's a lot of social commentary here too, a lot of which went over my head, being British the heavy commentary on American life doesn't make a whole lot of sense to me, but that didn't take too much away from my enjoyment of the film, at a base level it's still a straightforward us vs monsters horror set-up, it's only when you want to look deeper that you see the context, and while that does add a little bit of spice to proceedings, you don't feel as though you need a primer before you watch the film.

I think Peele shows an incredible know-how for constructing certain scenes and shots so early into his career, it's more evident here, as each scene has a certain artistic flourish, as if painted by Leonardo Da Vinci, with the title sequence being especially memorable and surprisingly unsettling.

He also has a sophisticated grip on the horror genre that many people spend years learning. It is far better spending time building tension and unrest in the viewer than it is startling them with a jump-scare, and Peele knows this, the jumps are almost non-existent, instead there's a feeling of creeping dread that hangs over the film, like a cloud you suspect might be bringing rain.

There's an emphasis on characterisation too, getting people to care about people in a horror film is no easy task, most horror films I watch have such vapid characters that it's usually a relief when Jason Voorhies introduces their skull to a machete with great force.

A strong cast also holds up Us, with Oscar winner Lupita Nyong'o leads the cast with an astonishing dual part, as both traumatised mother Adelaide and her doppelgänger, this is probably the best Nyong'o has been since 12 Years a Slave, which is quite an accomplishment for an actress of her ability. Supporting her is Winston Duke, who plays Gabe, the patriarch of the central family around which the plot revolves, who film fans may know as M'Baku from the MCU, he's affable and likeable in this film, I can't help but see a more substantial dramatic performance in his future though. There are also some very impressive performances from the film's child actors (Shahadi Wright Joseph as Zora and Evan Alex as Jason, the children of Gabe and Adelaide).

All of these actor's balance two distinct characters effortlessly, which is no mean feat for any actor, never mind a child. So on the performance side, the film is pretty flawless.

Just like in Get Out however, Peele lures you into feeling connected with these characters, and then plays with your expectations towards the third act, there are many twists and turns to this tale.

The risk is there for the film to twist and turn once too often, however, it nimbly, yet narrowly, avoids this hazard, dropping the curtain on the narrative just as it was starting to run out of ideas, it's final twist may seem like an overstretch to some, but it took me completely by surprise and is making me rethink the film all over again after seeing it.

As for the important question of 'is it scary?' The answer is a tough one. I've said in the past that I don't really get scared by films, they startle if a hated jump-scare is involved, but never enough to really make me scared, and while I wasn't scared of Us, I was intrigued and immersed enough in the world to not need to be scared, its narrative was interesting enough without the fear factor, I had the all-important sense of dread and tension, but not the fright.

Overall then, a deep, tense experience sums up Jordan Peele's sophomore film. An interesting narrative, interwoven with unnerving characters and just enough twists to make the narrative seem fresh, all with a healthy garnish of a tense atmosphere make up a terrific experience, I'd say an improvement over Get Out, even. Jordan Peele here proves that lightening can indeed strike twice,

Shazam! (Originally published March 28th, 2019)
Directed by David F. Sandberg
Starring: Zachary Levi, Mark Strong, Asher Angel and Jack Dylan Grazer

Since the DCEU started focusing on solo stories, I feel the franchise has been better for it, Wonder Woman was great, Aquaman was entertaining and now Shazam has come along to see if it can keep up the streak.

Shazam has an interesting enough history even before considering the film adaptation, the hero was in fact first called Captain Marvel, so, in a way, this month has seen TWO Captain Marvel films.

A lot of the films appeal seems to lie in its lightness of tone, which considering where the DCEU started is a bold step, not a new one though, as Aquaman was also a step in a lighter direction for the franchise, but where Aquaman leave the baton, Shazam runs with it like Usain Bolt after a Red Bull.

Story

Billy Batson is a 15-year-old foster child on the look-out for his birth mother. One day after a confrontation at school, he is transported to a different realm where the ancient wizard Shazam transfers his powers to him. From there Billy learns the meaning of being a superhero and being in a family.

Verdict

My usual rule of exposing myself to as little knowledge about the film worked a treat again, as without knowing much about Billy Batson and Shazam, I found myself almost instantly endeared to the outcast teenager suddenly given superpowers.

There's a tendency for films surrounding the narrative of family, and specifically finding a family, to come across as cliched and overly sentimental, and while Shazam doesn't fully escape these trappings, it makes up for it by providing a broad palate of characters to grow into a family that makes it impossible to hate.

This is juxtaposed by the villain's story arc in many ways, in fact the villain almost comes close to sympathetic in some respects, but he's just too much of a wicked bastard to feel sympathetic for, not that that's a point against it, I very much enjoyed the irredeemable power-hungry tyrant, in many ways he is like Killmonger from Black Panther, but without even the slimmest of justifications.

While the story isn't mind-blowingly original, it's delivered with such life a tenacity that makes it impossible to not enjoy. The characters are well-rounded, the dialogue is snappy and often very funny, and the action set pieces are very stylish. Even the effects, which many find lacking in the DCEU, were a huge improvement, they weren't perfect, and if I'm being very pedantic they were a touch over-designed, but their designs were eye-catching (or stomach-churning, depending on your outlook) and it felt as though they were adding to the narrative rather than taking away from it.

The performances were another impressive aspect of the film. Lead by the incredibly charismatic Zachary Levi as the titular hero, he oozes likeability and every witticism bounces from him very effectively, he shares a very effective chemistry with one of the cast's teen actors Jack Dylan Grazer (who cinema-goers will recognise as Eddie from The Losers Club in IT) who was one of my favourite characters in the film I must admit, he was almost an audience surrogate the way he idolises this universes heroes, it's a winning combination for a film relying on the lighter aspects of DC canon.

Elsewhere, Mark Strong is the lead antagonist, certainly a step up from 2011's abomination Green Lantern, his character isn't particularly deep, but he brings a cool menace to his performance, and seems to revel in it, his fight scenes with Levi's hero are incredibly watchable, and they too share an interesting chemistry.

The direction remains clean and sharp throughout, when compared with the dark and dingier scenes from the franchise they shine all the brighter, the climactic battle in particular was very well shot, if a tad over-long, and the film as a whole just radiates a bright, jovial nature, even during its darker moments.

Overall then, Shazam is a massive triumph for the DCEU. It found a niche that the franchise needed and made the most of it while it could, I expect follow-ups to not be far behind, and with this debut outing for the hero, I'd say the excitement was worth it, it might not be the biggest comic book movie release this year, or the most hyped, but it may well be the most charming.

Chapter Thirteen: April 2019

Pet Sematary (Originally published April 4th, 2019)
Directed by Kevin Kolsch and Dennis Widmyer
Starring: Jason Clarke, Amy Seimetz and John Lithgow

A few years ago, I gave a glowing review to the engaging adaptation of Stephen King's IT (which is now retroactively referred to as IT: Chapter One) which once again ignited interest in Mr King's works.

There really seems to be no middle ground with Stephen King adaptations, they're either very, very good (Green Mile, Shawshank Redemption and the original Carrie) or really, really bad (Christine, Maximum Overdrive and 2013's Carrie) there's a Yin and a Yang, so if IT is the Yin, does that give away my opinion of Pet Sematary?

Story

The Creed family move from Boston to the smaller town of Ludlow and find that their house is situated right next to a pet cemetery, and that the town has a ritual of burying their pets there, unfortunately, the dead don't stay dead in this graveyard.

Verdict

There's a line of dialogue in this film which I find sums the film up perfectly: "sometimes, Dead is better."

Okay so with my hand laid down so hard that I've knocked over the poker table, I might as well come out and say it: I really, really, really did not like this film.

Remember a few weeks ago, when reviewing Us when I said the best horror builds atmosphere and doesn't rely on cheap jump scares? Well, the screenwriters of this film could have done well to have read that. A broom falling over in the wind can make people jump, doing so in a horror film is as appealing as a Gary Glitter comeback tour.

I remember thinking that IT had reasons to exist, it updated the story and did some new films, with Pet Sematary, however, it feels as though we've seen everything it has to offer at least a handful of times. Firstly, it's to do with things coming back from the dead, which is as familiar a setting as my living room at this point, yes, they're not strictly speaking zombies, but are there any logical differences?

I feel bad for mauling this film as severely so far, as the acting performances are the shining diamond in the turd mountain. Jason Clarke is leading the film, while he can seem a bit bland, there is something I like about him, he seems very adaptable, I remember liking him in The Aftermath, not long ago. John Lithgow also plays Jud, the closest this film comes to an interesting character.

The direction is also very uninspired, adding very little to the films atmosphere with its visuals instead going for a cheap shocking visual, there's a particular scene involving some guy whose brain is hanging out and it looks like he has a bowl of jelly in the side of his head. It's immediate comparison to IT again does it no favours, and that was very tactfully shot for maximum tension, this just offers uninspired, hackneyed visuals.

So, we have: the undead, jump scares, and a creepy child, and what does this combination lead us to? A film without a single original thought in its head, much less an entertaining one. It has no concept of tension or pacing, it just blasts you in the face as soon as you walk in, like an obnoxious roommate.

Upon doing some research, I discovered that this is the first of many Stephen King adaptations to be released this year, and it sets a pretty depressingly low bar, a bar that I hope can be easily surpassed later this year by IT: Chapter Two, as for this film; well, some adaptations are best left buried.

Dumbo (Originally published April 5th, 2019)
Directed by Tim Burton
Starring: Colin Farrell, Michael Keaton, Danny DeVito and Eva Green

It is my considered (and mildly educated) opinion that Tim Burton is one of the most overrated directors of his generation. Most of the films he is revered for would all be legally allowed to drink if they were people, and his contestant aesthetic over narrative approach is sometimes quite nauseating.

His last film that I am willing to say is good would be 2008's Sweeney Todd, and even them I am being generous, arguably, so when a new film comes along purporting to be 'from the imagination of Tim Burton' that sets off one of my cynical warning lights, as Tim Burton's imagination hasn't evolved in 30 years.

But it's also a Disney film, and Disney have a respectable record of not letting just any old tat into cinemas (usually, the tat is released straight-to-DVD) so we shall see if Disney manage to rein in the more obnoxious aspects of Burton's films.

Story

It's the late 1910's and theatre owner, Max Medici (Danny DeVito) welcomes back his former top act back from service in the army, Holt Farrier (Colin Farrell). He quickly puts him to work in training the elephants, including one special new arrival with an extraordinary ability.

Verdict

While, as the first few paragraphs state, I am not a great fan of Tim Burton, when he gets it right, it is something special, while he was in his stride making films in his vision he was a leading light, and while Dumbo does not reach the heights (no pun intended) of his peak, it's a step in the right direction. A shaky step, but a step, nonetheless.

The biggest question when it comes to this film is: did it need a remake? Which is a difficult question in itself, as updating an old film property does have potential, simply remaking it without updating it doesn't really serve a purpose. Simply remaking a film in live action isn't enough, to me, it needs more of a reason to exist.

To that end, it isn't a direct remake, but much rather a re-imagining of the story that was first brought to the screen almost 80 years ago. Much more than a visual re-imagining, it being live action now, but there are several story differences also, there's no talking animals, the dismissive talking elephants are replaced with dismissive humans, who are even more unlikable for it.

The story has its peaks and troughs, some moments reach for an emotional impact, some hit and some miss, he parts between Dumbo and his mum hit the hardest, which is impressive for two exclusively CG'd characters. Where it over-reaches is in the human side of the story, it establishes that the children's mother, Holt's mother, had died, and it's so classic cliched Disney that it's almost painful, it's not as if they do anything new with that concept either, it's quite dreary, as a matter of fact, almost like they've been lifted out of a catalogue.

Where Burton does excel is in his visual style, even when his films are less than stellar, they're interesting to look at. If I had to describe Dumbo's visual style in one word it would be: busy.

It's filled with colour, life and brightness, in many ways it juxtaposes some of his past, more Gothic work, and it works when the colours are saturated and drained in the run-down Medici circus, it becomes overly busy when the plot shifts to Wonder Land, the park owned by Michael Keaton's character, V. A. Vandevere, it starts to become almost nauseating, when you go from the starchy feeling of the older circus, to the modern, shiny world of tomorrow, filled with bright lights and visually-clashing styles.

The acting in the film is another thing that is very hit, and miss, Danny DeVito and Colin Farrell are the highlights, DeVito is so effortlessly charming in everything he does, even the shades of grey in his character seem lovable. Michael Keaton however, chews so much scenery that I was surprised there was any of Wonder Land left. His over-acting in some scenes was almost painful, especially opposite the naturally likeable Farrell. His character is written to be deplorable, but his performance is probably the weakest thing about him.

So, in conclusion, it's not a home run for Burton or Disney, while it has its charms and nice moments, it's nothing really 'special' about it that sets Disney films apart, it lacks the spark of other successes. You wouldn't miss much if you missed it, but there might be something in there for people to enjoy.

Eighth Grade (Originally published April 9th, 2019)
Directed by Bo Burnham
Starring: Elsie Fisher, Josh Hamilton, Emily Robinson and Jake Ryan

I'm going to guess that if you're reading this, you've gone through puberty at some point. If you haven't then I'm very impressed at your burgeoning interest in film but get out now so you don't become as cynical as me.

Joking aside, puberty is a tough time for us all; our hormones are in complete disarray, we suddenly turn from a normal human being, into a gremlin that only communicates through sarcasm and grunting, and we're just generally not nice people to be around. Granted, some of this is because there are a million nagging thoughts going through your head at any one time, but as a rule, teenagers are uncommunicative, and nowadays, extremely superficial.

As I can well grasp, puberty is much harder if you're female, something I can entirely sympathise with, even if I'm ignorant to its realities, and there have been many portrayals of puberty in film, but none as seemingly honest as this one.

I was drawn to this film by its writer/director, Bo Burnham, whose work I am a huge fan of, the times I have waxed lyrical about his comedy performances don't bear thinking about and Make Happy might just be the greatest comedy special in the past 20 years, so to say I was intrigued by his debut film was an understatement. Coupled with the good-will it seems to have from everywhere else it has been shown, and it made me very excited for its eventual arrival here in the UK, but how does Bo make the transition?

Story

Kayla (Elsie Fisher) is an introverted teenage girl, giving advice on YouTube videos, advice she doesn't usually take herself. She is going into the last week of eighth grade and has to contend with the usual social hurdles of being a teenage girl in a social media-dominated world.

Verdict

For those who aren't aware, Bo Burnham started his career on YouTube over 10 years ago, with that in mind, seeing him incorporate YouTube and social media into his films is bizarre, but oddly refreshing, as here's someone with first-hand experience of this new age of social media, presenting an honest account of what it's like.

The fault of more recent coming-of-age films is their use of social media as a plot device, many don't seem to have a handle of its influence and prevalence on teenage society, your life is lived through your Instagram followers, or your Snapchat friends.

What Burnham has managed to capture here, is a brutally honest look at modern teenage life, in all its superficial charm. Firstly you have Kayla, an introverted girl who makes YouTube videos seemingly no-one watches, she spends a good amount of run-time of the film on her phone, be it on Instagram, Twitter, or Snapchat, she lives her life through her phone, and what's more, the people she's trying to impress do too.

There's a great amount of characterisation in this film too, I don't know how much of himself Bo put into the character of Kayla, but I always seemed to gleam from his comedy shows that he was a lot like she was when he was younger, in fact, most of his act, especially in his early days, was based around the fact he was an outcast, he built on this later, with a song that reflected on how your popularity goes up with fame, and it feels like he's putting a lot of his struggles onto his main character, using her as an avatar for his bottled-up, barely-contained angst.

This isn't to say she's your textbook 'nerdy girl' you see in other high school films, she pushes herself into new situations, often visibly uncomfortable, and her overcoming her struggles no matter how gingerly, makes her endearing, and I dare she will strike a chord with those of my generation who feels the same angst.

The dialogue is also inch perfect for the subject material. I've heard dialogue which is so accurately representative of how teenagers speak. There's a lot of trepidation, the repeated use of the word 'like' and 'erm' especially when Kayla is recording her videos, which is great because that's how people sound, especially when they're nervous, and it's balanced perfectly across the film, the adults get a fairer spread, but try too hard to be 'cool' in the way teenagers hate, it's a masterclass in dialogue writing.

The dialogue isn't the only strength to the screenplay however, as there are certain scenes in which you can feel the anxiousness from the characters, there's an expertly weighted scene in the films second act, in which Kayla is almost forced into doing something she doesn't want too, and it made her, and the audience, visibly uncomfortable, and not in a bad way, the execution wasn't heavy handed, it put the protagonist in a situation she was uncomfortable in, and because we'd grown attached to her, we felt her anguish.

There's so much to love about this movie that to list them all would become a laborious read, but so much of it is so well-judged; from the way in which adults patronisingly try and make themselves empathise with teenagers, to the films use of music, to the deft and striking direction, but if there's one thing that I will take away, it is Elsie Fisher's performance.

For such a young actress to so skilfully embody a role such as Kayla is staggering, but for all the weight of the script, the character quirks, the delivery, Fisher nails everything, Eighth Grade is an astonishingly good debut for Burnham, but it is helped tremendously by an incredibly engaging and dynamic leading performance.

It's been a long time since I've seen a film that I struggle to think of criticism for, and I bet if I thought long and hard enough, I'd at least think of one thing, but to do so would do a disservice to the film, and the message it brings.

Overall then, a staggering first directorial effort from Bo Burnham, I don't know what the future holds fo him, but I'm sure his future is bright, and as for Elsie Fisher, the sky is the limit. Eighth Grade came with a lot of praise, and it more than lives up to every bit of it.

Hellboy (Originally published April 11th, 2019)
Directed by Neil Marshall
Starring: David Harbour, Milla Jovovich, Ian McShane and Sasha Lane

Hellboy is an indictment of all that is wrong in Hollywood. A completely short-sighted attempt to re-write a series that is neither good enough, nor old enough, to demand one.

I apologise, as I usually take longer to get to my ultimate opinion, but my disdain for this film cannot be contained for even a paragraph of build-up.

I wasn't even a big fan of the original two Hellboy films, but they were at least interesting to look at, and were never given a chance to breathe under the influence of Guillermo Del Toro, their visual style was probably the best thing about it, which given GDT's reputation is hardly a surprise, but this is one of the many, many things that didn't make the journey back from hell, where this film should have stayed.

Story

Half-human and half-demon Hellboy works for a government institution investigating the paranormal, often working with people who openly hate him (can't say I blame them). He is called to England after an immortal 5th Century witch is resurrected, intent on destroying humanity.

Verdict

So, I pretty much gave the game away in the introduction, I hated this film. Hated every stupid, ugly, unnecessary minute of it. Its sins are numerous, but its biggest sin is just being so crushingly dull.

It's barely been a decade since the last Hellboy film, was there really a need to revisit this series so soon? If at all?

Without even getting into the morals of whether this film should exist (it shouldn't) but even as a movie it's so offensively bad that it makes you forget what goodwill you had for the series and replaces it with pure, vitriolic hatred.

The visual style which was so well-implemented? Gone, and replaced with special effects that would barrenness a video game from the late 90's. Seriously, I give less of a toss about VFX than

Pavarotti did about keeping a low-carb diet, but I won't apologise for expecting them to look at least presentable. To put it bluntly, the film is down-right ugly. Even though the creatures are supposed to be ugly, they aren't ugly in an interesting way, they're lucky if the look like a reject from a later Hobbit film, over-designed yet incredibly dull.

The story is drab and awful, and the dialogue seems like it's written by someone with saucepans for hands, if I had a pound for every dreadful one-liner, every unnecessary swear word, worked in about as well as one would work a killer whale into an oven and every line that didn't make sense, I'd be a millionaire, several times over.

The film spends its entire run-time building a third act confrontation that it never pays off; its fight scenes are straining so hard to be 'cool' that you can practically hear the screen-writers tense. It layers each fight with loud, rock music, hoping to seem cool and edgy, instead it just pulls the drab action into focus and seems tone-deaf.

As for the acting, it's up and down. I feel sorry for David Harbour and Ian McShane as they seem like the only actors who gave a damn, and frankly, who can blame them? Milla Jovovich wouldn't look out of place on a straight-to-DVD release, chewing so much scenery that I'm surprised there's any left, Daniel Dae Kim delivers his lines like an android with a low battery, but given the piffle they were given, I can hardly expect an Oscar-worthy performance.

As I've said before, the worst sin a film can commit is being boring, and Hellboy isn't just boring, it's obnoxious. Its plot develops without incorporating nuance, events happen disjointedly, without a rhyme or reason, and to make things worse, you can barely see what's going on because it's so terribly lit. Although at this rate, I'm willing to count that as a plus.

Also, I'm no prude for violence, but this film verges on fetishism. Someone can't be shot in the head unless their blood and brains can splatter over a wall, and fair enough if there's a reason but there just isn't. The tone flickers between wacky comedic quips, to harrowing, gritty violence, with barely a time to breath, revealing its threadbare script for exactly what it is. It has to rely on shock rather than tell a good story.

I've never felt like a film has wasted my time as much as Hellboy. It's been a long time since I've seen such a boring, idiotic, incomprehensible, ugly, poorly conceived mess. I would list all the things I would rather do than re-watch Hellboy, things that include anaesthetised dental surgery, and castrating myself with a rusty spoon, but I fear we'd be hear all day. If you value your time, do not watch this film, even if you don't value your time, don't watch it. This is a film that was born in hell and should never have risen again.

Missing Link (Originally published April 11th, 2019)
Directed by Chris Butler
Starring: Hugh Jackman, Zach Galifianakis, Zoe Saldana and Emma Thomson

I saw this on the same day as Hellboy, two films that could really not be further apart. Hellboy is a cynical and transparent attempt to cash-in on a long-dormant series. While this is a charming, artful film from a very consistent animation studio.

Laika Animation are the studio in question. They debuted in 2006 with Coraline (although they did some work on Corpse Bride before this), a very enjoyable and stylish stop-motion tale, and stop-motion has been their comfort zone ever since. Their last film was the incredible Kubo and the Two Strings, an absorbing tale influenced by Japanese mythology.

So here comes their latest offering, with an all-star cast and their usual charming visual flair, do Laika have another success on their hands?

Story

Sir Lionel Frost is a world-travelling adventurer in the 19th century. Rejected from the 'respectable' adventuring community, he embarks on a journey to discover the legendary Sasquatch, but upon finding him, gets more than he bargained for.

Verdict

One word I used in the introduction that I feel fits this movie well, is charming. Everything about it is pleasant to the senses, from the animation style, to the voice performances, everything comes together to create a world that radiates atmosphere and love.

While the plot keeps a brisk pace, often relegating the travel segments of the adventure to very short montages, it is as loaded as it needs to be. It doesn't over-load itself with cheap jokes, instead drawing us in with characters with believable and sympathetic arcs. It's not completely above making a juvenile joke or two, but that is forgivable if it is earned, if it comes along a substantial plot, and it does.

The characters are really where the film shines, the titular character of Mr Link (later renamed to Susan, for comedic purposes of course. Voiced by Zach Galifianakis) is a tragic character, despite his outwardly beastly appearance, he hides a soft, lonely heart.

Lionel Frost (Hugh Jackman) almost undergoes the exact opposite arc, starting as a respectable, yet slightly dim-witted, member of the upper classes, his intention to gain more respect soon changes when he realises that a man's heart makes him great.

Yes, that is a bit of a hackneyed, cliched premise, but even a cliched plot can be enjoyable when delivered well, and this is well.

Helped immensely by the animation style that hold on to its stop-motion roots, when it starts to look more computer rendered it encounters trouble. This might not be the case, but it looks as though different characters were made in different ways, and it can be jarring. For example, Lionel Frost and Mr Link look sleek and well realised, whereas Adelina (Zoe Saldana) looks too machine-like. Again, this may be completely false, but that's what it looked like.

But, despite these visual-based gripes, on a whole it looks great, specifically speaking towards the end, the design of the environments look great, as well of the characters.

While the plot is a bit old-hat, and the character design is a bit wobbly, there is a lot to love in Missing Link, when its animation style works, it looks phenomenal, the characters are well-rounded, and for a family audience, it deals with some challenging themes. There are a lot worse films you could take your kids to see this Easter.

Wild Rose (Originally published April 15th, 2019)
Directed by Tom Harper
Starring: Jessie Buckley, Sophie Okonedo and Julie Walters

I have a soft spot for the small working-class British narrative. Maybe it's because I can empathise certain aspects to my own life, maybe it's just nice to see stories that don't take place in ideal worlds, with idealised characters.

My favourite of this kind of film is Fish Tank, a film I studied during my first year of university; it span a narrative that could have only been told within its own situation. In many ways, Wild Rose reminds me of Fish Tank, with its underdog characters and smaller, focused narrative.

The differences are numerous however, it isn't all that similar, just barely in style, and the comparison only really makes sense in my head, the settings are similar, but not overwhelmingly, Wild Rose is set in Glasgow, within the incredibly varied world of the Glaswegian working-class, an ever-changing world from what it was, Wild Rose tries to find its spot in and amongst the many foibles of working class life there.

So, with this all set before us, is Wild Rose another great example of a working-class story on the big screen?

Story

Rose-Lyn Harlan (Jessie Buckley) has just finished a 12-month prison sentence, and returns to her life as a young mum, under the watchful eye of her stern mother (Julie Walters). She aspires farther afield from Glasgow however, and dreams of becoming a country singer, in Nashville, but as her mother keeps pointing out, life isn't always ideal.

Verdict

What I love about this type of film, what I loved about Fish Tank too come to think of it, is the characters. There's characters you meet in a working-class setting that rarely get seen in mainstream cinema. Ones that if you live in certain areas in certain parts of the world you would instantly recognise, this is what Wild Rose gets so, so right.

Firstly, a character must be portrayed by a skilful actor to bring them to life, and Wild Rose has that. Anchored by an engaging, and at times mesmerising, performance from Jessie Buckley, she brings to life each aspect of her character's emotions. The outbreaks of frustrations, the giddy highs of ecstasy, and the gut-punch disappointment when it all comes tumbling down.

Rose-Lynn is as human as characters get. She's flawed, and prone to alienating those closest to her, in particular her kids, in some of the films more effective scenes. There's even an underlying selfishness to her, which in some cases could make her unliveable, but rather than coming across as selfishness, it instead appears to be dogged determination to follow her calling, and she's impossible to dislike for that.

Julie Walters is also great as Rose-Lynn's mother, a woman with a sharp tongue and even sharper opinions, she too brings a spikiness to her character rarely seen in film. There is a loving relationship between the two, but the simmering tension between them often wins out, as she starts to tire of Rose's wide-eyed fantasies of far-off adventures.

A film that bases itself around such a music-centric story relies on the music in question to deliver, and there is certainly no shortage of country music to go around. I wouldn't call Wild Rose a musical as such, rather than a film music is involved in, and I know that statement sounds rather redundant, but what I mean is; the central drama is based around the characters and their struggles. The goal of getting to Nashville seems a distant fantasy, only getting further away the more you chase it, for the bulk of the run-time we are wrapped up in the ins-and-outs of Rose's life, and all of those surrounding her.

The soundtrack is the kind that serves its purpose to the point where it is enjoyable while it's there, but forgettable once it's over. There's no real ear worm along the lines of Shallow from A Star is Born, but it hardly needs to, as I say, it does its job while it's there, and it's used very effectively in some moments, which is all that can be asked of a soundtrack.

The direction is also very skilful, the tendency in films such as this is to let the drama unfold in front of the camera as naturally as possible, without pushing boundaries cinematography-wise. While it certainly isn't ground-breaking in its photography, there are a great deal of very artful shots and framing in this film, one that sticks in my mind is a birds-eye shot of Rose walking away from a party, all alone, separated from the bustling party by a wall, it works effectively as a shot, but also as a visual metaphor, if one was to think about it that deeply.

As far as criticism goes, it does at times feel a touch over-long and self-indulgent, there are certain scenes, and even a character, that could have been cut entirely without affecting the film in any major way. Although it never feels as though it drags, there are things that seem unnecessary upon further evaluation. That being said, the characterisation outside of Rose and her mum does sometimes feel a bit thin on the ground, perhaps a larger family unit might have fleshed out the story, but now I'm just being picky.

Overall, Wild Rose is a great example of British filmmaking, telling a story with a tone unique to its inner identity, and enhanced by incredibly engaging performances, definitely one to look out for if you get the chance, it might just surprise you.

Avengers: Endgame (Originally published April 25th, 2019)
Directed by Joe and Anthony Russo
Starring: Robert Downey Jr, Chris Evans, Chris Hemsworth and Mark Ruffalo (et al)

It's fair to say this film had a lot riding on its shoulders. Not only a sequel to a universally beloved epic, but the finale of an eleven-year cinematic journey that has taken us all across the universe.

Boasting an eye-wateringly huge cast and promising to be a once-in-a-lifetime film, that is sure to be phenomenon, but following from Infinity War is no small task in itself, let alone its standing as the finale of this long journey, a lot of expectations lay on the shoulders on the Russo Brothers and their bumper cast and crew, this had to blow everyone away to justify the hype, so let's find out if it did.

Story

After the events of Infinity War, half of all humanity has been wiped out. The remaining Avengers, struggling to come to terms with their failure, try to concoct a plan to reverse that damage, but is the sacrifice worth it?

Verdict

The Russo Brothers must possess nerves of steel, as once again, they do not meet expectations, the surpass them. The sheer weight of the task in hand doesn't seem to bother them, instead it motivates them to push them further into paying off the greatest cinematic journey in the absolute best way possible. They might not have started this journey, but they damn well finished it with style.

It's not only a film that surpasses anything anyone imagined, but it's also an incredibly surprising film. Most fans have spent the past year formulating theories as to what happens next, and while I am most definitely not going to disclose what does happen in the end, there are a few very surprising story beats in the setup of the epic story.

At the heart of the film is a beating emotional heart, rarely seen in big superhero franchises such as this. Dealing with such complex issues as grief, loss, and love, it delves much deeper than just epic action and over-the-top characters. Quite the opposite, the characters are the most human they've ever been, they haven't experienced failure on this level before, not only are they grieving for what they've lost, but they're blaming themselves for failing to stop Thanos, and that's a very complex thing, and it brings out the most human side of these characters, characters we've seen battle epic threats and succeed time and time again, but we've never seen them fail, at least not like this.

I had taken the option of watching the double bill of Infinity War and Endgame, and while I have seen Infinity War multiple times before, seeing them in close proximity really helps with recognising the story beats that both films share, in some ways they are two parts of one story, but in many ways they are two completely different films, operating on two completely different levels.

One aspect that worked in Infinity War that is managed once again here is the great balance of screen time between its many different locations and characters. Infinity War spanned the universe and so does this, as well as so much more, and yet, it never feels over-stuffed or over-stretched. The three-hour run-time is entirely justified here, as such a deep and complex story needs time to breathe and develop in its own time, it is a three-hour film that never seems to drag, its pace keeps up at such a rate that it doesn't feel as long as it is.

The film also boasts one of the greatest third acts in comic-book movie history, perhaps in film history full stop. Several satisfying moments that pay-off a moment set up many years ago. The moment that sticks in the mind from Infinity War that was a significant upturn moment in the film, is Thor's arrival on Wakanda. This film has several moments that give that feeling of euphoria that that moment did, and then some, things we've been waiting years for, unfold in front of our eyes, in the most crowd-pleasing way possible.

By this time analysing these characters should seem such a lost cause, considering how long we have been acquainted with them, but in some cases, it is almost like they are new characters, their evolution is believable, their motives clear-cut. After such a catastrophic event, we couldn't expect these characters to remain in the same state of mind as they were a year ago, many of them are broken people, some have hope, and some think all is lost, each with their own reasons for whatever they do, some arcs are deeply emotional and are often difficult to watch, talking about these is very difficult without spoiling the plot, but suffice to say these are not the same Avengers we've come to know and love.

However, as much as talking about the characters would give too much away about the plot movements, I can say without hesitation that the performances are universally excellent. Everyone brings their absolute 'A' game, especially the old favourites such as RDJ,

Chris Evans and Jeremy Renner, but to point out specific performances would be immensely unfair, as everyone concerned were excellent, it is worth pointing out the stand-outs however, and as well as the above three, Josh Brolin is also outstanding as the mad Titan, Thanos, I would say showing us more of Thanos' vulnerability this time around, which, given his character is no mean feat.

The direction is also very accomplished, given the busy nature of the script, it would have been very easy for the action to lose its focus, but the incredible action scenes are always focused in such a way that one can easily follow the action. Away from the action, the film really excels in its quieter moments, its action scenes shine all the brighter when they are book-ended by character development, and quieter moments of contemplation.

There is not much criticism I can levy at Endgame, by the end of the film I was left incredibly satisfied with everything that had happened, emotionally drained, but satisfied. I would say, however, that the usual criticism of contrived humour that has been aimed at the MCU is present here, although it never got too intrusive, it did seem incongruous with the tone at times, but as I say, it never draws you away from the film as much as others I could mention.

All in all then, Avengers: Endgame is a masterpiece of comic-book storytelling, and a masterpiece of a film in all. Before Infinity War, we all had high hopes, and that surpassed them, and the same happened before this, and they've done it again, our expectations have been surpassed completely and utterly, this is the perfect end to a saga that began eleven films ago and will be cherished for many years to come. To repeat my point from the start of this paragraph; Avengers: Endgame is a stone-cold masterpiece.

Chapter Fourteen: Exclusive Reviews

Star Wars: The Force Awakens

Directed by JJ Abrams

Starring: Daisy Ridley, John Boyega, Harrison Ford and Carrie Fisher

It's safe to say that the hype for The Force Awakens had all the subtlety of a one-man-band playing at full volume at 2am. Not only did it have the job of following the original trilogy's story, but it had to follow the incredibly disappointing Prequel Trilogy and improving on it of course.

It had the job of introducing new characters, and bringing back old ones, taking us to new planets, and establishing a new galaxy-spanning threat. It also had the hopes of many Disney representatives riding on it, they wanted as much from their new gravy train as possible, naturally.

So, almost forty years on from A New Hope, we revisit the galaxy far, far away to see what a new generation has to offer.

Story

Roughly thirty years after the fall of the Empire, the First Order has risen in its place, and is terrorising the galaxy anew. Leia Organa leads a resistance against this new threat, but with Luke Skywalker missing, it falls to new heroes to rise to re-take the galaxy.

Verdict

Leaving the midnight showing the first time I saw Force Awakens left me feeling the same sense of wonder I felt when I first watched Star Wars as a kid, and more importantly, what I felt when I watched The Empire Strikes Back, my favourite Star Wars film.

So, with that lofty feeling the first-time round, is it a feeling that holds up now, almost four years later? Well, kind of, yeah.

I still love the film for what it is, but my enthusiasm has died down in the past few years. Part of that is due to it doesn't feel as special as it did when it first arrived, way back in 2015 we were starved of Star Wars, we hadn't seen one in ten years (well, seven if you count the Clone Wars, but we don't talk about that film) it felt fresh to be back in the Star Wars universe, immersed in new characters and places, and now we're kind of spoiled when it comes to Star Wars, to an almost detrimental degree.

But, at the time, when Force Awakens was riding high, before everything was over-analysed (or before it was to such an extent) it was enjoyed for what it was, an extremely exciting new chapter in the Skywalker saga, with new threats and new characters to get behind.

For example, we're introduced to the series new big villain, Kylo Ren, an extremely complex character, conflicted and turned against his parents, and uncle, Han, Leia and Luke respectively by the over-powering Supreme Leader Snoke, his allegiance is never portrayed as set in stone, throughout the two current new trilogy films his arc has taken many turns, and will undoubtably take more in the concluding chapter.

The acting in the film is pretty consistent, all the new faces bring their A-game, and the old crew look happy to be there, at the very least, it is truly Harrison Ford's film however, as he steals every moment, whether it be as a disaffected father, or galactic hero. It was nice to see Carrie Fisher again too, even if her expression is somewhat affected by years of substance abuse and Botox, but she does her best within her return to her most iconic role.

But really, these films are all about the new blood, not only Kylo, but new lead protagonists Rey (Daisy Ridley) and Finn (John Boyega) it reverses our expectations of what the characters were going to be; in the run up, it's fair to say we expected Finn to be our new hero, but were pleasantly surprised by the emergence of Rey as the galaxies newest hope.

JJ Abrams was an inspired choice to shepherd this beloved franchise back to the big screen, after two films in the Star Trek franchise, he had earned his sci-fi stripes, as well as experience with reviving classic series, he was a reliably hand to guide the film, and he did a very good job in building an exciting adventure within a franchise that had long been stagnant, while filling the quieter moments with character development that a lot of people weren't expecting.

What a lot of people find detracts from the Force Awakens is its similarity to A New Hope in its story; I understand this position and agree with it to a degree, although I see the similarities as being more 'homages' than straightforward adaptation, I would say there is enough differences in the film that to call it a straight rip-off would be fanciful and foolish, but will acknowledge that its similarities are pronounced, perhaps intentionally, but I wouldn't like to speculate.

In conclusion, The Force Awakens was a welcome return to form of a franchise we thought long dead, but one we were glad of seeing revived. It paid its homages to the past while forging a path for its future and setting the scene for many years to come. It will be regarded as one of the best instalments within years to come, I'm sure.

John Wick

Directed by Chad Stahelski (and David Leitch)

Starring: Keanu Reeves, Michael Nyqvist, Alfie Allen and Ian McShane

This is one of those films that gets more interesting the more you learn about it. I was reading an article on the upcoming third instalment of this franchise recently, and it detailed the origins of John Wick as a film, and it made for very interesting reading.

The apparent aim was to make a film where 'Keanu Reeves kills 84 people' why this figure is so precise I don't know, and it wasn't always written with Keanu in mind, as backwards as that seems, but eventually it was pitched as Keanu's big action comeback, after a recent career slump, and it gave his career the shot in the arm it sorely needed.

Shot on a small budget, and only just managing to get a distributor, it's a miracle it was such as success that it spawned further sequels, and a proposed spin-off. But is it as good as people remember?

Story

Retired mob hitman John Wick is in mourning after losing his wife, when he receives a package from his late wife that instantly turns his life around: a puppy. After a confrontation with a mob boss' son, John finds himself the victim of a robbery, and his dog is murdered, setting him on a bloody revenge mission.

Verdict

Every once in a while, an action film comes along and takes everyone by surprise, a decade ago it was Taken, but Taken was never this cathartic or stylish.

Keanu Reeves has never been blessed with mastery of dramatic acting, what he can do is cold anti-hero's, the directors of this saw this and made advantage of what they had, and made Keanu into a stone-cold killer with a sharp suit, and even sharper fighting style, with a swift pace and classic revenge tale, John Wick is a winner on almost every conceivable level.

What it adds to the time-tested archetypes it makes frequent use of is an undercurrent of noir stylishness, bathing scenes in bright neon, as if they were in Blade Runner, as opposed to a relatively low-budget action flick. It adds a crease of originality that spices up an otherwise run-of-the-mill action film.

It also stands out by making use of a wide range of fight scene, from frantic and claustrophobic hand-to-hand duels to fast and frantic gun battles, John Wick mixes its styles and tips its hat to many films that came before it, in a way that doesn't pander to any particular style.

As mentioned earlier, Keanu Reeves is hardly going to be in Oscars contention any time soon, but he flourishes in the kind of environment that plays to his strengths, and I believe John Wick to be the best character for demonstrating Reeves' skills. Neo in The Matrix was a bit of a blank slate, onto which Keanu's limited charisma was projected, here he seems motivated and focused on bringing this character to life.

He is helped by the writing of the character, not only his characters, but those that surround him; Alfie Allen plays the perfect over-confident, easily hateable antagonist, he makes him so easily detestable that you can't wait to see him meet his fate. Also, honourable mentions must go to experienced hands Willem Dafoe and Ian McShane, whose characters gives us a glimpse into the wider world this film created, and one that was elaborated upon in the sequel.

In conclusion, John Wick is not just an enjoyable time, it's stylish and vibrant enough to make it a worthwhile artistic statement, rather than just another popcorn film. It sets out its stall and leaves ample opportunity for the world to be expanded, which it duly was in Chapter Two, but that's another review, for another time.

South Park: Bigger, Longer and Uncut

Directed by Trey Parker

Starring: Matt Stone, Trey Parker, Mary Kay Bergman and Isaac Hayes

South Park was a natural escalation in the increasing trend of animation aimed towards adults. What the Simpsons had started in 1989 had been slowly building over the course of the 90's series such as Beavis and Butthead took the prerogative, but it wasn't until South Park that the escalation reached its peak.

Challenging taboo will always have a shelf life, as it is only ever a taboo for so long, then it becomes just another thing, and South Park knew this, and it challenged every social norm it possibly could, riling people up every week with its irreverent humour, and it still does to this day twenty-two seasons in.

By comparison; Bigger, Longer and Uncut was early into South Park's life, coming out during the third season of the show, it had not yet hit its stride as the right-wing reactionary news bait it would become in years to come, and the film took aim at those very same reactionaries in the only way they knew how, by making them look as stupid as possible.

Story

After the release of a new Terrance and Phillip movie corrupts the minds of the children of South Park, their mothers force the U.S. into a war with Canada, and arrest Terrance and Phillip as war criminals, do so will have dire consequences however, as if they are killed, Satan and Saddam Hussein will rise from hell and conquer Earth.

Verdict

I'm not the biggest South Park fan in the world, I think some episodes are fantastic satires, and there is no better series for pushing boundaries, but I find some of its humour juvenile (deliberately so, I'm aware) and sometimes a tad preachy, but the movie version is a perfectly balanced gem of a film.

Yes there are still fart jokes, yes Kenny dies a completely predictable death (again) but for it's incredible resolve in making a point in as hilarious a way as possible, it casts its net wide and catches itself a whopper.

What sets it apart from the series is in the catchy and witty soundtrack, one of the most surprising musical films of all time, whoever expected South Park to become a musical? Well Matt and Trey must have gotten a taste for the musical after this, judging by their future work on Book of Mormon, and the early roots of that is evident here, with jaunty tunes such as 'Uncle Fucka' and 'Blame Canada' (which was nominated for an Oscar) it's the perfect bow on top of the well-wrapped parcel that is this film.

The fact that this film is pretty much just a massive middle finger to all the series' critics over the years does not go unnoticed, as they skewer the hypocrisy of right-wing moral panic (my particular favourite line is 'violence is okay, as long as no-one uses any bad words') that had savaged their show since the start, and they go out of their way to show them as being massive fools, this whole film is a protest in itself of censorship, perfectly paralleling the films plot shows the film to be smarter than first thought.

So with whip-sharp wit, hilarious and catchy soundtrack, the film combines this with stellar voice performances from the usual cast (most characters are voiced by the series creators Matt Stone and Trey Parker) with just two people making different kid voices, they create several distinctive personalities that carry over from the show wonderfully.

In conclusion then, while South Park is not for everyone, it' foul-mouthed and occasionally mean-spirited, its film is a shining example of both satire, and adult animation, challenging boundaries with humour and wit, it still holds up as a high watermark for the series.

Mary Poppins Returns

Directed by Rob Marshall

Starring: Emily Blunt, Ben Whishaw, Lin-Manuel Miranda and Emily Mortimer

There's always a risk when returning to a long-dormant franchise of tainting the originals legacy. Yet it seems fashionable now to revisit series thought long-dead in the hopes of attaching a pair of jump leads to its corpse and wringing a few more million dollars from it.

It probably sounds from that opening paragraph that I was down on Mary Poppins Returns from the outset, which isn't quite true. I was heartened from the trailers to see that they had seemingly captured the originals charm, even half a century on, as twee as that seemed in 2018, it was a welcome change of pace from the usual blockbuster fodder.

There may have also been a hope of cashing in on the niche that The Greatest Showman had left behind, that of the monstrously successful soundtrack. As much as Greatest Showman failed to woo critics, audiences couldn't get enough and maybe Mary Poppins Returns was hoping for similar returns (pun intended). Still, it had a reputation to live up to and a long, long history, so the opportunity to fail was vast, but was the return to Cherry Tree Lane as practically perfect as the original?

Story

The grown-up Banks children, Michael and Jane, (Ben Whishaw and Emily Mortimer, respectively) are facing financial difficulties during The Great Depression. Michael faces losing his family home in the wake of his wife's passing, when Mary Poppins, their childhood nanny returns to lend a helping hand.

Verdict

One of the greatest concerns going into MPR was that of the inevitable re-casting of Mary Poppins. While Julie Andrews is very much still with us, she is not particularly suited to such a taxing part at her advanced age. That being said, they really couldn't have done a better job in finding a Mary for the modern era.

Emily Blunt towers as the maypole around which the film dances, being the film's musical and emotional heart throughout, and while she isn't the only stand-out, she throws herself into the role with such admirable aplomb that you begin to forget there was ever another Mary.

The appeal of this film lies within its devotion to the nostalgia that surrounds it. The film is brimming with call-backs to the original and its style is shockingly close to what would have been the norm 50 years ago, it sets out to make you forget there has been close to 55 years between these two films, immersing you in its unique sense of nostalgia from the outset.

Its setting may have moved on to the 1930's but its heart remains the same, set in a lovingly re-imagined London, you spend most of the film with a sense of wonder that you probably felt watching the original, revisiting a world that is now so foreign and alien to modern eyes, yet warm and comforting at the same time.

It helps the film immensely to be helmed by someone with as much musical experience as Rob Marshall, now a veteran of the Hollywood musical, with a resume including Chicago (for which he won multiple Oscars) and Into The Woods (he is also scheduled to direct the forthcoming Little Mermaid remake) his steady hand is a welcome addition to the formula, you really get a sense that the film comes from a place of love, creatively, in the way the world is realised, and in its visual style, the animation section being a particular stand-out.

It is not only Emily Blunt that carries this film from an acting perspective however, as the supporting cast is littered with such talent as the mercurial Lin-Manuel Miranda, slipping into the dancing shoes left behind by Dick Van Dyke, who also appears in a cameo role, Ben Whishaw as the disaffected Michael Banks, visibly hurting with grief, and the appealing slimy villain role filled smartly by Colin Firth, it's an all-star cast filled to the brim with life and charm.

The main issue I harboured with Mary Poppins Returns was also an acting issue, as unavoidable as it seems, I found the child actors to be very below-par. Now, I know it's very difficult for a child actor to compare in any way to their adult counterparts, but there have been stand-outs in the past, and their occasionally wooden performances drag down the lively and colourful cast somewhat.

That aside, I feel there should be special praise directed at the film's soundtrack, which also had pretty sizeable shoes to fill following the iconic score of The Sherman Brothers, but again, Disney turned to an experienced hand, and it paid off. Marc Shaiman (best known for being the musical mind behind Hairspray) delivers a score that matches the performance and visuals, it's light, vibrant and memorable, with enough call-backs to the classic songs to reward the long-time fans without every feeling like it's pandering to the past. It especially delivers in its larger production numbers; 'Trip a Little Light Fantastic' and 'Nowhere to Go but Up' being good examples of this, taking a cue from the past and running forward with it, with sensational results.

In conclusion then, an exercise in nostalgia can offer just the tonic for a cinema-going crowd, and Mary Poppins Returns delivers that in spades. Wonderful performances, Memorable songs and some breath-taking visual set-pieces make Mary Poppins Returns another supercalifragilisticexpialidocious journey into the past.

Good Will Hunting

Directed by Gus Van Sant

Starring: Robin Williams, Matt Damon, Ben Affleck and Minnie Driver

I have, in the past, stated my grief at the passing of Robin Williams. As a performer, he brought great personal joy into millions of lives, whether as an eccentric alien in Mork and Mindy, or in his more serious roles like

Dead Poets Society, or indeed Good Will Hunting, he was a unique and powerful presence and he is missed dearly.

When it comes to his greatest performances, there are a lot to choose from, it all comes down to personal taste. Some remember him as Mrs Doubtfire, or the Genie, but where I feel he has most stood out, is in his more tender performances, which is why I chose this to review. What I consider to be his greatest gift to the world.

When Good Will Hunting was released, it made stars of writer/actors Matt Damon and Ben Affleck, it was actually a final college assignment for Damon, it was only completed when Affleck came on board, and had a troubled journey to the big screen. After its release though, Hollywood saw the promise of these two young fledgling actors and made them stars, and the rest as they say, is history.

Story

Will Hunting (Damon) is a troubled young Maths prodigy, working at a local school as a janitor, and who through a brush with the law, ends up as the patient of an unorthodox therapist (Williams) through these sessions, Will re-evaluates his life and relationships, as well as confronting his past.

Verdict

Good Will Hunting is one of those challenging films to review. A film that is so universally considered to be good, that anything I could write about it has been written a hundred times, but never mind because I'm going to write about it anyway.

The main emotional draw of this film for me is the characters and their relationships. Especially the relationship between Will and Sean, his therapist. Will doesn't feel like a character in a film, he feels like a human being, with flaws and struggles, as does Sean, they're both mourning a past life and seeking comfort, Sean finds his in helping others, and Will is yet to figure out where his future lies, and each choice he makes up to that point is progressively worse.

The performances of these two bring the characters to life in a believable and engrossing way. Damon is emotional and reactionary, not knowing where to lay the blame for what has happened in his life, now given this rare chance to turn his life around. Whereas Williams dials back his usual frenetic energy into a contained, emotional performance, one that still shows glimpses of his usual elf, but in a controlled way. Sean McGuire is a man with his own troubles, and that is evident in the film, but portrayed in a million subtle ways so masterfully that it makes his more emotional moments all the more affecting.

Just look at the now famous 'it's not your fault' scene for this sense of escalation, the exchange changes in pitch and intensity to such an emotional peak that it causes a much-needed explosion of emotion from Will, and a sense of breakthrough for the audience, all delivered in such level and controlled tones that it's hard to believe the man behind it once played an alien that sat on its head.

Aside from the much-admired acting, the film is tactfully shot by talented and experienced director Gus Van Sant, a man whose career has blown hot and cold, but is at the top of his game here. Always finding the right shot to aid the story, to give us the full picture, to see each side of an argument. Such a knack of filming is underappreciated as a whole, and I feel Van Sant does an excellent job of aiding the story with the camera.

All things considered then; this is a complete gem of a film. Perfectly balanced and not a minute too long. All the emotions hit home, and it finishes with an incredibly satisfying and uplifting conclusion. A brilliant script helped along with masterful performances and expert direction, and you have yourself a masterpiece of cinema, a piece of art that solidifies not only what cinema can be, but, soberly, what the world has lost in Robin Williams. He not only delivers a towering emotional masterclass, but generously supports Damon in delivering his own tour-de-force. A truly brilliant film.

Titanic

Directed by James Cameron

Starring: Leonardo DiCaprio, Kate Winslet, Billy Zane and Kathy Bates

There are very few things in this life that I hate. Inequality, violence, and talking in the cinemas rank highly in the very short list, but sitting atop the list, like an eviction notice written on a pile of cow dung on the welcome mat of my life, is Titanic.

Now, I get that this may seem extreme, it is not, after all the worst film in execution, it at least looks nice some ties and makes sense, but it is not that which makes me hate it, it's what it represents.

To me, Titanic is a representation of everything wrong with cinema. An emphasis on visual effects over story, cardboard cut-out characters, and a marketing budget roughly equivalent to the GDP of Belgium. It astounds me that this film was ever the highest-grossing film of all time, but I shall save my frustration for the main bulk of the review, let's get the over with.

Story

On the doomed maiden voyage of HMS Titanic, an unlikely romance blossoms between Rose (Kate Winslet) a first-class passenger, and Jack (Leonardo DiCaprio) a third-class passenger. Will their forbidden love take flight before the comparisons to Romeo and Juliet can be established, or more likely when the boat finally, and mercifully, sinks?

Verdict

In case you couldn't tell by that incredibly sarcastic synopsis, I find this whole film incredibly tedious.

The story of the Titanic is interesting enough in and of itself, it's a perfect example of the 'Icarus flight' someone with high ambitions comes crashing down, and there's plenty of mileage in that, but no, let's go for the D-grade romance novel instead, shall we?

I don't know what's more annoying, the fact that they wheeled out this tired cliché, or the fact that it worked, and millions of people paid their hard-earned money to see people with the depth of a teaspoon and charismas of a balloon with a smiley face drawn on it try and fail to stay alive long enough to be compared to Romeo and Juliet.

It's so aggressively dull that when the ship finally gets around to sinking, I couldn't care less. Hell, I want it to sink just so I don't have to watch this film anymore, I find myself cackling with glee as people fall into the propellers, and I'm pretty sure that wasn't the intended reaction. But when all of your deaths are like the 'what happens next' freeze frame on You've Been Framed, then you've definitely done something wrong.

So, let's get 'round to the characters, shall we? There's Jack and Rose, who only count as characters if a shop-window dummy counts as a supermodel, there's Rose's mum, who's a walking cliché of 'rich Victorian-era woman' right down to the ridiculously large hat, and Rose's fiancé, who is such a massive twat that the Eiffel Tower could use him as a sex aid. These characters all have explosive chemistry, in the way that I badly want to see them all dissolved in acid.

I'm pretty sure I'm right in saying that we all went to see the story of the ship, not the story of two emotionless automatons learning what love is. Yet it takes so long to get to that it's hardly worth bothering, when I would much rather be watching a boat sinking, rather than sit through another minute of your predictable romance plot, I'd say some re-evaluation was needed.

How about direction? Well, I say direction, I really mean animation, as most of the film isn't really there. Jim Cameron has a knack for this, and I feel sorry for his actors. All the years of training to emotionally connect with their characters and others, and now they have to go pretend to be on a boat in front of a green screen. Aside from that though, the sets they do use can be quite nice, so good job there.

Also, to stop this review from basically being a tirade against the film, I should probably note some positives. You have to admire the dedication put into making the Titanic look as authentic as possible at least, Cameron actually led expeditions down to the boat itself, an angle which was used in the final film, and I find looking at the wreck on the ocean floor much more interesting than the low grade Mills and Boon romance plot.

In the end though, dedication will only get you so far, yes Cameron re-created a pretty damn spot-on re-creation of the Titanic, but he also created a phenomenally tedious film, with characters straight out of the oldest cliché book in the business, and plot lifted wholesale from the works of Catherine Cookson, it's a film I wish would join its namesake at the bottom of the ocean for all eternity.

The Lion King

Directed by Roger Allers and Rob Minkoff

Starring: Jonathan Taylor Thomas, Matthew Broderick, James Earl Jones and Jeremy Irons

For any child of the 90's, our generation of Disney will always be the best. I know all generations will claim this; but we have possibly the most legitimate claim to 'best Disney era.' Depending on when in the 90's you were born, you were in the cusp of the 'Renaissance era' of Disney history, which spanned the best part of a decade from the late 80's until the late 90's.

Kids were spoilt for choice when it came to their favourite films; there's well-remembered classics like Aladdin and The Little Mermaid, and under-rated gems such as Mulan and Hunchback of Notre Dame.

But right in the middle of this spectacular run of films was perhaps the era's biggest hit, The Lion King. Released in 1994, it is fondly remembered as one of, if not the, greatest animated film of all time. So, with this lofty legacy in mind, let's dive in.

Story

Set against the rolling African savannah, a kingdom is divided when the king's scheming brother brings about the demise of the king. It is left for his Son to emerge and take back the throne that is rightfully his.

Verdict

There are many reasons why this film is so fondly remembered, a lot has to do with the films merits as a staggering piece of emotional animation, but just as prevalent is the sense of nostalgia surrounding this period in history, now that all of the children of that time are adults trying to remember happier times.

This can manifest in many ways, and truthfully, there are many movies that we find ourselves nostalgic about which don't truly hold up to scrutiny years later. We always view the objects of our youth through rose-tinted spectacles.

Thankfully, however, The Lion King is not such an example of this, in fact, I think I would go so far as to say that The Lion King would be held up as a masterwork no matter what era it was released. Of course it helps its case with the timing of its release, all the pieces were in the right place at that time, but the same film would have been great no matter what year it was released.

I have long gone to bat for Disney's ability to play with the audiences' emotions just as well as any live-action film can. The great thing about animation is it has the ability to tell stories that would otherwise be impossible. The world didn't realise that they wanted an adaptation of Hamlet but with animals until Disney gave it to us, and then we all wanted more.

The animation, as you'd expect, is flawless. Painstaking scenes depicting gathering animals with different lighting effects all seem to have come from a place of love and passion, the landscapes drawn for the animation could be works of art in and of themselves, and the character animation brims with personality, showing each characters mannerisms in subtle ways, like the way Scar walks, or more accurately skulks, about, giving the impression that this is a character not to be trusted.

The music is another reason for Lion King's staying power; and recruiting someone of Elton John's profile was always going to be a big coup for Disney and boy did he deliver. Along with Tim Rice, who provided the lyrics, he delivers one of Disney's greatest soundtracks, each song is memorable and warranted, driving across characterisation with each number, Scar's villainy in 'Be Prepared', Simba's brash, youthful arrogance in 'I Just Can't Wait To Be King' not a second is wasted, and no song outstays its welcome. It's a soundtrack as beloved as the film itself for good reason.

 The voice cast is also a stellar part of this film. James Earl Jones as Mufasa is so iconic that they've brought him back for the upcoming remake.

Jeremy Irons' menacing overtones fit Scar perfectly, and Nathan Lane and Ernie Sabella are perfectly cast as Timon and Pumbaa, respectively. It's a widely varied and terrifically talented cast that bring everything they have for the very best final product.

In conclusion, there is very little original left to write about The Lion King. It's beloved by generations of filmgoers and for good reason. It's beautiful animation, memorable soundtrack, and tremendous cast are enough to not only win you over, but keep you coming back for more.

Alien

Directed by Ridley Scott

Starring: Sigourney Weaver, Tom Skerritt, Veronica Cartwright and John Hurt

When it comes to great directors, very few have a perfect record. Stanley Kubrick may have been a masterful filmmaker, but he also made Eyes Wide Shut, Steven Spielberg has War of the Worlds, and Quentin Tarantino has Death Proof. No-one is perfect, much less film directors.

Ridley Scott is a great example of this. Throughout his long illustrious career, he has earned his reputation as a cinema legend, but even he is not immune to making a bad film. Exodus, Hannibal and Robin Hood (the 2010 one) all carry his name, and all of them are varying flavours of awful.

But when he gets it right, the result can end up inspiring generations of filmmakers. Much like 2001 laid the groundwork for many future sci-fi films, Blade Runner did the same for dystopian sci-fi, and this film firmly established the rules for horror in a sci-fi setting; the mystery, the denseness, and the claustrophobia.

This film recently celebrated its 40th anniversary, and it still ranks in many critic's top films of all time, it's widely respected and revered by cinephiles the world over, even if its legacy was somewhat tarnished by future instalments. But for now, let's forget about that, and take a look at the original, and see how it holds up 40 years later.

Story

The crew of the Nostromo are awaken from cryo-sleep in deep-space to find their craft besieged by a murderous alien threat.

Verdict

The story synopsis may be shorter than usual, but it is a film that is difficult to write about without spoiling its contents. Even though this film is 40 years old, I still find it best that films are experienced for the first time with no prior knowledge of plot events.

The winning formula at the core of Alien lies in its atmosphere. The sense of building dread set in an enclosed environment with an unknown threat will always be thousands of times more tense than monsters jumping out from behind every corner.

What helps this dread build and finally peak later is the knowledge that all of these characters have lived in the space that is now under attack for some time, it feels like a place people have lived, rather than just survived, and the characters and their interactions hint at several relationship dynamics that are lying just below the surface, which helps us buy into these characters as people, they all have flaws and relationships, making them sympathetic and making us sad when the Alien eats their brains with a side of garlic mayo.

This sense of pacing shows in the films restraint in revealing the Xenomorph also; in many less subtle horror films the threat would be introduced in a way to show as much of it as possible, highlighting everything about it and instantly making it less threatening. Paradoxically, the Xenomorph is rarely seen fully lit, it's in shadows, or moves so quickly that it's hard to tell what it looks like, only that it's something you wouldn't fancy meeting in a dark alley.

Aside from the atmosphere, the film's characters lie at the heart of its story, and while a few can drift into stereotype territory, the choice of a female protagonist must have been a bold move in 1979. No longer is the female character there to just do the screaming, in fact Ripley is probably the most capable character right from the start, which must have been a breath of fresh air forty years ago, and is still somewhat noble today, even in our 'enlightened' times.

Ridley Scott's abilities as a director also shine brightly in this film. He seems to work best with visually striking environments, creating the neon-soaked atmosphere of Blade Runner, and juxtaposing it here with a cramped, dull spaceship environment, with low-res monitors and stark drab colours, it gives the feel that this is an extraordinary thing happening in such an ordinary setting, which is such a bizarre thought when the thing in question is a spaceship.

The film is remembered mostly for a number of iconic moments within it that have stood the test of time, and are still being homage, or outright parodied, to this day. While these moments are a pay-off to a great building of tension, I find myself more enthralled in the building tension, the quieter moments where the characters are gathering their thoughts, that speak so much to their characters. All of these should be rightly remembered alongside the usual scenes as reasons why this film is so great.

In conclusion then, Alien is not just a great film on its own merits but left a legacy that so many films have tried to replicate that it pretty much set the standard that is still to be beaten. A masterfully shot, paced and acted piece of cinema, genuinely tense and unnerving and with one of the greatest cinematic threats in history, I imagine its influence will still be felt for many years to come.

Space Jam

Directed by Joe Pytka

Starring: Michael Jordan, Wayne Knight, Theresa Randle and Danny DeVito

A few reviews ago, I warned against the dangers of nostalgia when it comes to films. Then I was talking about a film that does hold up in hindsight – The Lion King – now let's look at the flip side of this particular coin.

The Looney Tunes are practically animation royalty nowadays, they've been around since the 1930's and generations of children have come to love Bugs, Daffy, and all the other wacky characters that make up the Looney Tunes roster. Their longevity is testament to their popularity, as there are still TV series running now that carry on the lineage of the Looney Tunes.

Their dalliance with feature-length films were exclusively compilations of classic cartoons up until the release of Space Jam in 1996, their first feature-length, single-narrative film, and there would only ever be another one after it, why is this? Well there could be a number of reasons, chief among them being the disappointing return of this film's successor, Back in Action, which was only a fraction of the success that this film was (despite being, in my opinion, the better film).

So with the potential for nostalgia routinely warned, let's dive into Space Jam.

Story

Legendary basketball player Michael Jordan announces his decision to retire from basketball, and transition into a baseball career, during this transition, he is unwittingly transported to the world of the Looney Tunes, where he gets caught up in an attempt to steal the Looney Tunes to be attractions at a failing amusement park.

Verdict

What I would really like to know is what sort of powerful drugs were going around the Warner Brothers writer's room at the time of Space Jam.

What bold visionary said: 'Hey, let's do a Looney Tunes film, where Michael Jordan saves the world by being good at basketball.' To which an entire room said: 'Brilliant!'.

Strange, and somewhat jarring plot aside for a while, you really have to admire the sheer effort of combining the worlds of live-action and animation together in this film, at times it makes it look seamless, as if Michael Jordan is actually interacting with an anthropomorphic rabbit.

Granted, there are times when it looks cheesy and out-of-place, specifically when any characters from the two worlds have to touch.

All in all it's an inoffensive film, it doesn't know what it wants to do at times, and flits wildly between whacky times in Toon-land and serious basketball players (who I assume are actually basketball players, as they act like they're coming off seriously strong anaesthetic) in counselling due to them losing their powers after some tiny aliens stole it with a basketball. This plot gets weirder the more you talk about it doesn't it?

Never is this frantic tone more evident than in the casting of Michael Jordan, look, I know Michael probably wasn't trained at Julliard, but can anyone think of a single athlete that has transitioned into acting, and been good at it? In Jordan's case it's a definite no. He has the same delivery and expression for every emotion, like he's reading from a teleprompter and he forgot to wear his glasses. It's especially noticeable when he's paired with actual actors, who make him look like a competition winner.

It really is a shame as the animation is also extremely slick and stylised in that Looney Tunes way we've come to know and love. It is more in line with the house style than Back in Action would be, which focuses more on real-world interactions, most of this takes place within the world of the Looney Tunes, which works in its favour as anything is possible in Looney Tunes world, and the world outside just seems drab and dull, no scene better typifies this than the scene before Michael Jordan is taken to the cartoon world, in which our human characters play golf, not known for being the most exciting sport, a significant chunk of screen-time is devoted to this before the plot properly kicks in, and it really shows where the priorities truly lie.

In truth, I can't stay particularly mad at this film. Sure, Michael Jordan's acting is so awful it makes Sofia Coppola look like Meryl Streep, and his basketball playing buddies fare even worse. But there are some fun moments with the Looney Tunes themselves, as well as a delightfully over-the-top Bill Murray at the peak of his Bill Murray-ness.

I can't really recommend Space Jam on its merits as a film, if you're about my age and remember it being a fun time as a kid, keep it as that memory, it will do you no favours re-watching it. Some things are best left in the 90's.

David Brent: Life on the Road

Directed by Ricky Gervais

Starring: Ricky Gervais and Ben Bailey Smith

Ricky Gervais is what you might call an acquired taste. He has been known to let his mouth get him into trouble, but however outspoken and opinionated he might be, there's one thing that cannot be taken away from him, and that's his writing talent.

His first big exposure was The Office, a somewhat ground-breaking sitcom in its own right, and the spawning point for this film, he then moved on to shows like Extras and Derek. However, his biggest creation is arguably his character from The Office, David Brent.

Brent is a concentration of all the worst traits a boss can have. Overly confident and feigning concern about his team to make himself look better, he was played to look foolish, yet recognisable, everyone has had a boss they hate, and Brent was an exemplar of that.

So, over a decade on, Gervais re-visits his most famous character, but under different circumstances…

Story

Fifteen years after finding fame on The Office, David Brent is once again chasing fame. He takes time off work to go on a music tour, one last shot at the 'big time' he feels he deserves. He brings a band along for the journey, as well as a promising young rapper, who he is supposed to manage.

Verdict

The Office was, for want of a better term, cringe humour. You cringed at whatever David Brent did or said, but in a way that made you laugh. To some, this is unbearable to watch, and to others it's comedy gold. It has since had life outside The Office, Peep Show is perhaps the best example, but no character comes close to being as cringingly hilarious as David Brent.

The real winner of the character is the sincerity in which Gervais plays him. It would be easy to over play his ignorance, but he subtly makes the character believable by having the character BELIEVE what he says and does. He doesn't intend to offend people, but he also doesn't realise WHY he is offending someone. He believes in his own hype, even if no-one else does.

Life on the Road is not Gervais' best work, not by a long-shot, and truth be told, it's a bit of an odd duck. You see, he's known for moving on from past characters and projects, always just making two series and a special, each of his series has followed this pattern, it is only Brent he has re-visited. There could be many reasons for this, of course, but it also makes the film feel derivative of the original series. It feels like we've already seen Brent at his best (or worst) so giving us more takes some of the shine off the characters appeal.

Not to say that there's no fun to be had. There are some genuinely great moments that are on-par with The Office, specifically in his interactions with his newest co-workers. That and the songs in the film offer some real surprises in both their quality, and their humour.

There are some that represent Brent's heavy-handed attempts to be seen as the 'nice guy' songs like 'Please Don't Make Fun of Disableds' and no, I didn't make that title up, again these are not played as jokes by Gervais, it's pretty clear that Brent takes these songs very seriously, as he does with his music career, we know he's terrible, his band knows he's terrible, but he doesn't, and that's what makes it so funny.

I genuinely don't think anyone could direct Gervais' writing other than Ricky himself however, and although this is not his best work as a director (or as a writer, After Life and Derek both trump this by a fair distance) there is skill in his shots, and because he knows the character and material so well, he knows how to get the best out of them like no-one else. I don't think I've ever enjoyed Gervais unless he's directing himself, he's just that kind of performer.

A surprise gem in this film is Ben Bailey Smith, who is best known as writer/rapper Doc Brown, who plays Brent's protégé in this film, but is shown to be a superior performer in every conceivable way, he adds a new dimension to the film and to Brent's character, he also provides the soundtracks best track; Cards We're Dealt, which is all of his characters frustrations emerging in rap form, it's a delight.

In conclusion then, while it is nowhere near prime Gervais material, it is still fun to spend time with the Brent character, and it offers just enough original scenarios and laughs to not feel like a cash-grab. Think of it as cinematic popcorn, you can consume it and enjoy it, but you're not likely to think much about it afterwards.

Schindler's List

Directed by Steven Spielberg

Starring: Liam Neeson, Ben Kingsley, Ralph Fiennes and Caroline Goodall

Sometimes it's really hard to write something funny about a film. In some cases it can be so inconsequential that it's hard to think of anything interesting to say about it, and in some cases, especially this one, it's just a matter of tone.

I hadn't seen Schindler's List until quite recently, when it was re-released to mark its 25th anniversary. I had known its reputation as a real cinematic masterpiece, and as Spielberg's peak, but the opportunity did not present itself at the right time until now.

Now, as I have said in the past, World War II is hardly fresh ground in cinema, even in 1993, it was somewhat old hat to produce a film about the era, but the difference here was how personal this story was to its director. Spielberg, being Jewish, could have opened some personal wounds for himself while making this film, but maybe he felt like it was a story that demanded to be told.

So, with expectations high, and tissues at the ready, lets dive into Schindler's List.

Story

During the Second World War, businessman and trusted member of the Nazi hierarchy, Oskar Schindler, secretly hatches a scheme to rescue a great number of Jewish prisoners, through putting them to work in his factories.

Verdict

Now, I am no historian. I know enough about the war to know the true horrors that took place, and the truly horrible people in the Nazi regime, there is a lot to tell about these people, even in grave curiosity, but there was so little I knew about this remarkable story, and the man behind it.

I know it isn't a documentary, and undoubtably, there will be inaccuracies and embellishments, but that is par for the course in the long run. This is a war story that deserved to be told, a story, not of evil and genocide (although there's a fair amount of that about) but of heroism, in the face of death and danger, Oskar Schindler defied the system.

The sheer contrast of tone and style in this film is truly breath-taking. Spielberg does not shy away from portraying the brutality of the regime, unspeakably violent acts take place in such beautifully sharp black-and-white cinematography, each bullet fired and drop of blood spilt is viscerally portrayed on-screen. As exemplified by a beautiful, yet heart-breaking, shot of the one-armed man, executed by the Nazis, spilling blood on the perfect, crisp snow. It succeeds in being both harrowing, and beautiful.

The decision to shoot in black-and-white could have quite easily backfired. Making that decision in modern times can be incredibly pretentious, but used here, it instead invokes the feeling of the era, as well as juxtaposing the brutal violence with it's sharp, eye-catching palate.

This is a film that feels like it was told for a reason, like Spielberg was on a mission to bring this to the screen, he wanted to show us how every single person died, families were ripped apart, and atrocities committed with no compromise. There are scenes in the ghetto and concentration camps that genuinely come close to being hard to watch, such is his devotion to not compromising his vison, and subsequentially creating a feeling of dread in his audience, a feeling of suspense that, at any moment, the big, bad wolf that was the Nazi regime could break down the door and bring this story to an end.

There are very few films that effectively capture the Nazis as the scourge that they were, that showed them as completely irredeemable sociopaths, instead sometimes portraying them as somewhat of a pantomime villain, an unbelievable, outlandishly evil force, when in reality, they were very real, and so much worse than any fairy tale villain. It is rare for a film to give you a feeling of dread whenever a character appears on screen, perhaps apart from this Inglorious Basterds comes closest, but even then, it struggles to come close to the portrayal of Amon Göth (Ralph Fiennes).

The acting in this film is as close to perfect as you're likely to get. I have rarely hated a character quite like I hated Göth, and rarely am I so satisfied when a character gets their comeuppance, Fiennes is scheming, violent and utterly reprehensible, it is a masterful performance, in any other film, he would steal the show, but here, he is just one of many great performances.

Liam Neeson leads the cast and is the best he has ever been. His arc is so well realised, his change of character so complete, that by the end, you are crying along with him. He goes from seeing the Jewish slave labour as a valuable resource to seeing it as the lifesaver that it was, he learns to see his workers as people, and in doing so, turns his back on the regime. He goes from being just another Nazi, to a Jewish hero, all within the three-hour runtime, and not one bit of it feels forced, his performance is simply peerless.

In conclusion, this is as close to perfect as a film, neigh a work of art, can be. Heart wrenching story, combined with gorgeous camera work, and masterful acting makes Schindler's List a cinematic dream, it comes with much praise, and it deserves every bit of it.

The Godfather

Directed by Francis Ford Coppola

Starring: Marlon Brando, Al Pacino, James Caan and Richard Castellano

I have been surprised by many films. Surprised by how good, bad, or indifferent they are. I've sat through some utter dross, and some utter gems. But I have never been so surprised to fall in love with a film as much as I fell in love with The Godfather.

That's not to say I don't admire Francis Ford Coppola, or the gangster genre. It's just the baggage that follows a film around. Being called the 'greatest film of all time' can do many things for a film, it can create a legacy, make it a film enjoyed by generations to come, but it can also make it a target.

Every critic has a film they consider the best, and I imagine every critic has a film that others consider the best, but they don't rate so much. For me that film is Citizen Kane, and it taught me to be wary of anything labelled the 'greatest' because if it is anything other than perfect, it can feel like a disappointment.

But, for all those that fall short, there are inevitably going to be films that surpass expectations, and The Godfather is that, in so many ways.

Story

Trouble is brewing within the organised crime world. Heads of families are at war with each other and people are getting gunned down in the street, and at the top of it all is Vito Corleone, the Godfather. But when an attempt is made on his life, the family's life is turned upside down.

Verdict

In the last review, I said that Schindler's List is 'as close to perfect' as you can get, well, I was wrong. The Godfather IS cinematic perfection.

Everything about it, from its direction, to its set design is perfectly considered and executed, it creates a tone of an important, once-in-a-lifetime film. There are many films that make illusions to being epic stories, well The Godfather feels epic without even trying to.

Each twist and turn in the story is considered, and perfectly placed, it has peaks and troughs, it goes from a sedate wedding scene to a bloodbath at a toll booth. For every moment of perfectly shot gunfight, there is a quieter moment, filled with story and character development, no character is filler, they all have a purpose.

The direction is astounding in its scope, taking us from the bustling streets of New York to the sprawling rustic landscape of the Sicilian countryside, its changes in scene representing stages within Michael's arc, while Vito's arc is mapped out in New York.

The most intriguing arc of this film, and the series as a whole, is that of Michael Corleone, going from a World War II veteran, uninterested in the life of organised crime his father and brothers find themselves in, into a ruthless crime boss, who orders the deaths of his enemies in cold blood.

This is portrayed smartly by Al Pacino, who completely owns the role of Michael, whose character will go through big changes in both this film and in Part II, but along each step of the way, he is believable. He does not join the mob because of blind loyalty, he is forced to due to his brother murder, he only starts to change when he claims his first kill and becomes a different man.

The film really is a showcase for some of the best performances in Hollywood history, not only Al Pacino, but Marlon Brando, who gives, in my opinion, the best acting performance in film history as Vito. You get the feeling that Vito is ruthless, but this is balanced by moments such as the iconic 'they slaughtered my boy' scene. He manages to be both violent and emotional within the same film, and it doesn't feel forced or disjointed, his emotion is seen when his family is threatened, and then everything after is the violence.

The cast as a whole are phenomenal, James Caan is fantastic as Sonny, Talia Shire is great as Connie and Robert Duvall is understated, yet notable in his role as adopted Corleone, Tom.

All of this is helmed with such artistic direction, that more than once it completely took my breath away. The attempted assassination of Vito and the Christening scene spring to mind, both of which could make good cases as the best sequences in film history, but it is not just artistic angles and framing that make these scenes, it's the pacing and timing in the script, they're big events of the narrative timeline, that spans two films, both of which clock in at more than three hours, creating enough memorable scenes to see us through the mammoth run-time is no mean feat.

I don't like to make tall claims or sweeping statements. I don't think I am qualified to name a film as the best; no-one really is. But I can say with confidence that The Godfather is the greatest film I have ever seen. No film has ever surpassed its reputation quite like it, and I really cannot think of adequate amounts of praise; if you're a film fan, and you haven't seen it, you owe it to yourself to set aside time to experience it. I just wish I could experience it for the first time all over again.

Mr Opinionated's Top 25 Films

25. Man on the Moon

24. Les Misérables

23. Beauty and the Beast

22. Django Unchained

21. Dead Poets Society

20. Rain Man

19. One Flew Over the Cuckoo's Nest

18. It's A Wonderful Life

17. Avengers: Endgame

16. Rocky

15. The Shawshank Redemption

14. Taxi Driver

13. Monty Python and the Holy Grail

12. The Lion King

11. 2001: A Space Odyssey

10. The Empire Strikes Back

9. Dunkirk

8. Pulp Fiction

7. Good Will Hunting

6. Logan

5. Three Billboards Outside Ebbing, Missouri

4. The Dark Knight

3. Schindler's List

2. Forrest Gump

1. The Godfather

Acknowledgements

There's so many people who were a factor in the road leading up to this book that I could write a second one just thanking people, so I'll keep it brief.

Thanks to my family, first and foremost, obviously, for supporting me in anything I do, even if I did turn out to be a snotty critic.

To my better half, Khyra, for making me a better person. Without her, I wouldn't have even started the blog, much less publish this book.

I'd like to thank a few people who inspired me to become a critic, people who will probably never meet me, but I'd like to give a special mention to Mark Kermode and Ben 'Yahtzee' Croshaw. One is a famous film critic and the other a video game critic, but a lot of my critical style can be traced to them. So thanks, guys.

Special thanks also to Graham Musk, who created the caricatured version of me you see on the front cover, and thanks to Elizabeth Carter, who took the headshot you can see on the back cover. All of their social media links and websites can be found on the next page.

Last, but not least, I'd like to thank you, yes you! The person with the book/kindle in their hands, reading this to the end, I suspect I have annoyed you enough throughout these pages, but you have my thanks either way, whether a long-time reader, or new reader, without anyone to read my reviews, I'd just be a mad man, shouting into the abyss.

Collaborator Links

Elizabeth Carter: Facebook - https://www.facebook.com/elizabethcartermedia/

Website - https://elizabethgcarterme.wixsite.com/portraits

Graham Musk: Facebook -